ıg Ireland

Deconstructing Ireland

Identity, Theory, Culture

Colin Graham

Edinburgh University Press

© Colin Graham, 2001

Edinburgh University Press Ltd
22 George Square, Edinburgh

Typeset in Melior
by Pioneer Associates, Perthshire, and
printed and bound in Great Britain by
MPG Books Ltd, Bodmin, Cornwall

A CIP Record for this book is available from the British Library

ISBN 0 7486 0975 X (hardback)
ISBN 0 7486 0976 8 (paperback)

Contents

Series Editor's Introduction

Contemporary history continues to witness a series of momentous changes, altering what was only recently familiar ideological, political and economic terrain. These changes have prompted a new awareness of subjective, sexual, ethnic, racial, religious and cultural identities and of the ways these are constructed in metropolitan centres, regions and nations at a time when these spheres are themselves undergoing a period of critical transition. Recent theory has simultaneously encouraged a scepticism towards the supposed authenticity of personal or common histories, making identity the site of textualised narrative constructions and reconstructions rather than of transparent record. In addition, new developments in communication and information technology appear to be altering our fundamental perceptions of knowledge, of time and space, of relations between the real and the virtual, and of the local and the global.

The varied discourses of literature and media culture have sought to explore these changes, presenting life as it is negotiated on the borderlines of new, hybridised, performative, migrant and marginalised identities, with all the mixed potential and tensions these involve. What emerge are new, sometimes contradictory perceptions of subjectivity or of relations between individuals, social groups, ideologies and nations, as the inner and public life are rewritten in a cultural environment caught up in religious and political conflict and the networks of global consumption, control and communication.

The series *Tendencies: Identities, Texts, Cultures* follows these debates and shows how the formations of identity are being articulated in contemporary literary and cultural texts, often as significantly in their hybridised language and modes as in their manifest content.

Volumes in the series concentrate upon tendencies in contemporary writing and cultural forms, principally in the work of writers, artists and cultural producers over the last two decades. Throughout, its consistent interest lies in the making and unmaking of individual, social and national identities. Each volume draws on relevant theory and critical debate in its discussion *inter alia* of questions of gender and sexuality, race and ethnicity, class, creed and nation, in the structuring of contemporary subjectivities.

The kinds of texts selected for study vary from volume to volume, but most often comprise written or visual texts available in English or widely distributed in English translation. Since identities are most often confirmed or redefined within the structures of story and narrative, the series is especially interested in the use of narrative forms, including fiction, autobiography, travel and historical writing, journalism, film and television.

Authors are encouraged to pursue intertextual relations between these forms, to examine the relations between cultural texts and relevant theoretical or political discourse, and to consider cross-generic and intermedia forms where these too bear upon the main concerns of the series.

Peter Brooker
University College, Northampton

Preface and Acknowledgements

Bart Simpson gets drunk for the first time on St Patrick's Day. Surrounded by the glorious trappings of Irish America and in the middle of a parade which memorably includes a James Joyce lookalike on the 'Drunken Irish Novelists of Springfield' float, Bart's plastic horn is accidentally the conduit for a spray of free stout. The parade turns from raucous carnival to silent outrage; 'Stop the celebrations, that small boy's drunk,' says an onlooker.

During the writing of this book I've worried at times that either my reader or I will have an experience parallel to Bart's. Caught up in the cacophony of Irish culture, it's easy to lose a sense of perspective. This book attempts to examine how that note of celebration gets attached to 'Ireland' and then perpetuates itself. It addresses the teleology which becomes superimposed on the structures of Irish culture through the concept of the nation, through the processes of modernisation and through the progressive ideal inherent in colonisation. Whether manifested in a desire to be synchronically and completely a nation, or in a need to 'authenticate' the past, or in a continual turn to the pledge of future time, the signs of Ireland find themselves imbricated again and again in what Declan Kiberd calls 'the foreglow of a golden future'. *Deconstructing Ireland* suggests that 'Ireland' is a future which is always posited and never attained. The book does not seek to find a final paradigmatic or historical cause for the state of 'play' in which Ireland exists. Rather it tracks the processes by which Ireland becomes 'Ireland', a 'cited', quoted version of itself which is both excessive and phantasmal.

Despite its title, *Deconstructing Ireland* is not a strict application of Jacques Derrida's philosophy to Irish studies. Derrida and his ideas appear at various times in the text, and their influence will be apparent to readers who are familiar with deconstructive thought.

Where *Deconstructing Ireland* follows Derrida at all, it is in the interest it has in examining the logic by which 'Ireland' and the 'Ireland' of Irish studies constitute themselves, looking for underlying forms of thought and conception, and reading through their faultlines. The conclusion which the book edges towards is that 'Ireland' stages its own deconstruction and that at every turn the idea unravels and reforms itself, always in anticipation of the next act of definition and criticism which, like this one, will be inadequately applied to it. The spirit of this book is one which analyses, celebrates and enjoys the fact that 'Ireland' is a deconstructing Ireland.

This book is organised around topics which describe points at which Irish studies currently places its own limits. The book begins with a chapter introducing the notion of a free-floating 'Ireland' intent on escaping the archival and defining intentions of its pursuers; from John Mitchel's vision of an Ireland which can be met in the exile's imagination to Ignatius Donnelly's Atlantean Ireland and Seán Hillen's 'Irelantis', this chapter attempts to argue that 'Ireland' is underwritten by a utopian trope which propels its completion always into the future. The result of this is, on the one hand, an emptiness of signification, as if Ireland has been drained of meaning until that future comes, and on the other hand, a repletion of meaning which allows a perpetual movement towards that future as a time when the plethora of signifiers will have settled back onto their proper objects of signification.

The suggestion that this *promise* of future harmony and wholeness is a persistent state of affairs is examined as a formative aspect of the history of Irish literary criticism in the twentieth century in Chapter 2. Discussing a series of moments in critical thinking in Ireland over the past century, this chapter suggests that the undelivered future of the nation induces a continual sense of 'crisis' in Irish criticism. Chapter 3 finds a particular cause of that crisis in the unresolved relationship between the Irish critical voice and 'the people' of which, and for whom, it implicitly wishes to speak. The chapter examines this dilemma of articulation using Roland Barthes' writing on Michelet as a starting point for a discussion of Irish criticism of James Joyce, and more particularly Joyce's own analysis of the same crisis of the intellectual voice in the 'Ithaca' episode of *Ulysses*.

Chapters 4 and 5 attempt the same kind of archaeology of the critical for postcolonial critiques of Ireland. Chapter 4 examines how postcolonial theory has begun to interact with Irish criticism, focusing on the moments at which the idea of the 'nation' operates as a force of recalcitrance in critical thinking and arguing that the postcolonial might be 'applied' to Ireland in ways which interrogate rather than shy away from the hold which the nation has on Irish critical thought. A similar knot exists in 'post-nationalist' thought on Ireland and the chapter suggests that there is a productive tension to be found in recognising the often stubborn centrality of the nation-concept in Irish criticism. Chapter 5 takes this examination of the postcolonial into the more specific terms of theories of subalternity and gender-as-subaltern, discussing the placing of women as subaltern in relation to 'national' politics in two male-authored fictional accounts (by Gerry Adams and Frank Delaney respectively) of the sectarian politics of Northern Ireland. Delaney's novel *Telling the Pictures* also points the way towards the final section of the book in that its recognition of the power and pervasiveness of the 'popular' becomes crucial to the last two chapters.

The final chapters of this book suggest that in 'popular' culture 'Ireland' can be seen to have a 'liminal', affiliated and active existence at once within and without the systems which try to define the concept 'Ireland'. Chapter 6 argues that the search for 'authenticity' is a pervasive feature of Irish culture and attempts to show that when the authentic is sought for it moves further away from its supposedly authentic and unselfconscious object of reference. The chapter scrutinises layers of 'authenticity' as constructed through literary culture, tourism and advertising, noting a progression towards the acceptance of a heavily ironised form of the authentic which questions the very idea of authenticity. The final chapter begins by disputing the way in which Irish studies has so far used 'popular' culture as a material base to support historical and cultural analysis and insists that the variety, eccentricity and complexity of popular images of Ireland is an untapped and invaluable resource in understanding how Irish culture has formulated itself. The book ends with a discussion and celebration of Irish kitsch as a cultural form which brand-names 'Ireland' as always utopian and always in the phantasmal future.

Deconstructing Ireland questions the boundary markers which Irish studies has set itself on a variety of sensitive issues: the political commitment of the critical voice, the assumptions of authenticity which support our critical premises, the generic line where the canon of Irish studies has been drawn, the future which 'Ireland' pulls us towards. In this it attempts to articulate a largely unspoken and contemporary moment when a postcolonial Ireland meets a postmodern Ireland. The consequences of this particular crossover for Irish culture and Irish criticism are still underexamined and may induce another and familiar crisis as 'Ireland' participates in a future which its criticism lags behind. This book seeks to anticipate that gap by suggesting that the crisis which the postcolonial/postmodern juncture induces is one with which 'Ireland' is familiar and which it has dealt with before. And yet deconstruction should also remind us that any act of criticism is only another link in a 'chain of supplements' 'multiplying the supplementary meditations that produce the sense of the very thing they defer'. So *Deconstructing Ireland*, willingly caught up itself in the supplementary chain, claims no originality in signifying what 'Ireland' is; however, it does ask that we look along the chain of supplementation and see that Ireland's origins and futures are produced and reproduced again and again as mirages and as impossible, but tantalising, utopian presences.

ACKNOWLEDGEMENTS

Parts and earlier versions of some of the material in this book have been previously published in the *Journal of Gender Studies*, the *Irish Studies Review*, *The Irish Review*, *Circa* and in *Ireland and Cultural Theory* (Macmillan). I am grateful to the editors and publishers for allowing revised material to be reprinted here.

Work on this book was begun during a Junior Research Fellowship at the Institute of Irish Studies at the Queen's University of Belfast; I owe a great debt to the Institute for its generosity during that time, and particularly to Brian Walker, Sophia Hillan King and John Fairleigh. I would like to express my thanks to my colleagues at the University of Huddersfield for their support during my years teaching there, and to Andrea Croxford, Deborah Shires and Sarah Williams who brightened many Yorkshire days. Thanks to Cartan Finegan of Heritage Ireland for sending me a copy of his paper on tourism, James McAleavy for lending me his dissertation, McConnell's advertising for generously supplying a copy of 'Ireland', and Susan Smith of the Museum of Childhood, Bethnal Green, London, for information and photographs. Peter Brooker, series editor, and Nicola Carr of Edinburgh University Press have been extremely supportive and patient throughout the writing process. My particular gratitude goes to Seán Hillen for permission to reproduce images of 'Irelantis'.

I have been very fortunate in writing this book to have met continually with an immense generosity, both critical and personal, from friends and colleagues; thanks are due to many including Janice Allan, Michael Allen, Rosita Boland, Fran Brearton, Feargal Cochrane, Stewart Crehan, Ewan Fernie, Roy Foster, Breda Gray, Tom Herron, Geraldine Higgins and Robert Shaw-Smith, Glenn Hooper, Eamonn

Hughes, Margaret Kelleher, Liam Kennedy, Edna Longley, Brian Maidment, Willy Maley, Sinéad Garrigan Mattar, John McDonagh, James H. Murphy, Lance Pettitt, Shaun Richards, Klaus Gunnar-Schneider, Neil Sammells, Gerry Smyth, Bruce Stewart and Oonagh Walsh. My gratitude to Claire Connolly and Kathy Cremin for reading drafts of various chapters, and to Richard Kirkland for his friendship and for sharing his acute critical insights. All opinions expressed in this book and any errors are, of course, my own.

My wonderful children, Joanna, Seamus and Melanie, have taught me unfailingly about play and about Ireland, though they'll know I've still more to learn. My parents, Dorothy and David Graham, have been constant in their support and care.

This book is dedicated to Selina Guinness, whose conversation, ideas, friendship and love have been continually liberating and sustaining.

List of Illustrations

'Ireland, east of Atlantis'[1]

Ireland's a dreadful country! I heartily wish it was in the middle of the Atlantic. (Alfred, Lord Tennyson to William Allingham[2])

PHANTASM AND EXCESS

Launching Ireland into a mid-Atlantic abyss was one solution Tennyson came up with as a salve to his irritation with the place. He also asked Allingham: 'Couldn't they blow up that horrible island with dynamite and carry it off in pieces – a long way off?'.[3] The frustration which leads Tennyson to imagine a violent terminality for Ireland is not just the typical fulmination of an English, Victorian conservative, who saw the Irish as 'charming and sweet and poetic' but 'utterly unreasonable'.[4] Tennyson's vision of Ireland in the 'middle of the Atlantic' is more prescient than the dullness his dismissive prejudice suggests. The phantasmic,[5] disappearing Ireland which Tennyson can barely bring himself to articulate pre-exists and pre-empts him. It is an Ireland which has anticipated its attempted destruction and which finds one strategy for survival in moving off into an impossible cultural geography at the very moment when it seems ready to submit to scrutiny.

As if calling his bluff, Tennyson's seafaring, moveable Ireland had already been symbolically met with earlier in the century by the transported rebel John Mitchel who, on his way to Van Diemen's Land via Bermuda in 1848, found himself the victim of a peculiarly meaningless form of national simulation:

At last we arrived at the anchorage in front of the government island, where the dock-yard is established. This island is at the extreme northwest of the whole group, and its name is nothing less than *Ireland*.[6]

While this second 'Ireland' is 'nothing less' than its almost cruelly resonant name, its irony does fit Mitchel's narrative. Ireland meets a cross-Atlantic mirror image of itself as sign and, at this stage in the story of Mitchel's exile, 'Ireland' is on the point of setting out on a journey which parallels Mitchel's own – exiled from its grounded self, it will start to appear everywhere, in an 'overabundance of signs',[7] so that it soon becomes much more than its name, while being less certainly a definable, unitary site. Sailing towards Bermuda, Mitchel attempts to fix the Caribbean island in his mind by calling up its associations; in succession he remembers connections through Bishop Berkeley, Prospero and Ariel, and Thomas Moore, a curiously apt amalgam of the religious, the colonial and an Irish sentimentality. Docked in the bay of Ireland Island, Mitchel finds that the ship next to his has on board Lord Dundonald, whose Irish name and revolutionary tendencies cannot dissuade Mitchel that the admiral 'regards Irish revolutionists as [anything other than] highly immoral characters'.[8]

Mitchel's transportation initiates what Engels, describing the out of control 'gallop' of capitalist overproduction, calls a 'crise pléthorique' (a term Engels borrows from Fourier).[9] This crisis begins to infect the semantics of the very word 'Ireland' itself, so that Mitchel stumbles in his attempts to keep these two Irelands apart, as when he writes: 'There is no such naval establishment as this in Ireland – I mean the other Ireland'.[10] Caught between an Ireland of desired return and an imprisoning Ireland which mocks that return, Mitchel's ability to define what is 'other' to his Ireland becomes more teasingly difficult to control. His dilemma is compounded by the 'Irishness' he cannot help but see around him and the Ireland he must construct from second-hand rumour and out-of-date newspaper reports. Mitchel is an early victim of a process which Fintan O'Toole identifies as a late twentieth-century phenomenon, in which Ireland dissipates into 'disappeared Irelands', so that:

While the place itself persists, the map, the visual and ideological convention that allows us to call that place 'Ireland' has been slipping away. Its coordinates, its longitudes and latitudes, refuse to hold their shape.[11]

Ireland becomes a plenitude of images, replicating itself for continual consumption and at times achieving an oversatiation. It is here that the 'Ireland' which is excessive topples into an Ireland of ceaseless reproduction and commodification. David Harvey, describing such a 'crise pléthorique' in terms more fatalistically postmodern than Engels', sees this as a time when other paths to relieve over-accumulation seem blocked. Ephemerality and instantaneous communicability over space then become virtues to be explored and appropriated.[12]

Sure enough, Mitchel's solution to this promiscuity of Irelands, in which images and signs of Ireland circulate while attachment to the object itself wanes, is a phantasmagoric form of 'instantaneous communicability' which oddly parallels Tennyson's. Mitchel writes: 'Often while I sit by the sea, facing that north-eastern *arc*, my eyes, and ears, and heart are all far, far':

and by intense gazing I can behold, in vision, the misty peaks of a far-off land – yea, round the gibbous shoulder of the great oblate spheroid, my wistful eyes can see, looming, floating in the sapphire empyrean, that green Hy Brasil of my dreams and memories.[13]

Under the intensity of the condition of exile, and pulling on the resources of the past ('memories') and the future ('dreams'), Mitchel's Ireland becomes more 'other' than it has ever been, as it leaves it moorings and enters the realm of mythology, defying the curve of the earth through the power of his imagination. Tennyson was inevitably quicker to similarly turn Ireland into a 'floating sign', but Mitchel's pained and pressurised imagination replays the same process. And while for Tennyson the goal is to find an end to having to talk of Ireland, Mitchel's desire is to perpetuate 'Ireland', to hold it in his mind as a place beyond the materiality of a world which is untrustworthy. For Mitchel, at once politically visionary and practical, the process involves and *uses* the very instruments of overdetermined signification which are also symptomatic of the crisis he faces;[14] so as he fixes Ireland in his mind he does it through Keatsian, autumnal and bucolic images which verge on the kitsch ('rivers . . . go brawling over their pebbly beds . . . and chide the echoes with a hoarse murmur', for example[15]) – the memory of Moore, and the model of his sentimental backward look, become all the more important now. The clichés of unspoilt rurality, like 'that green Hy Brasil', are given significance and justification by their existence inside 'dreams and memories'. Mitchel's vision ends with the words:

I see it, I hear it all – for by the wondrous power of imagination, informed by strong love, I do indeed live more truly in Ireland than on these unblessed rocks.[16]

This visionary liberation is followed by the recognition that the 'Queen of England' has 'banished me from the land where my mother bore me', and the moment ends. The next day's entry starts: 'Asthma! Asthma! The enemy is upon me'[17] – the panic of meaninglessness becomes physical and psychosomatic, turning the difficulty of establishing uncompromised intellectual contact with 'Ireland' into a corporeal effect (a trope discussed later in Chapter 3).

The Ireland which Mitchel can hear and see temporarily, coming to meet him over the Atlantic horizon, is a conjuration in the sense which Derrida describes:

A conjuration, then, is first of all an alliance, to be sure, sometimes a matter of political allegiance, more or less secret, if not tacit, a plot or a conspiracy. It is a matter of neutralizing a hegemony or overturning some power.[18]

Mitchel's floating, Atlantic Ireland is more than an act of desperate, exilic imagination. Detaching Ireland from its real place, he can re-place himself there, in an Ireland in keeping with the Ireland which circulates around him on Ireland Island – his summoning of Hy Brasil retains, as Derrida's comments would suggest, a sense of the political, and inwardly he 'plots' an overturning of the laws of nature, conspiring against the imperical in its conspiracy with the imperial. Mitchel conspires to do to Ireland exactly what Tennyson wishes for Ireland's fate. Faced with a repletion of signs, Mitchel's radicalism becomes truly revolutionary in that it turns signifier and signified loose from each other, awaiting the time when they can be properly reunited. Harmony can only be restored to the sign 'Ireland' when the individual is there to accommodate the duality of this 'two sided psychological entity'.[19]

Tennyson is obviously no revolutionary, yet his Ireland also imaginatively takes to the seas. So for all that a definable politics underlies Mitchel's pained outcast state from Ireland and Tennyson's irritability, there is something else linking the strange immateriality which they differently represent – a projection into the future of an Ireland which can only tendentiously be called into an imagined state *because* of its nascent putativeness. An Ireland can then be traced which evades totality by turning 'Ireland' into a place which, just as it is about to be placed, moves; as it is about to be destroyed, as with Tennyson's dynamite, it seems to explode itself, only to reappear reformed elsewhere. Mitchel, wondering what Bermuda will be like, constructs it beforehand on the basis of Irish associations – when he gets there he finds that it is already 'Ireland', that it has anticipated his associative yearning and that it offers him a near-mystical path back to its origin, which is in turn only accessible as a 'conjuration'. This is close to the 'real Irish Republic' which Hubert Butler contemplates, in appropriately aqueous terms, in his essay 'Am I an Irish Republican?':

A real Irish Republic? Would it contract and fade, if we were to grasp it, like an anenome dragged from a rock-pool? Undoubtedly, but that is what happens to all the ideas with which we try to regulate the stubborn world. But if we believe persistently in things that seem unrealizable and faraway, they shape themselves a little closer to reality.[20]

Mitchel's second, phantasmic 'Ireland Island' is in a sense a 'supplement [which] lays bare an additive substitution';[21] while it may logically appear to stand in for an Ireland which, at one pathetic remove, it resignifies, it is more properly a marker of 'the place of initial doubling', 'supplanting' and compensating for that which it signifies as its origin.[22] In this it is symbolic of the launching of a sign, 'Ireland', on the kind of path which Mitchel himself is following: exiled from grounded meaning, and as a result 'now predominantly concerned with the production of signs, images, and sign systems'.[23] Tacitly counteracting this tendency, the Ireland which 'contracts and fades' here is, crucially, also the Ireland of the future and of idealism. The evasion of definition which Butler identifies is not just a strategy to annoy, nor is it solely an attempt to form a kind of exclusivity. Undoubtedly both of these are aspects of the national story which structurally underpins any attempted definition of what Ireland is; the evasion is certainly a form of anti-colonial resistance and the exclusivism a claim to uniqueness which could have the same source. But also here is the need for the 'unrealizable and faraway'; in basic terms, Ireland's dissipation into a plethora of images and its formation of itself as a fantasy island are both aspects of a continually projected utopianism which acts as a bait and as a promise. Ireland is continually in the course of 'delay, delegation, sending back, detour, holding up, or putting in reserve',[24] a sign on the cusp of lost control, in danger of 'becoming the property of everyone'.[25] Saussure describes a language trying to fix itself for posterity as always doomed to failure because it will be 'borne along, willy-nilly, by the current that engulfs all languages'.[26] Whether the causes are identified as inherent in the strict teleology of nationalism, in the call to past and future which colonialism demands of the anti-colonial, or in the conditions of production inescapable in modern and postmodern capitalism,

Ireland finds itself, in Mitchel, in Tennyson, and, I will argue, else-where, a concept trapped in, and trying to free itself by deploying, a complex utopianism; accepting, for now, the current of unfixability, 'Ireland' sails symbolically on the Gulf Stream, awaiting a docking with itself at some future (always future) moment.

For Saint-Simon, utopia was a process incumbent on the present: 'Our fathers have not seen it; our children will arrive there one day, and it is for us to clear the way for them'.[27] Utopia is thus a mixture of the 'memory' and 'dream' which Mitchel uses as the means to see Hy Brasil – explaining the emptiness of the past by the glory of the future, the present moment is continually pulled forward and made weighty. Nation and nationalism, projecting themselves famously along the lines of history and destiny,[28] tempt understandings of the future into utopian schemes while apparently insisting on a smooth line which accommodates the past. Yet understandings of Ireland have too often seen its obsession with history as a sign of (the will to) a 'continuity of history', thus failing 'to locate the alienating time of the arbitrary sign' as 'the moment of anteriority of the nation's sign that entirely changes our understanding of the pastness of the past'.[29] When Ireland convinces us that it is only knowable through teleology, even when told against the nation narrative, we can miss the crucial disjunction which the deferral of the nation, and the very concept of Ireland itself, entails. Even Seán Ó Faoláin's attempt, in *The Irish*, to undo histories which are 'nationalist, patriotic, political, sentimental' describes its method as telling 'the story of the develop-ment of a national civilization', and ends with a wry, but essentially unadulterated, utopian vision:

How beautiful, as Chekov used to say of his Russia, life in Ireland will be in two hundred years' time![30]

This chapter begins an examination of the play between a haunting aporetic Ireland and an excessive, replicating plenitude of Ireland by acknowledging that both tropes play off the fundamental linearity of what Ireland is. Propelled into the future, 'Ireland' takes on both phantasmal and excessive utopian characteristics: both are ironic parallels to the future nation-state, and parodies of utopia itself, yet they parody only to preserve utopia and not to destroy it. While using facets of the mechanics of utopias (aware of the need to modernise the means of production; a clear social order; the convic-tion of a flourishing of culture), 'Ireland' as utopia, in its eternal delay, also shows itself to be aware of George Kateb's warning that the 'very wish to compose a utopia, to set forth in detail a utopian way of life, may in fact be repressive'.[31] 'Ireland' is a utopia twice removed by deferral, delegating details to the future.

My argument throughout this chapter, and the rest of this book, is that, while historical change is apparent in the conditions of production which affect what 'Ireland' is, there are consistently recalcitrant tropes which embody the ever-present tensions of narrating the nation, of promising a future, of informing and being a culture without appearing to be produced. The remainder of this chapter attempts to particularise these tropes by discussing examples which illustrate the utopian tendencies in nineteenth- and twentieth-century imagined Ireland Islands.

A ROUND TOWER ON COLLEGE GREEN

In 1932 a group of six biplanes flew over Dun Laoghaire Harbour, a few miles south of Dublin city centre, in crucifix formation. At the same time in College Green, facing the entrance to Trinity College, motorists negotiated a 'decorative' round tower rising above four storeys high (Figure 1). At night houses, streets and the temporary altar on O'Connell Bridge were brightly lit:

FIGURE 1 A decorative Round Tower in College Green, from the *Pictorial Record* of the Eucharistic Congress, 1932

The length of every street glimmered like the side of a huge liner with
hundreds of lighted port-holes. Powerful searchlights, pouring their rays
through lettered screens, projected mighty words across the sky. *Laudamus!*
Glorificamus! Adoramus! 'We praise, we glorify, we adore!' Out in the Bay
the pilgrims' ships – American, German, English, Italian, Canadian, Dutch –
were sparkling with light.

Dublin was luminous that night in every way and in the highest way.
Lights were on sea and on land, and in the people's hearts there was the
Light of the World.[32]

The Eucharistic Congress of 1932, the occasion for this mélange of
enthusiastic electrification and globalising ambition, was an expression of the increasing 'fusion of Catholic and national pride' in post-
Independence Ireland.[33] Terence Brown sees the Eucharistic Congress
as partial evidence for how the Church 'provided for the needs of the
Irish people', winning their 'unswerving loyalty' before using its
'authoritative position in Irish society to preach a sexual morality of
severe restrictiveness'.[34] In these historical views, the Congress stands
as symbolic augury of the new state's settling social and political
order, recognised internationally by Vatican endorsement. (In 1932
the Irish Free State also took over Presidency of the League of Nations,
further confirming its quickly establishing orthodoxy.) Declan Kiberd
echoes a similar warning about the ominous harmony of the Congress
when he notes that de Valera and Cosgrave were together bearers of
the papal legate's canopy, thus healing Civil War divisions under
the auspices of the Church, creating a *de facto* consensus around the
legislative role of religious morality, and in effect deradicalising the
potential of the still emergent state.[35]

Such views of the Congress are irrefutable when seen in the
overall context of the social and cultural history which succeeds its
moment, but they also tend to gloss over, perhaps instructively, the
diverse set of images (and the means by which they were dissemi-
nated) which the Congress used to give itself substance. Above all,
the Congress impressed observers by its use of technology, so aptly
expressed by the wonder of the correspondent quoted above, whose
metaphoric comparison of Dublin to an ocean liner we can add to
our list of floating Irelands. Icons of modernity, such as electrification, the searchlight, the ocean liner, the aeroplane, are the means by
which the rapture of the event is created. Its luminosity and its
ability to reach to and write itself on the heavens is very practically
dependent on the means of producing such special effects.

In the same year as the Congress, the *Soarstát Eireann Official*

Handbook was attempting to quantify the fledging state's achievements in the production and distribution of electricity. The *Handbook* also emphasised Ireland's strategic usefulness as a stopping point for 'transatlantic liners', and anticipated 'the near future' in stressing that in 'its geographical position the Irish Free State possesses great advantages for the development of air communication with the western world'.[36] The *Pictorial Record* of the Eucharistic Congress is similarly interested in proving its technophile credentials – among the newspaper reports, mainly blandly praising the devotion and/or organisation of the event, is a long extract from the *Overseas Engineer*. Detailing how one million people could simultaneously take part in a religious service, it explains the use of a public address system and points out that: 'Such a problem would have been insurmountable a comparatively few years ago, but thanks to modern electrical science it was solved to perfect satisfaction'.[37] Eliminating the possibility of 'a pronounced time lag' in the relaying of the mass, technology could be seen here in the service of the literal 'unisonance' of the nation which Benedict Anderson describes in *Imagined Communities* and which he too figures through synchronised song; technology therefore enabled the Congress to sound and appear as the 'physical realization of the imagined community'.[38] As the *Overseas Engineer* puts it, 'only by the use of a loudspeaker system could the singing of such a vast congregation be properly *controlled*'.[39] This ability to synchronise the nation, and so to embody its homogeneity as a corporeal, spiritual and communicative unity, is certainly, as the *Overseas Engineer* reveals, an indicator of the nation-state's need for conformity and control of its citizenship's subjectivity. In this context, the writing in the sky becomes a literal form of 'modern magic',[40] in which the event of the staged nation has its singularity and homogeneity guaranteed by the internationalist universalism of both the Church and the progress of modernity itself; and the writing in the sky is also a moment of synchronic reading, claiming the very clouds for both Church and state (which at the time was also in the process of staking its claim to other natural elements, including land and water).

But what of that round tower on College Green? Its role in such a modernising national synchronicity does not immediately seem as sonorously at one with the event as the skywriting or the loudspeaker system. Mark Maguire, in his excellent essay on the Ardnacrusha Hydroelectric Scheme, points out that the dam project 'emanated from somewhere in the space between nation and state, and wove

modernity into the archaic fabric of nationalist Ireland'.[41] In pushing
the project forward on its election in 1932 the new Fianna Fáil
government overrode the lifestyles of the Abbey fishermen, who
found themselves battling against the very party whose support they
might have expected. During the building of Ardnacrusha, as Maguire
shows, the state's solution was to turn the archaeological past to
heritage; the Abbey men placed themselves outside this trope, refusing heritage since it was the death of their livelihoods and with the
'nationalist cry of "up Garryowen"' attacked the forces of the state. In
this conflict

The state sought to destroy the very kind of group which its nationalist
rhetoric celebrated, and did so in the name of the nation.[42]

While the archaeological past could be accounted for in the
Ardnacrusha project, lived and recent ideas of the rebellious nation
had a suddenly awkward, dislocated relationship to the nation itself,
so that the onward march of the nation into statehood actually closed
the space of one subset of the people while erecting a modernised
space for the nation. The nation in formation elides its own constitutive materials and peoples. In the onward rush to prove itself in
the contemporary world the nation here makes the mistakes which
Frantz Fanon anticipates for postcolonial nationalisms:

The national government, before concerning itself about international
prestige, ought first to give their dignity to all citizens, fill their minds and
feast their eyes with human things.[43]

There are then, despite Benedict Anderson's notion of unisonance,
gaps in the nation-state as it finds itself pulled towards the future,
as it settles its nationality into the international. These aporias, one
of which is explored by Maguire, can be theorised in terms of postcolonial agency, and most specifically in Irish terms through the
subaltern model (as discussed later in Chapters 4 and 5). But the
tower on College Green is an altogether more passive rendition of a
non-modern Ireland[44] made to seem anomalous in the events of state
formation and religious affirmation. The analogy between the tower
and the history of Ardnacrusha is only a partial one, and the blankness of the tower as symbol in comparison to the attempts at agency
by the Abbey fishermen is crucial to bear in mind. Nevertheless, the
tower can be read as an exposure of the 'alienating time' which is
the potential rupture in the nation-state's self-conception and as

further evidence, fallen out of the iconic sign-system of the nation, of the myopia of the ideal of progress which Fanon warns against.

The history of the symbol of the round tower in nineteenth-century Ireland has been charted by Joep Leerssen, who notes that towers

were used, and overused, as part of national-cultural iconography, so profusely present on kitschy Victorian title-pages and printers' embellishments, alongside shamrocks, harps, wolf hounds, druids and maiden-icons.[45]

Leerssen also shows how the round tower became available as an icon through the century, piecing together the antiquarian debates which raged on the subject, until George Petrie's academic victory on the matter was finalised when he 'designed' the tower which now stands at Glasnevin cemetry in Dublin. The round tower was then securely part of 'national-cultural iconography' because it had been materially fixed, explored and explained by the discourse of antiquarianism – then it could be let loose in the field of kitsch, which in Leerssen's critique appears as a rather empty proliferation of second-hand, washed-out signs of the national culture. Late Victorian follies which imitate the round tower are equally, in Leerssen's account, dependent on the national archive and seemingly neither add nor detract meaning from the original, but simply exist as weaker and comically blanched versions.

Given Leerssen's archaeology of the sign of the round tower, the version which stood on College Green in 1932 could be interpreted as an early piece of vulgar tourist kitsch, part of the Baudrillardian 'whole museum of junk',[46] paralleling at a remove the more serious museumifying of the nation which arises from the 'idea of accumulating everything, of establishing a sort of general archive, the will to enclose in one place all times'.[47] However, to accept this is to submit the sign itself and criticism of the sign to the will of this archival force. Earlier in this chapter we noted how Mitchel's 'Ireland' might be seen to float in an 'overabundance of signs', and how the overarching design of 'Ireland' blurs from the unitary to both the excessively multiple and the haunting emptiness of the future. Can the archive at the centre of the nation project escape this process? Can the image of the round tower on College Green in 1932 be simply sneered away as an overenthusiastic embarrassment, just another folly? My suggestion is that the tower's place in the Eucharistic Congress's material culture stands as sign in the same relation to the centripetal idea of 'Ireland' as the Abbey fishermen do to the Fianna Fáil government – the tower should, according to antiquarianism and its commodified version of the archive, safely signify Ireland unproblematically, just as the Abbey men should be in tune with Fianna Fáil policy. But the moment of 1932 for both, in its future-tendency, means that they are highlighted, or can be read, as ghosts of the nation which, from the nation's perspective 'risk coming back *post mortem*'.[48] The Abbey men are performatively subaltern; the round tower commodifies itself to the point where, as we saw earlier in the chapter, the sign 'Ireland' exists in parallel to itself. The two examples together raise the problematics of a postcolonial reading of kitsch as discussed in Chapter 7; for now my purpose is to pursue the possibilities which the round tower has as sign, despite its imbrication in the national archive and its apparently deadened meaning in kitsch.

In his book *The Imperial Archive*, Thomas Richards analyses how the impulse to catalogue, collect and place the data and signs of the material world in the sanctity of the archive winds and then unwinds itself through the colonial and postcolonial. Towards the end of his book Richards, discussing Thomas Pynchon's *Gravity's Rainbow*, summarises a phenomenon which might help us to liberate the potential of the anomalous round tower on College Green:

Positive knowledge recedes back into myth and religion. The superintend-ing states no longer even care what knowledge is, so long as they have it. The state is neutral about knowledge so long as knowledge belongs to the state ... The museum is no longer the privileged archive of culture; the archive, the sum total of what can or cannot be said or done, has become the very form of the modern state.[49]

At a moment of complacency, then, there is the possibility that the state assumes its success as 'superintendent' and that, in its Andersonian coevality with its marmorealised culture, the distinction between the moment of now and the sign of 'myth' is effaced. It is surely also possible to argue that such an unwariness on the part of the state is the very point at which the sign which seems to signify the nation can in fact, to return to Derrida's definition of the supplement used earlier, be a moment of 'doubling' which 'supplants' the originality of the signified. In this the 'mythic' sign is lost to the system which it is confidently assumed to be part of. Like Mitchel's 'Ireland' it connotes the solid entity while proclaiming its detachment, and its 'utopianism' is most clearly found in its resonance with the deferred future 'state' of the nation. When the nation has become the state (while still in partial abeyance), then the situation has to some extent altered, so that the 'floating' sign seems a lonelier and less likely entity. In the midst of the cohering process of the internationalism of the nation and the saturation of the space of the nation by a self-conscious avowal of modernity, the sign of myth has its fixture assumed in the established archive, which is now 'neutral', no longer 'privileged'. The round tower in College Green is the point at which the synchronic public address system of the nation has 'a pronounced time lag' reintroduced into it; the mythic erupts into the urban, the archive spills over meaninglessly out of the library, and above all the physical sign of this difference is, to return to David Harvey, a pure ephemerality in a time when 'instantaneous communicability over space' is desired. The tower is a temporary sign of permanence, an escapee from the nation's sign system, a reminder of past visions of the future at a time when the future is toyed with as already here in the modern present. Given this status, the tower arguably exists when the utopian trait discussed earlier is at its lowest ebb, when present and future are being collapsed into each other; yet we might see, in the tower's oddness, the space within the system of significa-tion in which the utopian, the alternative and the unfixable are both real (the picture of the tower in the *Pictorial Record* shows it above all to be an obstacle) and passingly marginal. The tower is a sign which retains, somewhere in the constricting new consensus, the 'looming, floating' vision of John Mitchel's 'dreams and memories', but in this case achieves that through commodification piled on commodification, emerging out the other side of kitsch as the unsellable and the impractical. To redeploy Saussure, the tower is a reminder that a system attempting to fix its synchronic meaning instigates its own disappointment: 'Whoever creates a language con-trols it only so long as it is not in circulation'.[50] Despite the 'control' which seems, theoretically and in terms of cultural history, to be the *raison d'être* of the unisonant moment of the nation at the time of the Eucharistic Congress, the 'circulation' of the sign of the tower, placed centrally yet 'out of joint' in the capital, is its circulation beyond control.

UTOPIA AND MODERNISATION

The Utopian value of a merely cultural modification is an ambiguous judgment, whose signs and symptoms can be read either way – fully as much as signs of systematic replication as of impending change.[51]

Fredric Jameson, in his continual scepticism about the condition of postmodernity, places the utopian impulse in postmodern culture at exactly the undecideable juncture between political meaning and self-reflexive, apolitically tending irony which might characterise the comparison just made between the Abbey men and the tower in College Green in their different relationships to the Ireland which asserts itself in 1932. Joep Leerssen's view of kitsch, if projected forward to the tower in 1932, would tend to see it simply as a larger version of the kitsch of the late nineteenth century, differentiated only by the fact of being a traffic hazard rather than a bibliophilic decoration. 'Systematic replication' is, in essence, too easily a self-contained phenomenon for the liking of various cultural critics, and Jameson himself sees such replication as systematic and empty, rather than being entirely convinced about the power of critique which resides in identifying a system which is being imitated ironically from inside itself.[52] Examining the utopian trope within concepts of Ireland, even as sketchily as is necessary in this chapter, allows for the examination of the outer reaches of this kind of debate (which can be figured in contemporary terms in a postcolonial/postmodern/post-nationalist choice). Utopia's need for visionary, extrasystemic epistemologies entwines the politics of nationalism and socialism, in whatever relationship, with the fetishisation of the 'modern' which began to emerge in the previous section. In this it problematises the concept of the 'modern' in relation to Ireland – and while it may seem self-reflexive and self-serving to site the critical voice in the midst of this problematic, the fundamental question for an analysis of the utopian and the modernising in relation to Ireland is how the voice which undertakes that analysis positions itself, both temporally and in its valorising language, in relation to the 'progress' it attempts to describe, decry or be thankful for.

The blunt polarities of these arguments are summarised in Conor McCarthy's recent book, which in its very title links modernisation and 'crisis':

Modernisation, in terms of modernisation theory, has been understood as standing in opposition to tradition, or effecting a radical break with it. In Ireland, the chief repository of tradition has come to be seen as the discourse of the *nation*, and the political movement known as *nationalism*.[53]

McCarthy goes on to argue, through Benedict Anderson's familiar dicta, that modernisation and the idea of the nation to some extent emerge together (for example, through the increasing simultaneity offered by print culture in general and newspapers in particular), and this in turn becomes a saving grace of nationalism; McCarthy argues that slighting nationalism by accusations of atavism, nostalgia and racism misses the note of 'hope and coherence' which the idea of the nation maintains. Of course, restoring 'to a subject or community its own potentiality'[54] may be one way of seeing the role of the nation, but it also immediately reintroduces the split-self (or split-community) model of modernity which nationalism supposedly evolves in tandem with – an inevitable result of the turn from the past and its atavism, and the future and its utopian pledge. The problem then is to figure Irish modernity in any positive kind of way: if modernity is under-stood as fragmentary and the nation as a futurology of the coherent, and the two have the same point of origin, then there is a somewhat desperate divergence which begins at that very point of origin and cannot therefore offer a previously existent form of its own future. Meanwhile the advance of capitalism through the modern period would seem to reduce the potency of the nation's claims to sover-eignty of all kinds, so that the nation's potential for self-realisation looks like an increasingly resistant, revolutionary hope(lessness) in the face of globalising capital. Alberto Melucci talks of the effects on concepts of ethnicity which are '[thrown] into the great machine of mass culture':

The multiplication of contacts and the constant flow of messages destroys the homogeneity of the individual cultures: the media transmits standardized models, while migration and mass tourism encourage the extinction of cultural practices bound up with specific territorial or social circumstances.[55]

And this view of the fate of identity is often shared in Irish cultural debate, epitomised since the beginning of the twentieth century by Douglas Hyde's advice that Irish households 'should have a copy of Moore and Davis' to counteract 'penny dreadfuls, shilling shockers, and still more, the garbage of vulgar English weeklies'.[56] Seamus Deane usefully ties the poverty of nationalism's future vision to its saturation by capitalism:

Once nationalism, although only partially triumphant, was faced with the future, it became little more than a species of accommodation to prevailing economic (predominantly British) forces. Its separation from socialism left it ideologically invertebrate.[57]

Deane leaves ajar the door of the future by seguing economic forces into British forces, and by his appeal to socialism's utopian alternative as the missing piece in a lost strategy. In a similar vein Luke Gibbons, responding to John Wilson Foster's assertion that the 'bourgeois humanist fantasy' is something that 'many of us in Ireland would like to enjoy . . . thank you very much', writes:

The fact that the modernization project has lost its way in Ireland is clear to all who are willing to disengage themselves from fantasy, 'bourgeois humanist' or otherwise.[58]

In the understandable heat of his response Gibbons perhaps glosses over the key dependency which both Irish and capitalist modernising projects have on 'fantasy', not only in turning cultural production into an increasingly fantastic form of science fiction in which human-ism becomes so obviously (to the radical critic) a delusion. In his essay 'Coming Out of Hibernation?', Gibbons presses firmly on that choice for the critical voice discussed above when he asserts 'that an industrial revolution in an electronic age need no longer be encumbered by a vision of social progress' and that '[if] there is any convergence between European nations in the run up to 1992, it is at the level of regressive social policies'.[59] This pre-Celtic Tiger assess-ment need not be measured against the movements of social policies in the two states on the island since its publication; what is more important for my purposes is the way in which Gibbons' critique alternates its teleological tropes with its object of study. 'Revolution' does not bring 'progress', 'convergence' is 'regressive' – Gibbons, like Deane, sets the social (and socialist) alongside the nation and its capitalist self-image, and so both critics have contradiction and the identification of hypocrisy as their best critical tools, heroically attempting to point to lacks in the ideology of progress while progress adapts to the future. This is not to deny the necessity of such critiques, nor their moral value. But it is to say that, in accepting the view that the economic base is inexorably and methodically progressive, these critical alternatives accept the grounds of their defeat before they begin.

There are ways of seeing the modernity of the nation which rely less on an absolute opposition between the social and capital (and which may at times be useful given the hegemony's ability to account for an argument before it is stated).[60] As Jameson reluctantly suggests, the signs of the future in postmodernism are interpretable 'fully as much as signs of systematic replication as of impending change' and by inserting the critical voice into the space of this ambiguity *between* the future and the dead simulacra of the present, it may be possible to see the ways in which the future becomes imagined and how that is necessarily part of the endless replication of the present, itself a kind of symptom of panic over the future.

To exemplify this kind of approach, we can look briefly at an Irish socialist future vision. In 1831, at Ralahine in County Clare, there *was* 'An Irish Utopia', at least according to James Connolly.[61] The Ralahine commune, or 'colony' as Diarmuid O Cobhthaigh described it,[62] was set up on the land of John Scott Vandeleur; Vandeleur had apparently heard Robert Owen in Dublin preaching his gospel of cooperative societies and, according to different accounts, he had either been converted to Owenite socialism or spotted a business opportunity and a way to quell the agrarian Terry Alt disturbances which threatened his landlord livelihood. The commune was organised by an Englishman, Edward Thomas Craig, who had experience of putting Owen's ideas into practice yet possessed a keen sense of the fragile nature of the utopianism involved in transferring the idea to Ireland:

My family was strongly opposed to the undertaking, and the possible sacrifice of future interest in a legacy was intimated. I was not swayed by any consideration as to the loss of the prospective legacy, nor did I appreciate the objections urged on account of the plan being impracticable, Utopian, and absurd, because it implied a rash, perverse, and obstinate spirit, instead of a calm and deliberate investigation of the conditions necessary to success. I fully appreciated the difficulties, and I had confidence that, with prudence and perserverance, these might be overcome.[63]

An earlier version of Matthew Arnold's Celt/Saxon dichotomy shadows Craig's account, and reminds us of the flaws always written into the Ralahine project. As Connolly points out, 'Mr Craig knew no Irish, and the people of Ralahine, as a rule, knew no English'. (Craig's distance from the Irishness of the commune members is notable in the way in which he objectifies Irish conditions in his narrative; however, his sense of dedicated comradeship never diminishes with hindsight.)[64] Added to these national tensions was the fact that Vandeleur retained ownership of the land on which the commune was settled and in this arrangement lay the end for Ralahine's ability to act as a fully functioning example which 'might have helped to make Ireland a paradise of peace'.[65] Just as the commune had become fully established, Vandeleur's gambling tendencies led him to bankruptcy and flight from Ireland, and the commune collapsed.

Ralahine then is bound to be seen, retrospectively, as a lost utopia. For AE, speaking from the perspective of the early twentieth-century cooperative movement, Vandeleur gambled away 'what may well have been a happier destiny for his country'.[66] For Connolly, the Owenite utopia of Ralahine preceded 'A Chapter of Horrors', but remains 'an

Irish point of interrogation erected amidst the wilderness of capitalist thought and feudal practice, challenging both in vain for an answer'.[67] Ralahine, for these strands of Irish socialism, is the glimmer of a non-modern utopian state which was also distinctly Irish; Ralahine, in other words, seemed to imply that rural and urban splits could be healed, while the future need not be slavishly modelled on either industrialisation or the old order. Leaving Ralahine, Craig finds himself describing the unravelling of a utopian landscape on which the history of sectarianism and British misrule inscribes itself as he passes through it:

Every prominent object seemed to awaken mingled feelings of pleasure, sadness, and regret. The old Castle, with its lofty grey tower, its massive archway, and its wild rocky surroundings, recalled scenes that had been enacted within its blind, windowless walls, from the days of its Milesian chiefs, the tribal septs, and Tanistry, when the bards sang the praises of their princes and the right of people to the land of their birth, in contrast with the brutal inroads of the grasping and bloody Normans, with their hard, cold, crushing exclusiveness and despotism, ending in the Union . . . and its crop of poisonous vipers! Ralahine had shown that it was possible to give peace to Ireland without force, by making the people agents in their own elevation out of poverty and discontent.[68]

In discussing Connolly's sense of national tradition and its place in his socialist project, Gregory Dobbins notes that Connolly tended to see past moments of 'primitive communism' as having a 'radical valency . . . [which] can be found within the specificity of that social order rather than the possibility that it could be recreated'.[69] Ralahine's 'utopian' existence, already disappearing into the fractious past as Craig departs, is a fine example of how this 'valency' functions in Connolly's thought; Ralahine is not a dead past but, to use Connolly's own term, works as an 'interrogation' of the forces of capitalism and feudalism, and hence of Irish hegemonic teleology. Connolly, in refusing to mourn Ralahine or to recreate it, leaves it to ask its own questions and undertake its own form of 'interrogation' in a way which allows the very notion of 'An Irish Utopia' to be interrogated also.

Connolly's Ralahine is then a kind of non-place in the history of Irish utopianism. It was a utopia, or rather would have been, Connolly suggests, if left to mature – now it stands as testimony to the potential of utopianism and a reminder of the ills of landlordism. For Connolly Ralahine *was* a utopia, but proves only that utopias are possible. Following Engels' warning about the dangers of socialist utopias, Connolly seems to have agreed that 'the more completely they were worked out in detail, the more they could not avoid drifting off into phantasies'.[70]

'THE IRISH COLONIES FROM ATLANTIS'

At http://www.stanford.edu/~meehan/donnelly/ Richard L. Meehan puts together an examination of apocalypse which covers everything from *Gilgamesh* to present-day 'diseases such as AIDS, instability of global markets, floods and other signs of climate deterioration, geophysical chaos'. You can also visit Jennifer Lee's Honor thesis analysis of the site which suggests that its non-linear structure reflects the nature of reading the web as media event (and presumably the deterioration of certainty which Meehan is obsessed with). Meehan's site is called 'Ignatius Donnelly and the End of the World', and its relation to Irish utopias is twisted, strange and fascinating.

Ignatius Donnelly was a second generation Irish-American, born in Philadelphia in 1831. Donnelly was a lawyer, politician and writer. At various points in his life he was governor of Minnesota and a Senator. Donnelly is sometimes remembered as a populariser of the theory that Bacon wrote Shakespeare's plays; his *The Great Cryptogram* (1887) showed in a painstaking way how Bacon encrypted his name throughout Shakespeare's *oeuvre* – Donnelly's later *The Cipher in the Plays and on the Tombstone* (1899) 'proved' Bacon to be author of the plays of Marlowe, Jonson and *The Pilgrim's Progress*.[71] Donnelly also wrote *Caesar's Column*, a futuristic novel set in late twentieth-century New York, but his relevance for present purposes lies in his 1882 book, *Atlantis: The Antediluvian World*.

Atlantis is in one sense the world of antiquarian research in the nineteenth century gone into freefall, described by its most recent editor as an 'unwitting act of fiction . . . a prolonged poetic trope'.[72] Donnelly's argument is disarmingly simple, and begins with Plato's dialogue with Critias in which Atlantis is described – Donnelly takes Plato at his word and Atlantis as fact. Using archaeological and anthropological evidence as his basis, Donnelly sets out to prove that the sinking of an entire civilisation is geophysically possible and that the culture of the Western world (and beyond) points to the plain fact that 'all the converging lines of civilization lead back to Atlantis'.[73] *Atlantis* has maps of the lost civilisation and its current position in (that is, under) the Atlantic Ocean; it reconstructs this lost paradise and fount of culture. Donnelly's method is typified by his incredulity that any sane person could look at the Egyptian pyramids and the

Peruvian pyramids and not deduce that somewhere between these two must be a place from which the idea sprang and from which it was exported. In this, Donnelly's imagination can be seen to use evidence in a very particular way; he says at one point that, before evolutionary theories, science tended to think of fossils as 'simply a way nature had of working out extraordinary coincidences in a kind of joke'.[74] Donnelly takes every living and dead piece of evidence seriously, so that all signs are real signs, and all signs point back to some unitary origin – Donnelly's method is to then find a singular coherence which can be traced back through a process of migration and dispersal, and this is crucial to seeing the significance of his bizarre book in terms of an Irish utopian imagination.

Ireland figures in *Atlantis* in a variety of ways, and as Donnelly says:

We would naturally expect, in view of the geographical position of the country, to find Ireland colonized at an early day by the overflowing population of Atlantis.[75]

Ireland's geographical place returns at the end of this chapter ('The Irish Colonies from Atlantis') in Donnelly's *Atlantis*. Preceding that, and throughout the book, Donnelly suggests that Irish material culture is replete with signs which connect with the common Atlantean root and its parallel signs throughout the world. Ireland has its own pyramids, for example, 'flattened on the top',[76] while the debate about Irish round towers is resurrected in a newly comparative form ('We find similar structures in America, Sardinia, and India'[77]). Other evidence is linguistic, geological (including evidence of recent volcanic eruption), fossilised (the great Irish elk) and cultural (down to Irish customs of playing jacks and saying 'God bless you!' when someone sneezes).

Donnelly's thesis is very obviously, in scientific terms, that of a crank, but it is also explicable through the accumulated tropes which this chapter has investigated. At the end of his analysis of how Ireland was 'drawn from the storehouse of Atlantis',[78] Donnelly turns to the voyage of the sixth-century Saint Brendan and his mythologised attempts to find, according to one's preference, the mystical land of Tir na nOg, or the Americas. Naturally, in Donnelly's scheme, Brendan was in fact 'guided' by 'the traditions of Atlantis among a people whose ancestors had been derived directly or at second-hand from that country'.[79] Brendan's voyaging was symbolically that of an Irishman in search of his lost Atlantean origins. Ireland is not now the land of origin itself, but a placed colonised by its inhabitants, and a place which must accept that those living on it have migration as their chief cultural and racial characteristic. Brendan is then almost a psychic preparation for Donnelly's last word on Ireland, which he hands over to his daughter, Miss Eleanor C. Donnelly and her poem 'The Sleeper's Sail'. In the poem, a 'starving boy dreams of the pleasant and plentiful land', uncannily echoing John Mitchel's Atlantic vision of Ireland. In this section of the poem, the boy tells his mother what he saw in his dream:

> 'And then I saw, the fairy city,
>   Far away o'er the waters deep;
> Towers and castles and chapels glowing,
>   Like bléssed dreams that we see in sleep.'

> 'What is its name?' 'Be still, *acushla*
>   (Thy hair is wet with the mists, my boy);
> Thou hast looked perchance on the Tir-no-n'oge,
>   Land of eternal youth and joy!'[80]

Donnelly's comment is rapturous and predictable:

This is the Greek story of Elysion; these are the Elysian Fields of the Egyptians; these are the Gardens of the Hesperides; this is the region in the West to which the peasant of Brittany looks from the shores of Cape Raz; this is Atlantis.[81]

From inside her genetic folk memory, Ignatius Donnelly sees Eleanor Donnelly summon a dream vision of the Irish dream country, poeticised through a third generation Irish emigrant's voice. And Donnelly's response is to universalise this 'evidence' like all else in his book. This Mitchel-like view back across the Atlantic brings Ireland into sight through its own myths, but Donnelly's impulse and interpretation moves a stage further than Mitchel's and, for all its eccentricity, it is a process intended to normalise the position of Eleanor Donnelly and Ignatius Donnelly himself. Donnelly's Ireland has ceased to be special and ceased to be the only possible, genealogical point of solid return. Instead, in the middle of the Atlantic, there is a now invisible place from which America and Ireland have a common root; by 'proving' the existence of Atlantis, Donnelly has turned the experience of emigration from one of isolated disjunction from a 'settled' place, to the only and universal global experience, including the Irish experience in no special way. So Tir na nOg is not exclusive, it is simply one among many metaphoric declensions of Atlantis. Ignatius Donnelly has a utopian drive which is complicated because the emptiness at the heart of his evidence is not the absent island of Atlantis but the unfulfillable desire to make the past converge on the present just as the present converges in the Atlantean past. Not surprisingly, his solution is to look forward to the future, to science[82] and to the museumification of Atlantis itself:

We are on the threshold. Scientific invesitigation is advancing with giant strides. Who shall say that one hundred years from now the great museums of the world may not be adorned with gems, statues, arms, and implements from Atlantis.[83]

For all its strangeness, *Atlantis* is in tune with, and to some extent running ahead of, the 'Ireland' discussed throughout this chapter. Atlantis ultimately escapes Donnelly's capacity to describe the sign systems which it enables (hence the need for a future museum). Global material culture is everywhere Atlantean, yet Atlantis is nowhere, no place. 'Ireland' floats (again) as part of this sign system, but is only a 'second order' sign, a mythology, signifying the absent transcendent which all culture signifies, 'that is Atlantis'. So 'Ireland' progresses from Mitchel's transcendent vision of it, which detaches the concept from the land but which retains a future hope by keeping in view, in Derrida's evocatively geographical phrase, 'the horizons of potential presence';[84] Donnelly's Ireland is not even able to retain the future promise of an Irish presence, since it is 'deconstructed' 'in its totality', by '*making* it *insecure* in its most assured evidences'[85] and by calling attention to the very temporality of the sign – Ireland as sign can never be decisively synchronic (as at the Eucharistic Congress) or diachronic (as in the teleological impulse of the nation story). Donnelly's 'Ireland' draws attention to the 'linearist concept of time [which] is ... one of the deepest adherences of the modern concept of the sign' and which leads to the inevitable evocation of a *res*, 'an entity created or at any rate first thought and spoken, thinkable and speakable, in the eternal present of the divine logos'.[86] Donnelly's madness is to name the logos and call it Atlantis – but in doing so he finds the faultlines in the idea of 'Ireland', in its past and future linearities, and in its equivocal synchronicity.

To put it simply, Donnelly's Irish-American view of Ireland makes emigration normal, makes 'Ireland' a migrating entity, and disallows the possibility of Irish culture helping the idea of Ireland secure itself to itself. It may be at the edges of logic, and at the margins of the logocentrism of nationalism, but Donnelly's Atlantis is an overblown exemplification of the dislocations of Irishness throughout its history. In its 'excess' of logic, its 'phantasms' of 'scientific' evidence and its vision of an Ireland which is not Ireland but a remnant of Atlantis, Donnelly's Ireland is the apotheosis of the utopianism which this chapter has discussed – Ireland is everywhere and nowhere, 'broken in pieces',[87] enveloped in a story in which its particularity and there-fore its definition will never be resolved. And if you go to Richard L. Meehan's website you will find that, despite the media, he cannot replicate Donnelly's Ireland. Chapter III of his web-book, '*Geraldis Cambrensis*: The Nature of the Westerly Regions', is narrated by 'Donnelly', who has returned to visit the late twentieth century. 'Donnelly' suggests that the Ireland of Gerald's days, with all its unlikely wonders, is like the California of today. And while Meehan is able to allow Donnelly to point out that 'The Irish[,] like the Jews and the Armenians and certain Asiatic peoples, consider themselves as exiles', Meehan's comparativism can never recapture the complex radicalism of what Donnelly's Ireland meant to his Atlantean scheme, or, more importantly, the way in which Donnelly's Atlantean scheme sits as a final dispersal of the signs of 'Ireland', deconstructing their linearity, dispersing the space they seem to signify.[88]

IRELANTIS

Following Althusserian thought, Jameson says of the postmodern that its utopianism 'can be seen . . . not so much as the production of some form of Utopian space but rather as the production of the *concept* of such space'.[89] The introduction of such metaspace into a metanarrative in Irish culture, means that 'Ireland' becomes emptied of Ireland, and Irish signs have a multiple 'valency' which effects an unsettling form of liberation from the object or *res*. Donnelly's Atlantis is a Utopian space which cannot be produced, except through con-tinually conceptualising its own metaspace, and so his 'Ireland' is a Tir na nOg which is fated never to return and never to be arrived at. Baudrillard describes this theoretical position thus:

Only affiliation to the model makes sense, and nothing flows any longer according to its end, but proceeds from the model, the 'signifier of reference', which is a kind of anterior finality and the only resemblance there is.[90]

The delay which is structural to utopian time is the flipside of 'anterior finality' and is thus always a reminder of the anteriority of the present moment. Added to this the utopian imperative leads to the consideration of a metaspace which questions boundaries, both geographic and epistemological. The effects of this utopian projection through the screen of 'Ireland' can be seen in all the texts discussed in this chapter: Tennyson's Ireland 'floats' and explodes, but he knows that it frustrates his destructive desires, and that frustrates him all the more; Mitchel's Ireland is exiled, a condition which means it must defy physics to be 'real' and then only achieves the status of the shadow of a presence; the round tower at the Eucharistic Congress is a form of pastiche and fakery, but its urban and historical position functions in such a way that its disjunctive anteriority can be said to remind the modern nation of its archaism, inserting teleology back into synchronicity and a kind of empty signifier into an attempted cogency which realises utopia now; James Connolly's version of the Ralahine commune implicitly recognises some of these traits, and his chapter title, 'An Irish Utopia', carries a deadpan irony which speaks of a refusal to allow Ralahine to dictate the future in its socio-economic detail, though it does cautiously preserve the idea of an 'Irish utopia' for the future. Donnelly's Ireland, I would suggest, is exemplary of the culminatory effects of all these possibilities, in which 'anterior finality', taken as a reverse utopianism, means that Ireland becomes subtended to the more powerful need for 'affiliation to the model' when all signifiers are 'of reference'. Donnelly's Ireland, like everything else in his book, is in danger of sinking into the sea in pursuit of Atlantis.

The 'Ireland' emerging in this chapter is made up of a variety of signifying possibilities: the anachronistic sign, the overinterpreted sign, the repletion of signs, the ironic sign; the sign made meaningful by its place in a pastiche; the sign, above all, which promises to mean fully, not now, but at some future date. At the meeting point of the particular, ambiguous colonial circumstances of Ireland and Irishness (the 'liminal space' discussed in Chapter 4) the teleological anti-colonialism of Irish nationalism is cross-hatched with an archaism and a western modernising drive, and one 'result' is the deferred utopianism which this chapter has sought to outline. This utopianism finds itself accommodating modernisation, industrialism, the mystical, the visionary, the exilic and the frankly lunatic, never committing itself to any, but always offering to redefine its space and its time for each. It is this capacity, to outstrip all that it contains, which makes Ireland enthralling as concept and as object of study.

In 1999 the artist Seán Hillen published a book of 'paper collages' entitled *Irelantis*.[91] The first image in the book is 'The Great Pyramids of Carlingford Lough', in which a John Hinde postcard landscape is surveyed by a man in a typically garish red jumper (Figure 2). The vista of 'Carlingford', which Hillen points out in his commentary 'neatly marks the border between the North and the Republic of Ireland',[92] is interrupted by three pyramids from Giza and on the horizon the world rises up (or continues to set) over the sea. This landscape is a new, conglomerated version of Donnelly's Atlantean Ireland, with the anteriority of the sign abandoned and anachronism celebrated, 'a kind of a joke'. Each of Hillen's images undoes space and time so that 'Irelantis' exists outside synchronicity and diachronicity, but remembers both. Whether 'Irelantis' is future or past is unclear, since it is sometimes archaically Edenic ('The Colosseum of Cork') and at others apocalyptic (as with 'The Great

FIGURE 2 'The Great Pyramids of Carlingford Lough', from Seán Hillen, *Irelantis* (Dublin: Irelantis, 1999). http://www.irelantis.com

Cliffs of Collage Green' and the two images which envisage the 'Great Eruption' in the Dublin mountains).

Hillen's work in *Irelantis* is described by Fintan O'Toole:

Irelantis is, of course, contemporary, globalised Ireland, a society that became postmodern before it ever quite managed to be modern, a cultural space that has gone, in the blink of an eye, from being defiantly closed to being completely porous to whatever dream is floating out there in the media ether. But this Ireland is also everywhere and nowhere. Hillen is dealing with displacement in a world where all borders – political, cultural and psychological – are permeable.[93]

This reading of *Irelantis* is indisputable in its identification of the 'everywhere and nowhere' nature of the work and its open permeability. But *Irelantis* is not necessarily proof of the course of Ireland's late entry to the race for postmodernisation. Given the texts examined above, we might wish to be less surprised by *Irelantis* and see it instead as a manifestation, in contemporary and ironic nuance, of the 'dreams' which have been 'floating out there' since and well before John Mitchel or Ignatius Donnelly. *Irelantis* has a knowing irony and an artistic agency that might separate it from the 'hyperreal'[94] world of John Hinde's postcards. But even Hinde's work, sometimes seen as the static equivalent of *Man of Aran* in its vain construction of an Ireland that never existed, gives us, as Luke Gibbons suggests, 'an uneasy feeling that we are getting a last glimpse of a world that is lost'.[95] The hint of the end-of-the-world in Hinde becomes a recorded scream in Hillen, but again anteriority and its alternate futurology are the taut edges of the images, and we should be wary of explaining the differences between the two only in terms of the progress of western modernity – that progress, after all, is what they both set themselves at a not entirely oppositional angle to. If Ireland can be a 'lost world' and an Atlantis, its status is not simply in the past but in a startlingly radical sense 'everywhere and nowhere'.

Writing on 'late capitalism' and its effects on the idea of the nation-state, the sociologist Robert J. Holton suggests that 'the nation-state cannot be regarded as being in decline or overrun by globalization . . . because global capital is mostly not of an anarchic variety and still requires state functions to be performed'.[96] This potentially non-allergic relationship between nation, statehood and capital points back to Benedict Anderson's *Imagined Communities* and its idea that the nation and the development of capitalism, in its various stages, twin the concepts of fragmentation now and coherence in the future as only-possible-illness and only-possible-medication. If global capital creates the cultural effects of modernisation but functionally needs the nation-state as part of its mechanism, then the symbiosis between the two is less anomalous, and the accommodation of the new technologies within the Celtic Tiger economy, for example, less of a surprise. But it is also the case that the divergence of the social and of capital does not create a settled future, either in national terms or in how the cultural image itself can be commodified. Dwayne Winseck has shown how the regulatory attempts of world bodies such as NAFTA and the World Trade Organisation to account for the flow of information in the electronic age have left ambiguities and contradictions which 'help explain the shifting balance between the use of communication policy as a means of social policy during one era, while concerns with realizing the economic value of communication predominate in another'.[97] Without entering the socio-politics of this debate, it is clear that in criticism (and perhaps particularly in Irish criticism) the nation and the postmodern are too often played out against each other, as insular atavism battling with the 'multi-', a sincere nostalgia blinkering itself to ironic pastiche. The interaction of nostalgia and future visions in a 'crise pléthorique' may not be a symptom of an Irish obsession with history. More likely it is evidence that, as Declan Kiberd argues, 'the Irish are futurologists of necessity'.[98] As this chapter has tried to show, not only does 'Ireland' cast itself into the future in order to be realised; it also turns inside-out the underlying need for the future, disarming the crisis of what the future might be by forcing it to exist in a 'plethora' of cultural images.

Notes

1. Ignatius Donnelly, *Atlantis: The Antediluvian World* (New York: Dover, 1976 [1882]), p. 43.
2. Quoted in William Allingham, *William Allingham's Diary*, intro. Geoffrey Grigson (London: Centaur, 1967), p. 293.
3. Quoted in Allingham, *William Allingham's Diary*, p. 297.
4. Quoted in Allingham, *William Allingham's Diary*, p. 298.
5. See the discussion of 'Phantasmal France' and 'Unreal Ireland', in Seamus Deane, *Strange Country: Modernity and Nationhood in Irish Writing Since 1790* (Oxford: Clarendon, 1997), pp. 1–48.
6. John Mitchel, *Jail Journal* (Dublin: M. & H. Gill, 1918), p. 34.
7. Jean Baudrillard, *Revenge of the Crystal: Selected Writings on the Modern Object and its Destiny, 1968–1983*, eds and trans. Paul Foss and Julian Pefanis (London: Pluto, 1990), p. 75.
8. Mitchel, *Jail Journal*, p. 35.

9. Frederick Engels, *Socialism: Utopian and Scientific*, trans. Edward Aveling (London: George Allen & Unwin, 1936), p. 65.
10. Mitchel, *Jail Journal*, p. 36.
11. Fintan O'Toole, *The Lie of the Land: Irish Identities* (Dublin: New Island, 1998), p. 2.
12. David Harvey, *The Condition of Postmodernity: An Enquiry into the Origins of Cultural Change* (Oxford: Blackwell, 1991), p. 288.
13. Mitchel, *Jail Journal*, p. 65.
14. For a reading of the 'absurd' geometry which the *Jail Journal* is capable of see Christopher Morash, 'The Rhetoric of Right in Mitchel's *Jail Journal*' in Joep Leerssen, A. H. van der Weel and Bart Westerweld (eds), *Forging in the Smithy: National Identity and Representation in Anglo-Irish Literary History* (Amsterdam: Rodopi, 1995), pp. 207–18.
15. Mitchel, *Jail Journal*, p. 65.
16. Mitchel, *Jail Journal*, p. 65.
17. Mitchel, *Jail Journal*, p. 65.
18. Jacques Derrida, *Spectres of Marx: The State of Debt, the Work of Mourning & the New International*, trans. by Peggy Kamuf, intro. Bernd Magnus and Stephen Cullenberg (London: Routledge, 1994), p. 47.
19. Ferdinand de Saussure, *Course in General Linguistics*, intro. Jonathan Culler (London: Fontana/Collins, 1978), p. 66.
20. Hubert Butler, 'Am I an Irish Republican?', in *In the Land of Nod* (Dublin: Lilliput, 1996), pp. 55–6.
21. Jacques Derrida, *Of Grammatology*, trans. Gayatri Chakravorty Spivak (London: Johns Hopkins University Press, 1976), p. 270.
22. See Derrida, *Of Grammatology*, pp. 280–1.
23. Harvey, *The Condition of Postmodernity*, p. 287.
24. Derrida from *Positions*, quoted in and translated by Chistopher Butler, *Interpretation, Deconstruction and Ideology* (Oxford: Clarendon, 1984), p. 62.
25. Saussure, *Course in General Linguistics*, p. 76.
26. Saussure, *Course in General Linguistics*, p. 76.
27. Cited in George Kateb, *Utopia and its Enemies* (New York: Schoken, 1972), p. 11.
28. The 'homogeneous empty time' concept as borrowed from Walter Benjamin by Benedict Anderson, and Anderson's belief that nationalism turns 'chance into destiny' in Anderson's *Imagined Communities: Reflections on the Origin and Spread of Nationalism*, revised edition (London: Verso, 1992), pp. 26 and 12.
29. Homi K. Bhabha, 'DissemiNation', in *Nation and Narration*, ed. Homi K. Bhabha (London: Routledge, 1990), pp. 310 and 311.
30. Seán Ó Faoláin, *The Irish* (Harmondsworth: Penguin, 1980 [1947]), pp. 9 and 169.
31. George Kateb, *Utopia and Its Enemies*, p. vi.
32. *Thirty First International Eucharistic Congress, Dublin 1932: Pictorial Record* (Dublin: Veritas, n.d.), p. 154.
33. See the entry on the Eucharistic Congress in S. J. Connolly (ed.), *The Oxford Companion to Irish History* (Oxford: Oxford University Press, 1999).
34. Terence Brown, *Ireland: A Social and Cultural History, 1922–1985* (London: Fontana, 1985), p. 39.

35. Declan Kiberd, *Inventing Ireland: The Literature of the Modern Nation* (London: Jonathan Cape, 1995), p. 360.
36. *Saorstát Eireann Official Handbook* (Dublin: Talbot, 1932), p. 169.
37. *Thirty First International Eucharistic Congress, Dublin 1932: Pictorial Record*, p. 165. Other accounts, however, suggest that all may not have been as technically perfect as the propaganda suggests. At the Papal High Mass the tenor John McCormack (by this time Count John McCormack) sang Franck's 'Panis Angelicus'. Gordon T. Ledbetter, writing on McCormack's performance on this occasion (which was filmed), notes 'the confusion caused by the lapse of the voice as it was broadcast through the local loudspeakers': Gordon T. Ledbetter, *The Great Irish Tenor* (London: Duckworth, 1977), p. 133. Typically, no such disharmony is recalled in Lily McCormack's *I Hear You Calling Me* (London: W. H. Allen, 1951), pp. 184–5.
38. Anderson, *Imagined Communities*, p. 145.
39. *Thirty First International Eucharistic Congress, Dublin 1932: Pictorial Record*, p. 165
40. This phrase from Mark Maguire, 'The Space of the Nation: History, Culture and a Conflict in Modern Ireland', *Irish Studies Review*, 6:2 (1998), 111.
41. Maguire, 'The Space of the Nation: History, Culture and a Conflict in Modern Ireland', 110.
42. Maguire, 'The Space of the Nation: History, Culture and a Conflict in Modern Ireland', 114.
43. Frantz Fanon, *The Wretched of the Earth* (Harmondsworth: Penguin, 1990), p. 165.
44. On the 'non-modern' as a characteristic feature of Irish subalternity see David Lloyd, *Ireland After History* (Cork: Cork University Press/Field Day, 1999).
45. Joep Leerssen, *Remembrance and Imagination: Patterns in the Historical and Literary Representation of Ireland in the Nineteenth Century* (Cork: Cork University Press/Field Day, 1996), p. 140.
46. Baudrillard, *Revenge of the Crystal*, p. 75.
47. Michel Foucault, from *Of Other Spaces*, quoted in Maguire, 'The Space of the Nation: History, Culture and a Conflict in Modern Ireland', 117.
48. Derrida, *Spectres of Marx*, p. 48.
49. Thomas Richards, *The Imperial Archive: Knowledge and the Fantasy of Empire* (London: Verso, 1993), p. 152.
50. Saussure, *Course in General Linguistics*, p. 76.
51. Fredric Jameson, *Postmodernism; or, the Cultural Logic of Late Capitalism* (London: Verso, 1993), p. 163.
52. In the context of postmodern utopianism Jameson discusses spatialization through installation art. His comparison of Hans Haacke and Robert Gober is instructive here. Fredric Jameson, *Postmodernism*, pp. 161–80.
53. Conor McCarthy, *Modernisation, Crisis and Culture in Ireland, 1969–1992* (Dublin: Four Courts, 2000), p. 15. Emphasis in original.
54. McCarthy, *Modernisation, Crisis and Culture in Ireland, 1969–1992*, p. 17.
55. Alberto Melucci, 'The Post-Modern Revival of Ethnicity', in John Hutchinson and Anthony D. Smith (eds), *Ethnicity* (Oxford: Oxford University Press, 1996), p. 367.
56. Douglas Hyde, from 'The Necessity for De-Anglicising Ireland', in Mark Storey (ed.), *Poetry and Ireland Since 1800: A Source Book* (London:

Routledge, 1988), p. 82.

57. Seamus Deane, *Celtic Revivals: Essays in Modern Irish Literature* (Winston-Salem, NC: Wake Forest University Press, 1987), p. 15.

58. Luke Gibbons, 'Challenging the Canon: Revisionism and Cultural Criticism' in Seamus Deane (ed.), *The Field Day Anthology of Irish Writing* (Derry: Field Day, 1991), III, p. 567.

59. Luke Gibbons, 'Coming Out of Hibernation? The Myth of Modernity in Irish Culture', in Richard Kearney (ed.), *Across the Frontiers: Ireland in the 1990s* (Dublin: Wolfhound, 1988), pp. 217 and 218.

60. At worst this teleological yet dissident criticism leads to an assertion such as Desmond Bell's: 'Such are the contradictions of Irish modernization that we have prematurely entered the post-modern era' while 'Modernism remains an untried project'. Bell obviously reduces the postmodern to a time-bound diagnosis while modernism is a 'project' potentially exceeding time itself, but also reduced, by the advent of postmodernism, to historical time. Bell here is also faintly echoing Jürgen Habermas's thinking as expressed, for example, in 'Modernity – An Incomplete Project', in *Postmodern Culture*, ed. Hal Foster (London: Pluto, 1985), pp. 3–15. See Desmond Bell, 'Ireland Without Frontiers? The Challenge of the Communications Revolution' in Richard Kearney (ed.), *Across the Frontiers*, p. 229.

61. See Chapter XI, 'An Irish Utopia', in James Connolly, *Labour in Irish History* (Dublin: New Books, 1983 [1910]), pp. 77–90.

62. See O Cobhthaigh's notes to Edward Thomas Craig, *An Irish Commune* (Dublin: Irish Academic Press, 1983 [*c.* 1920]), p. 169. On Ralahine see also Cormac Ó Gráda, 'The Owenite Commune at Ralahine, 1831–2', *Irish Economic and Social History* 1 (1974), 36–48.

63. Craig, *An Irish Commune*, pp. 7–8.

64. Connolly, *Labour in Irish History*, p. 82.

65. Craig, *An Irish Commune*, p. 147.

66. AE, 'Introduction' in Craig, *An Irish Commune*, p. xi.

67. Connolly, *Labour in Irish History*, p. 90.

68. Craig, *An Irish Commune*, p. 167.

69. Gregory Dobbins, '"Scenes of Tawdry Tribute": Modernism, Tradition and Connolly', in P. J. Mathews (ed.), *New Voices in Irish Criticism* (Dublin: Four Courts, 2000), p. 10.

70. Engels, *Socialism: Utopian and Scientific*, p. 12.

71. See E. F. Bleiler, 'Ignatius Donnelly and Atlantis', in Donnelly, *Atlantis*, pp. v–xx.

72. Bleiler, 'Ignatius Donnelly and Atlantis', p. xi.

73. Donnelly, *Atlantis*, p. 133.

74. Donnelly, *Atlantis*, p. 418.

75. Donnelly, *Atlantis*, p. 408.

76. Donnelly, *Atlantis*, p. 342. The reference here is to ancient burial mounds.

77. Donnelly, *Atlantis*, p. 417.

78. Donnelly, *Atlantis*, p. 414.

79. Donnelly, *Atlantis*, p. 420.

80. Donnelly, *Atlantis*, p. 421.

81. Donnelly, *Atlantis*, p. 421.

82. Donnelly's ideas were seen in exactly this way by Madame Blavatsky who, in *The Secret Doctrine*, used Donnelly extensively as a source for her own

writings on Atlantis: 'Even the clever work of Donnelly . . . is put aside, notwithstanding that its statements are all confined within a frame of strictly scientific proofs. But we write of the future': H. P. Blavatsky, *The Secret Doctrine: The Synthesis of Science, Religion, and Philosophy: Volume II – Anthropogenesis*, Third Point Loma Edition (Point Loma: Aryan Theosophical Press, 1925), p. 334. My thanks to Selina Guinness for pointing me to this use of Donnelly's work.

83. Donnelly, *Atlantis*, p. 480.
84. Derrida, *Of Grammatology*, p. 67.
85. Derrida, *Of Grammatology*, p. 73.
86. Derrida, *Of Grammatology*, pp. 72–3.
87. Phrase taken from a description of Ireland in C. J. O'Donnell, *The Irish Future, with the Lordship of the World* (London: Cecil Palmer, 1931), p. 17.
88. http://www.stanford.edu/~meehan/donnellyr/gerald.html
89. Jameson, *Postmodernism*, p. 165.
90. Jean Baudrillard, *Simulations*, trans. Paul Foss, Paul Patton and Philip Beitchman (New York: Semiotext(e), 1983), p. 101.
91. Seán Hillen, *Irelantis* (Dublin: Irelantis, 1999). On Hillen's art and its relationship to John Hinde's postcards see Mic Moroney, 'Postcards from the Edge', *Cara* (March/April 1998), 20–8. On *Irelantis* see Rosita Boland, 'Hillen's Hinde-sight', *The Irish Times* (Weekend Section), 9 October 1999, p. 5. My thanks to Rosita Boland for supplying me with copies of these articles.
92. Hillen, *Irelantis*, p. 6.
93. Fintan O'Toole, 'Introducing Irelantis' in Seán Hillen, *Irelantis*, p. 5.
94. Moroney, 'Postcards from the Edge', p. 20.
95. Luke Gibbons, *Transformations in Irish Culture* (Cork: Cork University Press/Field Day, 1996), p. 40.
96. Robert J. Holton, *Globalization and the Nation-State* (London: Macmillan, 1998), p. 155.
97. Dwayne Winseck, 'Contradictions in the Democratization of International Communication', *Media, Culture and Society*, 19:2 (1997), 221.
98. Declan Kiberd, 'Anglo-Irish Attitudes' in Field Day Theatre Company (ed.), *Ireland's Field Day* (London: Hutchinson, 1985), p. 95.

2

'Pillars of Cloud and of Fire': Irish Criticism in the Twentieth Century

BEGINNINGS

The Renaissance, with the discoveries of Copernicus and Galileo, the discoveries of Columbus and his followers; later such things as the discovery of the law of gravitation, the Cartesian philosophy, the French Revolution, Darwin's theory of evolution: these have profoundly affected European literature. They have not similarly affected literature in Ireland.[1]

Thomas MacDonagh's *Literature in Ireland* (1916), that seminal statement of the specificity of Irish criticism, momentarily turns the universe on its head in the pursuit of Irish difference. Gravity, genetics, subjectivity, European history and western science have their foundational status flung aside for a brief moment, as MacDonagh casts about for a terminology and set of concepts which can do justice to what he calls the 'Irish Mode'. Even when he goes about resetting western metaphysics on its accustomed plinths, MacDonagh leaves what we presume essential teetering on the edge of irrelevance:

This is not to say of course that in Ireland writers are still likely to write of the earth as the centre of the solar system, of epicycles and the rest. It is to say that literature here has not just that education which is common to the other literatures of western Europe.[2]

MacDonagh's largely unintended philosophical radicalism is on one plane, of course, simply an idiosyncrasy of his style; a poorly written overemphasis perhaps. But it is also profoundly revealing of the task faced by MacDonagh early in the century in his attempt to write an Irish criticism. That this might raise the possibility of an Ireland beyond the forces of evolution or Newtonian physics is provocatively surreal; however, it enforces for us, looking back to critical discourse

at the beginning of the twentieth century, the extent to which fundamentals were still seen to be in need of discussion so that 'Irish'
literature could be given shape and be written about. Having said
this, the rest of the century should not be characterised as one in
which such issues have been made tame, in which the laws of gravity
have been re-established – the definitions of both words in the
term Irish literature (What and who is meant by Irish? What is
its/their/our 'literature'?) have stayed under constant dispute. The
keenness of MacDonagh's dilemma is reflected in the metaphysical
aporia toyed with in his writing, but then such chasmic gaps have been
opened again and again through the century, sutured by the internal-
ities of national politics, sameness against difference, distinctiveness
against typicality, literature against culture. This chapter does not
attempt to chart the exact developmental history of Irish criticism in
the twentieth century (that is a history still to be authoritatively
written), but instead examines some of the schemata into which it
has repeatedly fallen, with or without the help of gravity, suggesting
that Irish *literary* criticism is defined in the century by a continuous
reversion to the model underlying MacDonagh's writing here, one
which can be roughly characterised as a noble struggle out of crisis,
in which each successive 'critical' moment asks for licence in the
remaking of itself out of the scatterings which are the inheritance left
by the previous order.[3] In this, Irish literary criticism in the twentieth
century might be said to go on repeating the staid narratives of the
nation-state as it conceived itself in the first part of the century (a story
which it was at least partly responsible for creating and confirming),
and to have anachronistically persisted in this unacknowledged
reflex until the end of the century, while its objects of study (Ireland,
forms of 'Irishness' and Irish literature) have gone through a variety
of experiences which the critical discourse studying them has
retroactively refigured into familiarity.

This chapter is only partially a narrative of Irish literary criticism
through the century; it can never hope to tell the whole story, partly
because of space, but also because Irish criticism's silence *about
itself* makes it so difficult to reconstruct. And yet the century began
with what initially seems to be that strongest of opinions about literature and criticism, the Revival. It is as fortuitous (and unfortunate)
for the history of Irish criticism as it is for Irish literary history that
the 'Revival' was a *fin de siècle* movement. The sense of a historical
breach which the term carries has tended to archaise the nineteenth
century, and Yeats's faint praise of 'Davis, Mangan, Ferguson' and the
authors he collects in *Representative Irish Tales* is paralleled by what

is partly a self-fulfilling search for critical discourse in Yeats's prose and in the Revival more generally. Quite where Irish criticism had got to by the 1890s has often been obscured by the heroic self-fashioning which Yeats undertakes, the implication most often being that he may as well make up his own criticism as he goes along. This relegates to historical near-redundancy the vast critical enterprises carried out, for example, in *Dublin University Magazine* or *The Nation* and in the antiquarian writings about the lyric tradition which emerged during the nineteenth century, building so many of the cultural assumptions which Yeats relied on in his own critical writing (even while he was reacting against their literary standards, as in 'What is Popular Poetry?': 'I knew in my heart that the most of them wrote badly'[4]). Yeats's dual sense of crisis is that Irish literature is firstly inaccessible and secondly untalked about. During the process of collecting the material for *Representative Irish Tales* Yeats complained to John O'Leary about the unreliability of the British Museum's catalogue: 'Plenty of Irish books are not in it'.[5] The editorial endeavours of compiling *Representative Irish Tales* are reflected in Yeats's 'Introduction' which, while making claims for those authors included, concedes towards the end that they fall into 'conventionality and caricature' and allows for the following statement of revivalism:

Meanwhile a true literary consciousness – national to the centre – seems gradually forming out of this disguising and prettifying, this penumbra of half-culture.[6]

Even when engaged in the process of providing the accessibility and overcoming the ignorance of nineteenth-century Irish literature implied by the British Library's elisions, Yeats is clearing a path to future enlightenment which effectively begins from his present moment. The retrospective view of 'A General Introduction to My Work' (1937) adds the late-Yeatsian twist that the Royal Irish Academy invented the study of Irish literature (before *The Nation*), but also suggests that '[when] modern Irish literature began, [Standish] O'Grady's influence predominated. He could delight us with an extravagance we were too critical to share'.[7] Thus the story of the Revival, almost fifty years after its beginnings, is still of a generation having to start afresh with material which was viewed as scant and inadequately unmodern; this trope, a kind of hollowed-out-history, and its accompanying sense of crisis, reappear throughout the century, so that it seems as if Irish critical discourse both thrives on a sense of its own failings and recuperates itself with the need for regeneration.

The '*mal d'archive*' which marks Irish criticism is, as Derrida suggests it must be, 'a token of the future'; this 'token' is, in turn, bound to 'the possibility of a forgetfulness'.[8] Criticism, in other words, is constitutionally a discourse which promises fulfilment and completion, fails to fulfil the promise, forgets that it has promised before, and goes on to promise again. In the Irish case, the archive strives to contain/explain/supplement 'Ireland', while the concept 'Ireland' becomes the reason for the existence of the archive. Archival 'token' and the futurology of 'Ireland' then find themselves caught in the supplemental cycle of promising and forgetting which is Irish criticism.

Yeats's constant assertion that his own generation were at a 'beginning' is at least relatively true (and has been convincing for generations of scholars); it is most clearly evident in the projects of the early Revival period which involved a gathering and cataloguing of a mass of literary 'evidence' as a base on which the superstructure of the Revival could be built and on which it only could be built. An example is the serious, if flawed, attempt to present a voluminous collectivity of Irish writing in Charles A. Read's *The Cabinet of Irish Literature* (1895).[9] Whatever its historical idiosyncrasies (it begins with Keating) and Anglo-Irish biases, *The Cabinet of Irish Literature* was a monument at the turn of the twentieth century asking to be used and questioned in the same way that *The Field Day Anthology of Irish Writing* (1991) has a practical presidency over the curriculum of Irish literary studies at the turn of the millennium. Such canon-forming (or confirming) impulses were also behind David J. O'Donoghue's *The Poets of Ireland* (1892), an effective dictionary of Irish poets. O'Donoghue's book might seem to qualify Yeats's notions of the paucity of Irish criticism since its eclectic and wide-ranging notion of what an Irish poet is (again Anglo-Irish centred, though wider-ranging than the *Cabinet*'s remit) means that Yeats himself gets a substantial entry (as does Oscar Wilde).[10] However, O'Donoghue's book (like Read's *Cabinet*) is also a statement of and for the Revival, since O'Donoghue ('a little clerk of much literary ardour' was Yeats's description[11]) was a member of the Southwark Irish Literary Club and a founder, with Yeats, of the Irish Literary Society in London in December 1891. Yeats's inclusion in *The Poets of Ireland* weds continuity to future prominence in a way that replicates, at an oblique angle, the emerging self-conception of the Revival.

Additionally, while downplaying the weight of the critical culture of the nineteenth century, the Revival has also marginalised an effectively *belle lettrist* branch of Irish criticism which was as crucial ideologically as its English counterpart.[12] In a related way, the popularity of a (re-)sentimentalised Irishness at the beginning of the century could be said to have engendered its own proliferation of writing about Irish literature. The critical fate of Maria Edgeworth, whose *Castle Rackrent* stands somewhat anomalously in *Representative Irish Tales*,[13] is instructive around the century's end, mainly for its buoyancy and constancy. Having had a 'portrait' included in E. Owens Blackburne's *Illustrious Irishwomen* (1877), Helen Zimmern's *Maria Edgeworth* was published in 1883. Edgeworth then had two books devoted to her at the beginning of the century: Emily Lawless's *Maria Edgeworth* (1904, which has the double irony of appearing in the series 'English Men of Letters') and Constance Hill's *Maria Edgeworth and Her Circle* (1910).[14] Edgeworth was, thus, publicly discussed and written about around the turn of the century in ways that are difficult to reconstruct now, especially through the haze which the Revival is in some ways responsible for. Through Lawless as an Irish woman author writing about another Irish woman author, through the title of Blackburne's book, through the shamrocks and harps which decorate the covers of Blackburne, and through Edgeworth's novels as (kitschly) republished by Dent in 1893, it is clear that Irish literature had, between 1890 and 1910, a definable and marketable existence beyond and at a remove from the Revival's rhetoric. It is also worth pausing to note that this momentary flourishing of an Irish proto-feminist criticism has been relentlessly subtended to the nation-narrative being constructed around it. The reversal pattern here, which turns the excess of difference into a lack which goes unnoticed, is constant throughout the twentieth century in Irish criticism, and most clearly comprehensible in the difficulty one would face in putting together a narrative of feminist literary history/theory in Ireland (if such a homogeneous history were desirable in feminist terms).

The conceptual blockage which Yeats and the Revivalists see themselves as labouring to shift is exemplified by Matthew Arnold in Yeats's essay 'The Celtic Element in Literature'. This is a neat reversal of the position described in *On the Study of Celtic Literature* (1867), in which Arnold had seen the 'Celts' as constructors of 'barriers'. Yeats's 'Celt' is a reviver rather than an obstructer, moving rather than fixing, and this very precisely undoes Arnold. As a result, and because of the way in which it negotiates Arnold away from the grasp on 'Celtic' definition which he has had, 'The Celtic Element' is a useful place to begin to look in more detail at the strategies of Irish criticism around the beginning of the century. 'The Celtic Element' also deploys patterns of thought and argument which are repeated as variations through, most significantly, Thomas MacDonagh and Daniel Corkery (discussed below). At the beginning of 'The Celtic Element' Yeats appears to accept the weight of learning and argument which has accumulated in Renan and Arnold, and he quotes both approvingly (Renan and Arnold placed together here signal more than their individual writings; they stand for a disciplinary way of speaking about the 'Celtic' and the 'Irish' which disables its subject). After noting that Arnold's Celt has an 'unaccountable, defiant and titanic' melancholy about 'him', Yeats writes:

How well one knows these sentences, better even than Renan's, and how well one knows the passages of prose and verse which he uses to prove that wherever English literature has the qualities these sentences describe, it has them from a Celtic source. Though I do not think any of us who write about Ireland have built any argument upon them, it is well to consider them a little, and see where they are helpful and where they are hurtful. If we do not, we may go mad some day, and the enemy root up our rose-garden and plant a cabbage-garden instead. Perhaps we must re-state a little Renan's and Arnold's argument.[15]

If the reader catches the double-edge of seeming scholarly respect yet dismissive boredom in the repeated 'how well one knows', that is confirmed later when the extent of this 're-statement' of Arnold becomes clear. That has also already begun in the essay's title. While Yeats's 'Celtic *Element*' is an element in an appropriately supernatural sense and in the sense of being a 'factor' in 'literature', a part of a greater entity, it is also elemental in that it is an irreducible essence. As a shift in terminology, 'element' immediately gains ground over Arnold's less solid, non-material 'genius'. It is linguistic sleight of hand of this kind, a quiet violence of terminological substitution introducing new definitions by subterfuge, which characterises Irish critical discourse at the beginning of the century as it contests its own inadequacy.

While the term 'element' aids Yeats in circumventing part of Arnold's hold on the critical vocabulary available at the time, Yeats also has to go about claiming back a form of history for the 'Celtic element' which directly wrests its control from Arnold. Yeats's strategy is instructive here, since, again, it is repeated in MacDonagh, Corkery and others. Yeats writes:

All folk literature has indeed a passion whose like is not in modern litera- ture and music and art, except where it has come by some straight or crooked way out of ancient times. Love was held to be a fatal sickness in ancient

Ireland, and there is a love-poem in the *Love Songs of Connaught* that is like a death cry.[16]

The crucial word here is 'except', since this opens the way for a process of transference over a history which is fully politicised and across which passage is given to 'ancient times'. 'Straight or crooked' describes neatly (and nearly self-effacingly) the access to the 'ancient' crafted by Hyde (and then implicitly by Yeats himself), and represents a deferral of the completeness of history which appears to be necessary in order for Irish criticism to give itself a beginning. Yeats tries out this emptying of history again when he writes, after quoting 'an Elizabethan Irish poet':

Such love and hatred seek no mortal thing but their own infinity, and such love and hatred soon become love and hatred of the idea. The lover who loves so passionately can soon sing to his beloved like the lover in the poem by A.E., 'A vast desire awakes and grows into forgetfulness of thee'.[17]

Here what explicitly defines the Celtic ('such love and hatred') is a detour around oppressive historical processes ('the idea'?) since the only goal in sight is 'their own infinity', the ultimate extrapolation of the utopian tendency discussed in the previous chapter. In its happy acceptance of infinity the authentically Celtic allows for a shift backwards to the ancient, and forward to modernity and a future. This enables AE's 'likeness' to the ancient to construct 'the little looking-glass of the modern and classical imagination',[18] reflecting practice across aeons, diminishing intervening history to the point where it is no obstacle. This reprocessing of history, which moves the Celtic Element out of the ravages of known time, facilitates the start of a gentle redefinition, edging towards an Irishness known through literature, ancient and modern, that is both an image and its reflection.[19] 'Cassandra and Helen and Deirdre, and Lear and Tristan' are of the 'primitive imagination', reflected in the 'modern and classical imagination',[20] and at this point the breach in historical time has allowed for the smuggling in of 'primitive' for Arnold's 'Celtic'. While Celtic is not, by any means, a term Yeats wants to reject, its meaning here needs modifying for his purpose, and its substitution by 'primitive' is always underwritten by a hint of Irish exceptionalism and particularity (as when the metaphor of the Celtic as the 'fountain' closest to the main river of European literature in exemplified by Renan's equally watery account of Lough Derg pilgrimage visions).

Yeats's 'The Celtic Element' reveals a necessity to deal with history by finding a mechanism which moves across time and at least puts off its laborious fullness; it also functions by efficiently wresting terms from their previous owners and turning their meaning towards more 'Irish' purposes. (It might be argued that the circulation of the almost equivalent terms in the essay, 'Celtic' and 'primitive', is itself a dance around the fullness of the term Irish, so that while Ireland can be explicitly the matter under discussion at the beginning of 'The Celtic Element', there is a certain trepidation and reluctance to settle on the nation at the end.[21]) We have already seen above how Thomas MacDonagh's *Literature in Ireland* also dramatically undertakes the reorientation of terminology under the auspices of what is 'Irish'. MacDonagh begins his book by saying:

These studies in Irish and Anglo-Irish Literature are frankly experimental. In them I have tried to clear away certain misconceptions, to fix certain standards, to define certain terms. I trust that as a result the Irish Mode will be better understood and appreciated than the Celtic Note for which I substitute it.[22]

MacDonagh's fascination with the shifting and cementing of critical terminology and forms of meaning is expressed more frankly than Yeats's method allows, and his confident disabling of old structures (which are barely discussed, but which are responsible for the notional 'Celtic Note' – Arnold is the main culprit again) is perhaps too easily put down to the revolutionary context of the book.[23] Like Yeats, MacDonagh can only gesture towards a useable definition of 'Irish' literature by a resetting of history which verges on the ahistorical, a faltering timelessness:

Intellectualism is the Renaissance. When in place of that clear standard we set those pillars of cloud and of fire known to the spiritual intuitions, the day of the Renaissance is done; the forms of Renaissance literature decay.

In Ireland some literature has kept the old way familiar to the Middle Ages.[24]

The dissolution of the Renaissance may be also a counter-Reformation instinct, but more centrally active here is the attraction for MacDonagh of the 'elemental' (again) fire and air which paradoxically proves itself to be more resilient than the materialism of rational history, subject to the decay of its own logic. As the Renaissance disintegrates, so the correspondence across history which Yeats envisages, while not exactly matching in MacDonagh, is structurally as important ('Ireland' in the present tense sees itself in the spiritualism of 'the Middle Ages'). It is MacDonagh's hollowed-out-history which earns the space to substitute 'Irish Mode' for 'Celtic Note'. It also enables a freedom from historical process which can imagine a future Irish literature in the English language, which does not see 'Irishness' everywhere, or Irishness as absolutely unique, and which openly disavows definition of what the nation and its literature are, since it is too early to know. MacDonagh's *Literature in Ireland* is revolutionary not only because of the author's (and the text's) participation in the Rising[25] but because of its willingness (perhaps resultant from its own mild chaos as a text) to really begin again and to defer to a future which is beyond knowledge but not speculation.

There are other critical texts from the early part of the century which would reveal variations on and contradictions to the pattern of terminological shifting and aporetic history[26] which I am suggesting here. Ernest Boyd might tell a different story,[27] as would John Eglinton.[28] But it is with Daniel Corkery's *The Hidden Ireland* (1924) that the imperatives of the post-Independence context necessitate a reorientation of critical discourse towards a freshly solidified base, attempting to reconcile the newness of the State with the linearities desired by literary history and the acts of discretion implied by 'criticism'. While the outcome of this in Corkery is obviously a historico-political analysis at odds with Yeats (and MacDonagh), *The Hidden Ireland* is also, perhaps surprisingly, a recantation of the tropes of terminological play and adjustment, and the atrophying of history, which appears in the earlier critiques.

Corkery's method has two important theoretical strands: one is the act of recovery (finding the 'Hidden' Ireland), the other is the definition of what that Ireland is as it blinks in the light of the history into which it has just emerged. *The Hidden Ireland*, in the main body of its text, becomes a catalogue of and paean to the Munster poets of the eighteenth century. Before that, it sets out a critical framework which polemicises literary discourse in Ireland in parallel to the birth of the new state and its exigencies; in that polemic there is a vying for predominance among various factors in literary Irishness which return throughout the century. For example, while the lack of critical recognition of the Munster poets animates Corkery's book, it is also more subtly underlain with a desire for completeness somewhat mismatched with a conviction of Irish excess and abundance. As is well known, *The Hidden Ireland* launches itself from the fury of an attack on Lecky's historiographical elisions as symptomatic of politicised versions of Irish culture. Of this relationship with Lecky (which continues to twist in paradoxical revulsion and dependency throughout the book) Corkery says:

[Lecky's] account of the life of the country as a whole needs many supple-mentary books, not one. Some indeed have already appeared; and this book aims at being simply one more.[29]

'Wholeness' and 'supplementarity' placed side by side here represent the dilemma which Corkery addresses, in that the 'Real' Ireland, once whole unto itself, once self-fulfillingly obvious, is now only accessible and explicable through commentary, exposition and endless addition. So one of the functions of *The Hidden Ireland* is then to embody, in itself as an example, the roles which critical discourse and literary scholarship have in the project of the nation. Corkery sets out to turn the supplement of criticism away from being a reminder of the doubled or split nation detached from access to its origin and hopes that criticism can become a form of national recuperation leading to repletion. *The Hidden Ireland* dramatises the dilemma which means that the acts of sincere recuperation which follow colonialism seem to waver and fall into an extension of the colonising process. Corkery treads tentatively in the knowledge that reaching back for what once was will push the 'wholeness' of the nation continually towards its need for the supplement, and the risk of turning its memory to dust. Hence Corkery vacillates between a desired-for organicism (and effective romanticism[30]) and the metadiscourse of the supplement; or, to put it more simply, between poetry and criticism, between the Munster poets and his own book about them.

Corkery in a sense reverses the process of emptying history which Yeats and MacDonagh find necessary. The aporia which recurs in Yeats and MacDonagh is structurally inverted in Corkery's excessive eighteenth century, which is to be added to, uncovered fully and remade, with the regrettably necessary addition of commentary. However, the reordering of history through literary criticism, whether as gap or supplement, does seem to have the same rippling effects on the standard linearities of history; for example, like MacDonagh, Corkery also does away with the Renaissance, viewing it as a blot on European history, and, with more certainty than MacDonagh can muster, Corkery effectively envisions the death of the stultifying legacy of the Renaissance, killed off by the resurgence of 'national standards' and the throwing off of 'borrowed alien modes'.[31] The insulation afforded by this national absoluteness leads to the extraordinary notion of Shakespeare as a pre-Renaissance writer ('Happy England! – so naively ignorant of the Renaissance at the close of the sixteenth century'[32]) and a view of European integration

which has the post-Independence mentalities and fears of Irish nationalism inscribed in its logic and rhetorical insistence:

It has to be insisted upon that Renaissance standards are not Greek standards. Greek standards in their own time and place were standards arrived at
by the Greek nation; they were national standards. Caught up at second-hand
into the art-mind of Europe – thus becoming international, their effect was
naturally to whiten the youthfully tender national cultures of Europe. That
is, the standards of a dead nation killed in other nations those aptitudes
through which they themselves had become memorable.[33]

The progress of history for Corkery is then one of artful forgetting
which needs to undergo a process of remembering and becoming
'memorable'. To find his Hidden Ireland we must, he says, 'leave
cities and towns behind', and what we will find there is an Ireland
which resists history in being unchanging. The radical, subaltern
status of the Hidden Ireland is, however, not one of unutterable
quietude, and in this Corkery provides models for late twentieth-
century postcolonial criticism which have not easily been taken up.
This is partly because, despite Corkery's condemnation of Lecky, he has
both a nostalgia for the eighteenth-century social order (including
elements of the Anglo-Irish) which produced the poets he studies,
and an enforced reliance on 'sources' which are either themselves
Anglo-Irish (Maria Edgeworth, for example) or anachronistic (Michael
Doheny's *The Felon's Track* set in 1848, Lady Chatterton writing in
1838 and a cabin Corkery himself visited in 1915 all serve as evidence).
Corkery in the end is caught in the same dilemma as Yeats and
MacDonagh. History as excess has the same effects as history as prob-
lematic-turned-chasmic; what is in excess of or is lacking in history
pressurises History. Corkery's continuous, determinedly unchanging
Hidden Ireland is lost from history and so preserved from alteration,
and yet it can, anti-teleologically, appear (because of its ineffable
constancy) in all possible places. Its subalternity may not be spoken
directly but can be heard, and then accessed through the poetry he
goes on to describe.

   It is all too easy to see and dismiss Corkery's work as the search for
a stability of undiluted nationality which is insular and in a sense
reactionary, in that it is nuanced by the newly forming State.[34] Yet
Corkery's is a much more porous criticism than a retrospective view
might suggest. His Wordsworthian romanticism and unquestioning
faith in the genius of Shakespeare show a coincidence of literature
and nation which is universal and fundamental to his understanding

of the literary *per se*, rather than being partisanly nationalistic. His view of the Big House and its residents is often ambiguous, as he condemns all others who subjugated the peasant but can at times remain silent on the role of the Anglo-Irish who were not absentees. But, as with Yeats and MacDonagh, it is in his manouevring around terminology that Corkery is at once unforgiving and yielding. Where Yeats and MacDonagh operate terminological switching quietly, Corkery frequently uses a word which describes this very process; for him words and ideas have the possibility of being 'coterminous': 'The Hidden Ireland was in a sense coterminous with Ireland itself' is, for example, followed quickly by 'Irish Ireland, then, while in a sense coterminous with Ireland itself', creating a swirl of self-definition typical of the discourse of the nation, but revealing for all that.[35] The final section of Chapter One of *The Hidden Ireland* completes the cycle, introducing the religious distinction which has been absent up to that point and thus comes unexpectedly abruptly: 'We have now glanced at Catholic Ireland in the eighteenth century'.[36] The coterminousness of 'Hidden', then 'Irish' and now 'Catholic' Ireland is cemented with the simplicity of the past tense, so that the reader is initially left with no choice but to give in to what has already ineluctably been.

While reading Corkery from our own time allows for the disentanglement of some of his thought, and above all allows us to see his project as sited in its own time, his influence as a typification of a perceived orthodoxy in the first decades after Independence makes his critical voice echo as a chastisement to those who come after him. Dissent against the potentially nullifying counter-revolutionary period, which at first glance seems to ideologically insist on a silence hanging over the metacritical in the early years of the state, can be found in Hugh Alexander Law's *Anglo-Irish Literature* (1926). Law is strident in defending a perceived denigration of Anglo-Irish literature (for which he partly blames MacDonagh). His defence is put in terms which are as politicised as Corkery's and which, while in one sense oppositional to state nationalism (to the point of echoing unionist rhetoric), are similarly about the recovery of a lost cultural strand (or, at least, one which is in the process of being submerged into history): 'the treasure of accumulation for us by generations of Anglo-Irish is great; and I, for one am not for surrendering any part of it'.[37] The debate beginning here is one which continued through the century over the purity of the canon of 'Irish literature' and the usefulness of the term 'Anglo-Irish' in this context. Law uses MacDonagh against himself very effectively in retaliation:

It is easy to be talking of the Celtic note or the Irish mode; not quite so easy to define or even detect it. Who has it, who lacks it?[38]

As with Law, Stephen Gwynn, writing *Irish Literature and Drama in the English Language: A Short History* (1936), finds his terms and histories already closely guarded against redefinition. In the criticism written by both Law and Gwynn the legacies of the Revival, and of MacDonagh and Corkery, are instructively stifling. Gwynn's criticism has a double vision of history. One strand covers his chosen literary period, which conveniently picks up in the nineteenth century where Corkery ends (thus ignoring Corkery's eighteenth century while bypassing engagement with the inescapable universality of Corkery's empty historical time):

Five generations cover it [that is, Irish 'national' literature], from Moore's *Melodies* down to O'Casey's *Juno and the Paycock*, or whatever else one takes as characteristic of Ireland since a revolution established the Free State.[39]

Initially Gwynn avoids identifying what is typical of the undecidedness of the present by not deciding, and his sense of literary history becomes hemmed in on both sides, by the State and by Corkery's eighteenth-century Munster. However, Gwynn's reluctance to obtrude into the difficult past, where the Irish and English of his book's title have already been claimed and formulated earlier in the century, is not long-lived. His secondary sense of history is less bound to literary trajectories and relies on a movement which pushes back towards an inclusivity inherent in the term the 'Anglo-Irish' which he initially seems to forgo (when, for example, he says that the 'whole position' of Irish literature 'has been altered out of knowledge . . . since Ireland came back in some measure to her own possessions'[40]). This is carried out through an imprecise cultural/historical version of literary transmission. Having rejected the Canadian model as a way of understanding the development of Irish literature, and seeing the Scottish as 'closer to reality' but bringing in 'no alien element', Gwynn writes:

In Ireland the case is very different. The special interest in the literature of which I have to write is that it *links up* the intimate expression of an Ireland which has *become* English-speaking, which for a century at least has thought in English, to a poetry and mythology that took literary shape centuries before English was a written or a spoken speech.[41]

Gwynn's book attempts to gently hijack MacDonagh and to bypass Corkery. The giving away of the eighteenth century is a tactic which can neutralise at least the historical impact of Corkery's critique, but MacDonagh's allowance of the possibility of English as a medium is pulled up through the practicalities of language history (the contention that Ireland 'thinks' in English at least buys time), while 'links up' describes that linguistic dawning which MacDonagh allowed for, though for him it was usefully far off, and repairs the divisions which Corkery draws (taking us back to his Big House/peasant organicism). This done, if transparently, Gwynn is able to resolve for himself the dilemmas which Law much more forcefully confronts. Partly because he is writing post-*Ulysses*, but also because of his more pluralistically inclined vision, Gwynn ends his book with the curiously amalgamated chapter title 'James Stephens, James Joyce and the Ulster Writers', in which the fact of Stephens and Joyce appearing alongside Shan Bullock, Lennox Robinson and St John Ervine is interestingly never explained; an implicit outsider status is lamented in regard to them all, along with Gwynn's own slight bemusement as to how to make Stephens (especially his *Crock of Gold*) and Joyce fit existing paradigms. Hence Joyce 'holds high rank undisputably' but is primarily a humorist, and one of some cruelty. When, towards the end of the chapter, Gwynn notes that Richard Rowley's *City Songs* of urban life in Belfast 'add to Irish literature something inspired by energies which are not memorable in the life of any Irish city but Belfast'[42] it then becomes apparent that emerging from the gaps (and the counterbalancing inclusivist impulse) of Gwynn's literary history is a set of alternatives (represented by Joyce's difference from all else and by Ulster's partition) which is not yet comprehended by literary criticism.

The final chapter of Gwynn's *Irish Literature and Drama* settles itself by returning to literature from 'After the Revolution', in which the line from Yeats and the Revival to, for example, O'Casey can be more smoothly rendered in terms of the emergence of the nation-state. Gwynn ends appropriately with ambiguous praise for the Irish Academy of Letters, which he sees as at once a sign of the national vitality of literature, and also as an institution inadvertently exclusive in its constitution (the omission of Kate O'Brien and Elizabeth Bowen are noted, to Gwynn's credit). Gwynn and Law are useful examples of differing responses in literary criticism to the emerging authority of statehood in post-revolutionary Ireland. It would be a caricature of Corkery to see him as the figure of new national consciousness haunting the varieties of Anglo-Irishness which Law and

Gwynn differently seek to defend and include, but Corkery is crucial in that his professional status as Professor of English at University College Cork and his ethics of national criticism combine to place an insistent grip on the terminologies of Irish criticism which must be responded to. Thus the institutionality which Gwynn ends with is not only seen in the Irish Academy of Letters, but in the academy which Corkery belongs to. Law makes a tetchily apologetic comment early in his book about his own amateur status ('It will, I am afraid, be only too plain that I have no pretensions to learning'[43]), which finds its inversion in Gwynn's praise for the two Dublin universities and the way in which they have cemented the status of literary study, while 'in the Queen's University of Belfast good work is being done on the special history of Ulster';[44] what both Law and Gwynn incidentally make clear is that literary study, post-Independence, is being professionalised in a way that is inflected by statehood (while also, it must be noted, being in line with the history of profession-alised literary study elsewhere).[45]

THE BELL AND THE NEW CRITICAL MOMENT

It is an irony then that the next site at which to look for movement and change in Irish criticism in the twentieth century should be the aggressively populist (and in that sense 'amateur') editorial policies declared by Seán Ó Faoláin in *The Bell*. Richard Kearney summarises *The Bell*'s philosophy thus:

Now that Ireland had reached its long-fought-for national Independence, the editors felt it possible to open Irish minds to life as it was lived in the present, that is, unencumbered by nostalgic abstractions from the past or millenial abstractions about the future. Ireland had come of age. The moment for critical stocktaking had arrived.[46]

For all its 'project of pluralistic, non-sectarian debate . . . [and] creation of a new cultural community',[47] and perhaps because of it, *The Bell*'s attempts to push into the new predetermined that it would continu-ally find itself collapsing into the old, characterised by what Gerry Smyth calls 'the specifically nationalist problematic which seemed to dominate the pages of *The Bell*'.[48] *The Bell* has traditionally, and rightly, been seen as the site of a dissent against post-Independence hegemonies (and censorship in particular); however, with the advan-tage of critical hindsight and distance, it is apparent that from its inception it would find near-impossible the pluralism with which it declared itself. Ó Faoláin's famous first editorial, 'This is Your Magazine', with its metaphors of organic (masculinised) growth into maturity certainly unconsciously register the very progress of national history which *The Bell* was attempting to disentangle itself from. The refusal 'to use the word Irish, or Ireland, in the title'[49] was the first step in the creation of the conceptually spectral presence of the nation in the journal which Smyth describes. The rejection of the nation-as-title is quickly followed by Ó Faoláin's wonderfully descriptive metaphor of *The Bell*'s role as liberalising irritant to the state: 'All over Ireland – this is the expression of our Faith – there are men and women with things itching them like a grain stuck in a tooth'.[50] The ready reintroduction of 'Ireland' as *the* remit for the journal, and the ironically used 'our Faith' indicate, at the very point of departure, the future disappointment which Ó Faoláin was to express in his equally well-known final editorial, 'Signing Off', before Peadar O'Donnell took over the editorship.[51]

Ó Faoláin's defence of *The Bell*'s record in 'Signing Off', which he makes against the 'pessimism' he is desperate to leave behind him and with the wish 'that we had more articles on literature, and aesthetics, and technique',[52] interestingly reverts to a dichotomy which is roughly amateur/professional. Ó Faoláin notes that 'people have made fun of our factual pieces' (he gives the slightly mischievous examples 'Myself and Some Ducks' and 'Myself and Some Rabbits'), and asserts that such writing 'seemed to me to be the parable of the heart's search for the heart'.[53] This is no small claim for the magazine which published parts of what became *The Tailor and Ansty*, a homage to a form of ordinariness and 'innocent laughter' which proved too much for the Censorship Board[54] and which quintessentially represented a public battle waged by an 'official' Ireland against what it left outside itself, the very antagonism which *The Bell* had from its beginning expected and desired.

Revelling in the inclusion of the 'amateur' and the marginalised (always made strange by the definitively writerly predominance of the journal), *The Bell*'s project was almost heroically self-stymied. Its inability in the end to reach its goal, 'that Ireland would have to abandon its obsessive absorption with its own past',[55] is another variation on the critical trope which reappears throughout the century, in which a fresh critical impetus picks itself up from the ruins of the immediate past ('the time when we growled in defeat and dreamed of the future' in contrast to the future which has 'arrived and, with its arrival, killed' 'the old symbolic words'[56]). The specific terms of *The Bell*'s continuing frustration are a partial explanation for a subsequent switch of energies from the investment in the amateur towards the increasing professionalisation of criticism; this, intertwined with the institutional cover offered by the universities, allowed for criticism which at least felt less trammelled by the overwhelming, publicly dissenting duties which for Ó Faoláin were so crucial to the project represented by *The Bell*.

So while *The Bell*'s contributors necessarily crossed the divisions between professional and amateur, critic and writer, in other parts of the world these boundaries were being made more solid, post-Modernism, by the rise of New Criticism. The arrival of New Criticism in Ireland was announced by a definitive debate over several issues of *Studies* in 1955–6 involving Denis Donoghue, Donald Davie and Vivian Mercier (a *Bell* contributor early in his career). Donoghue's feisty and crusading polemical argument for the adoption of New Critical methodologies, 'Notes Towards a Critical Method: Language as Order', urges Irish criticism to give up the attempt to define poetry and 'pursue description'. This said, Donoghue is deliberately unspecific, in typical New Critical fashion, about applying his doctrine to the politico-historical specifics of the Irish situation. So the injunction to critics is to recognise that

poems are made out of the poet's desire to create forms, entities, things of order with which to oppose the continued flux, change, transience of life.[57]

Donoghue's quest for the objectivity of New Criticism was taken as a direct comment on the state of Irish criticism by Davie and Mercier, despite the fact that when he discusses Yeats's 'The Blood and the Moon' under the subtitle 'The Source in History' there is still no overt reference to an Irish context. But the combination of the New Critical challenge to orthodox reading, the Jesuit origins of *Studies* and the fascinating speculation by Donoghue that American New Criticism was a Catholic enterprise,[58] were enough to deflect his critical polemic into an argument about the state of *Irish* criticism. Donoghue himself nudges this process when he finally makes a contentious cross-cultural (and cross-sectarian) argument for poetry read through New Critical methods, suggesting that this is the only form of reading 'which will allow "The Wreck of the Deutschland" to be appreciated by an atheist or the *Cantos* of Ezra Pound by a Jewish money-lender'.[59]

Donald Davie's response to Donoghue, 'Reflections of an English Writer in Ireland', is spiky yet ultimately unsure about what to make of Donoghue. Davie accuses Donoghue of assuming 'that Ireland is just lagging behind, twenty years out of step',[60] yet Davie himself, arguing that 'England has had critics', reflects on his experience of the Irish literary community: 'nothing is more striking in the Anglo-Irish literary tradition than the absence of any true critic at all, certainly of any critical tradition'.[61] The lack of real engagement between Donoghue and Davie is striking,[62] as Davie picks up on the missing element in Donoghue's critique (the Irish possibilities for New Criticism) yet swerves that into a crass debate over national criticisms which shows little knowledge of the situation in Ireland.

The intervention of Vivian Mercier begins to make fruitful sense out of what Davie and Donoghue have both tangentially attacked. Mercier firstly overturns the Catholicity of Donoghue's New Criticism by saying that Donoghue 'is in grave danger of swallowing that Puritan heresy, the New Criticism, hook, line and sinker': Puritan because New Criticism 'can never be content merely to enjoy... [but] must justify [this] enjoyment, whether it be of spiritual or fleshly pleasures'.[63] Having evened the balance of dubious religious analogies, Mercier places Donoghue's commitment to New Criticism as 'a natural and healthy reaction against the over-emphasis of Marxists and others on the political and social content of literature as well as on the political and social conditions in which it was produced'.[64] Mercier also puts Davie firmly in his place, noting that Davie's stay in Ireland has meant that he 'has learned to imitate our chief fault when he talks so glibly about the "absence of any true critic at all, certainly of any critical tradition"'.[65] Refuting Davie with the example of Yeats's criticism and his editing of the Irish nineteenth century, Mercier writes:

Ireland doesn't lack critics; she lacks publishers ... Our critics are too unscholarly, our scholars too uncritical or indifferent to the common reader.[66]

The thrust of Donoghue's New Critical agenda and its focus on textual reading seems to be passed by in the debate which followed it, but in an important way Mercier treats Donoghue and Davie as symptoms of a wider structural problem in Irish criticism which foregrounds the social and institutional place of the critic above the detail of their methodology. Mercier's question 'Why have we no literary history of Anglo-Ireland in its hey-day, the eighteenth century?',[67] may be answered by looking back to MacDonagh's and Corkery's strategic emaciation of historical and literary time. His answer to his own question pushes further though:

In the nineteenth- and twentieth-century Anglo-Irish literary history, the amateurs have it all their own way: Hugh Law, Stephen Gwynn, Ernest Boyd, Robert Farren (*The Course of Irish Verse in English*) – no native author of a comprehensive work has ever held a university post.[68]

The divided attitudes regarding the university-led study of Irish literature seen in Gwynn and Law (above) resurface here in Mercier with an unashamed belief in the professionalisation of literary criticism, tempered with the need to address 'the common reader'. Mercier's measured yet strident response to Donoghue and Davie takes the opportunity to go beyond the hesitancies of what he sees as 'amateur' criticism and to place the future of Irish literary criticism in a full-on, 'professionalised' and institutionalised facing up to the weight of history which Donoghue signals tangentially in his discussion of Yeats, and which Davie clumsily wades into in his dismissal of a critical tradition. In this sense Mercier's analysis is a seminal point of change for Irish criticism in the twentieth century, expressing exasperation with a lack of confidence (and a lack of procedural rigour) and looking to the state institutions of the universities to deliver an encompassing and liberal critical history to Irish readers.

THE NORTH AND 'NEW' POLARITIES

It is tempting then to see Mercier's essay as symbolic of a point at which Irish criticism takes on a previously impossible fullness (impossible because of both historical circumstances and the ways in which critical discourse tended to validate the 'amateur'). The new 'school of Irish criticism' which Mercier imagined certainly appeared to some extent, but it too inevitably had its constitutive elisions. Gwynn's surreal wedding of Joyce with new Northern writing in the penultimate chapter of *Irish Literature and Drama* is a useful reminder that the 'Ireland' which Mercier writes of and where he firmly places his criticism and its reception wavers with uncertainty at the border of two states. The North is, of course, not the only ghost at the feast (the issues of gender and, partly related to that, the canon, which Mercier sees as deficiently defined, are just two exemplary absences), but it is arguable that the issue of the North (often functioning as a convenient cipher for old debates) became the underlying political dynamic of much Irish criticism in the later part of the century, most obviously with the beginning of civil disruption from the late 1960s on. *The Bell*, in its joyful eclecticism, had brought the North within its remit through specific contributors (such as John

Hewitt and Louis MacNeice); what happened in the last three decades of the twentieth century in Irish criticism was the development of a series of polarities around the remnants of the 'national question' (nationalist critics versus liberal critics, postcolonial criticism versus revisionism, multiple versions and denials thereof) which, varying between embarrassed silence and excessive account-taking, found the unfolding of the Troubles to be whittling away quietly and continually at the most basic of critical assumptions.

Outlining the particular ways in which this 'crisis' manifested itself in Irish literary criticism is a task yet to be fully attempted; however, it would provide one way at least to understand many of the major literary critics of recent years (Terence Brown, Seamus Deane, Declan Kiberd, Edna Longley, David Lloyd, as initial examples). The most persuasive analysis of criticism in and about the North itself is to be found in Richard Kirkland's *Literature and Culture in Northern Ireland Since 1965: Moments of Danger*,[69] which shows how the pervasive sense of 'interregnum' within Northern literary institutions acted with an often narcissistic energy capable of allowing itself to be discussed only in terms of crisis. For Kirkland this is as much the case in literary criticism as it is in literary production, and his analysis in this regard is nearly unique in understanding the function of the critical contexts of Irish literature.

The recent schisms in Irish literary criticism around revisionism could certainly be mapped onto the tremors caused by the Northern 'crisis' and yet in this their return to issues of identity, affiliation and aesthetics replay the national problematics of criticism throughout the century. For example, there is a revealingly shared sense of an ending common to critics such as Declan Kiberd, Seamus Deane and Terry Eagleton (who are diverse in other ways); *Inventing Ireland* (1995), *Strange Country* (1997) and *Crazy John and the Bishop* (1998)[70] all conclude by attacking, dismissing or 'discussing' the impact of revisionism and using it to clarify and give boundaries to their own critical enterprises. A reversed but similar pattern of contentiousness occurs in the writings of Edna Longley, whose anti-structuralist stance in *Poetry in the Wars* (1986) becomes mapped onto the revisionist mode in *The Living Stream* (1994),[71] in which the Field Day Anthology in particular is symbolic of the repetition of nationalist tropes under the surface of the seemingly 'new'. The North is then often the ground on which these theories *fail* to meet, with Longley's famous statement that '[poetry] and politics, like church and state, should be separated'[72] starkly forcing the issue. It is too neat to see the ground covered in this ongoing exchange as an exact parallel of those crises which dominated Irish criticism earlier in the century. However, where MacDonagh required an emptied, phantasmal history, Deane requires a 'strange' and haunted country; where Corkery celebrates the finding and making of the fulsome nation, Kiberd's *Inventing Ireland* is a declension and celebration of the same process; and Longley's switches between polemic engagement and calls for inclusivity chart a territory which carries shadows of the differing strategies of Law and Gwynn. The comparisons can take little more weight than this and already reduce the work of all of these critics; however, the crucial point is that a series of arguments which proclaim themselves to be about aesthetics versus politics find that these supposedly adversarial positions become intertwined (and are cherished) on any two 'sides' in Irish criticism; aesthetics are naturally politicised, politics aestheticised, as a result.

Therefore, all this to and fro, and the substantial work it has been responsible for, has a certain reciprocity about it, and through this the unstated metadiscourses of Irish criticism work their repetitious patterns at the end of the century, just as they did at the beginning; as a result Irish literary criticism has been partially sheltered from the full force of the 'theory wars' which have engaged the energies of Anglo-American criticism to the point of exhaustion in the last three decades. 'The North', in its various critical guises, can now silently make the case that Yeats had set out at the beginning of the century: that Irish criticism is at best a shattered discourse in need of restitution. More than this, the underlying structures of that shattering dictate their own reconstruction in terms of the *national*, so that factors lying outside what is immediately recognisable as Irish criticism (Mercier's 'Marxists', for example, but currently and more pressingly feminist criticism, theory and literary history) remain beyond the purview of the mainstream of critical consciousness. The power of these repetitious patterns in Irish criticism is that in their phoenix narrative both the moments of destruction and restitution have a drama which postpones and drowns out other voices.[73]

A too frequently unacknowledged text, which calls to attention this dialectic, is David Cairns and Shaun Richard's *Writing Ireland: Colonialism, Nationalism and Culture* (1988).[74] Cairns and Richards deploy a Gramscian and Foucauldian-inflected poststructuralism which became the grounding of radical critical writing in the 1980s and which they rigorously, inventively and sympathetically apply to the history of Irish writing. Field Day's later interventions (including the introduction of voices from outside Ireland: Jameson, Eagleton, Said[75]) tended to direct the debates back to known patterns, and the radical newness offered by Cairns and Richards only really found its next major voice in David Lloyd's *Anomalous States: Irish Writing and the Post-Colonial Moment*.[76] Lloyd's writing in *Anomalous States* has many qualities (polemic, political drive, a sense of historicity which is not primarily in the thrall of literary history), but its acceptance of and demand for theoretical frameworks which force the articulation of critical premises and foundations threatened to put critical discourse in Ireland through a form of questioning which, for once, it had not already anticipated. However, Lloyd's most recent intervention in book form, *Ireland After History*,[77] goes backwards by going forwards in that his critical stance is now explicitly aligned with a dissident politics which can more easily be collapsed into existing antinomies. Corkery's confidence in finding the prevailing, authenticated voice of a real Ireland haunts contemporary versions of Irish postcolonial theory, and either reassuringly, or disturbingly depending on one's point of view, reiterates the difficulty of grounding Irish critical discourse in its own subject, since knowing what that subject is is always constitutively beyond the grasp of critical knowledge. Lloyd's Ireland replicates Corkery's in its subaltern, suppressed yet ultimately (putatively) cogent expressibility; however, the essays in Lloyd's *Ireland After History* lack the security of being able to show where that 'excessive' Ireland is exactly; this is a result of Lloyd's sense of history itself as always outside historiography, always marginal, while Corkery finds his Hidden Ireland inside the history and historiography which already pertains. Lloyd's continual and rigorous search circulates around 'the *possibility* that social and cultural forms which are necessarily relegated to residual status by dominant historiography *might* generate forms of emergent practices, even where their apparent content may be in some views simply conservative'.[78] So Lloyd's Ireland, existing 'after' history, always slips away into delayed promises of future statement, into 'gestures towards other possibilities';[79] like so many Irish critics before him, Lloyd digs in the rubble of what preceded him in the (heroic) hope and expectation of discovery, until what is a putative future becomes the end of criticism in itself; as with the utopian trope discussed in Chapter 1, the point here is that the future becomes structurally a necessity for criticism, and so, like Connolly's Ralahine, becomes necessarily only given definition as the unspecified future. To the extent that we can make any generalisations about the characteristics of twentieth-century Irish critical discourse, we can find them typified in Lloyd, even though it might at first seem that those principles are entirely altered by his methodology; the fetishised aporia that is

Ireland (and Irish literature) and the concomitant glance to future clarity are a feature of Yeats's criticism as they are of Lloyd's. MacDonagh's instinct to set Ireland outside Cartesian and Darwinian Europe may be historically questionable, but it finds its replication in Lloyd's notion of a version of Irishness which is (postcolonially) 'non-modern', 'out of kilter with modernity but none the less in a dynamic relation to it'.[80] The teasing gap between the modern and the 'non-modern', between concrete definition and continually deferred definition, has become such a trope of Irish criticism that we might wonder whether a fuller analysis of Irish criticism in the last century would not reveal this to be a self-fulfilling function of criticism itself, rather than the inevitable and serious game of pursuit of national and literary explication which it again and again reappears as.

This chapter has attempted to summarise a series of major trends and recurrent patterns in Irish criticism in the twentieth century. The most readily apparent, linking factor in all the critics discussed is the tenacious grip which the 'national' has on critical discourse in Irish literary studies (whether that be expressed through identity politics, future aspiration, celebration of the past and liberation, or by dissent against these). While this is a predictable enough model, its sense that a bifurcated existence is fundamental to literary-critical models of Ireland has often been viewed in more 'writerly' ways. In 1997 Neil Corcoran's *After Yeats and Joyce*[81] supplied students of Irish literature with a ready introduction to the subject in the twentieth century, and the title of Corcoran's book is an apt reminder that at times in writings on Irish literature Yeats and Joyce seem to be the points of inevitable return, paid homage to and then used as an explanatory context. In his essay, 'Yeats, Joyce and the Irish Critical Debate',[82] Terence Brown delineates a history of this oppositional dialectic as it crosses over into Irish criticism, from Irish Ireland up to Seamus Deane. Brown ends with a note of optimism on Deane's future discussions of Yeats, since the combination of Deane's introduction of a 'colonial' reading of Yeats (in *Heroic Styles*[83]), tempered with the new knowledge of Yeats's life which emerged with the first volume of the Yeats letters,[84] offered a way for Yeats to be 'recovered' in some sense for a modern Ireland from which he was being increasingly disenfranchised (in favour of Joyce's more 'authentically' modern, urban pluralities). It is debatable whether Brown's anticipation of a 'new' critical version of Yeats was fulfilled *within* the paradigms of Irish criticism, as he hoped; however, recent critical trends in readings of Yeats and Joyce might be instructive in seeing some elements of newness and change interrupting the ebb and flow of Irish critical discourse. Yeats and Joyce have, of course, always had a critical life outside 'Irish studies' and in recent years, as the equally rigid critical paradigms of 'modernism' have begun to falter under the weight of theorisation, there are signs that there is a strain on the ability of Irish criticism to hold its old positions too. So while Yeats studies and Joyce studies have retained a partial, almost esoterically aloof independence, the work of Marjorie Howes and Elizabeth Butler Cullingford on Yeats, and Vincent J. Cheng and Suzette A. Henke on Joyce,[85] are examples of how theoretical concerns around issues of gender, race and colonialism are beginning to reinflect critical thinking in ways which dissolve the supremacy of either a definitive Irishness or a literariness (Modernism) in reading the 'generally understood' 'contrast between Joyce and Yeats'.[86] The process which Brown identifies as an alteration in Irish readings of Yeats and Joyce may eventually be made inevitable and be overtaken in the twenty-first century by theoretically-informed (and near-heretical) critiques from 'outside' the folds of what is recognisably Irish criticism, finally starting the dissipation of the weary binaries which Denis Donoghue identifies when he says of Yeats: 'It is foolish, then, to recruit Yeats to a cause, he will go over to the enemy, if only to prolong the quarrel'.[87] Still, Donoghue's comment that 'a reader of Yeats finds himself living in an empire of feeling'[88] is now, at last, being symbolically reorientated towards a more material sense of 'empire' and a more gendered sense of both reader and writer. Or maybe this sense of a new beginning is the old sense of beginning come round again. Denis Donoghue certainly is confident in the abilities of Irish criticism to resist theory when, in commenting on the Field Day pamphlets collected in *Ireland's Field Day*, he ominously warns that 'The man to beat is Yeats'.[89]

The end of a century of Irish criticism allows us a privileged if arbitrary marker, a point from which to look back at the archive of writing about Irish writing which has been accumulated through the radical fulfilments and disappointments of the nation-narrative and through the tensions which have arisen between the nation and its literature. Derrida suggests that a 'science of the archive must include the theory of . . . institutionalisation, that is to say, the theory both of the law which begins by inscribing itself there and of the right which authorizes it'.[90] Irish criticism in the twentieth century is, as this chapter has sought to show, at once a noise of argument and a silence around the foundations of those arguments; its buried processes of institutionalisation make the archival science of saying what exactly Irish criticism has been even more complex. Still, the end of the century suggests an increasingly widespread recognition that:

There is no archive without a place of consignation, without a technique of repetition, and without a certain exteriority. No archive without outside.[91]

The as-yet unpublished fourth volume of the *Field Day Anthology* may be the most fundamental test of the strength yet endured by the Irish critical archive's laws and authority. Such public and sustained interventions at the boundaries of Irish criticism's self-'consignation' are overdue revelations that the 'techniques of repetition' which Irish criticism has fallen into are now (once again) wearing themselves out.

Notes

1. Thomas MacDonagh, *Literature in Ireland: Studies Irish & Anglo-Irish* (Talbot: Dublin, 1916), p. 5.
2. MacDonagh, *Literature in Ireland*, p. 5.
3. The closest text to a full history of Irish literary and cultural criticism, in the twentieth century and before, is Gerry Smyth, *Decolonisation and Criticism: The Construction of Irish Literature* (London: Pluto, 1998), to which I am indebted. While covering much ground from the nineteenth century to the present day, Smyth's focus is on the 1950s. The fullest, most informative and most lucid account of critical culture in late nineteenth- and early twentieth-century Ireland is in the Introduction to and anthologised extracts of Luke Gibbons, 'Constructing the Canon: Versions of National Identity', in Seamus Deane (ed.), *The Field Day Anthology of Irish Literature* (Derry: Field Day, 1991), II, pp. 950–1020.
4. W. B. Yeats, 'What is Popular Poetry?', in *Essays and Introductions* (Dublin: Gill and Macmillan, 1961), pp. 3–12 (p. 3).
5. John Kelly and Eric Domville (eds), *The Collected Letters of W. B. Yeats: Volume I, 1865–1895* (Oxford: Oxford University Press, 1986), p. 201.
6. W. B. Yeats (ed.), *Representative Irish Tales*, with a Foreword by Mary Helen Thuente (Gerrards Cross: Colin Smythe, [1891] 1979), p. 32.
7. W. B. Yeats, 'A General Introduction for My Work' in *Essays and Introductions*, p. 512.
8. Jacques Derrida, *Archive Fever: A Freudian Impression*, trans. Eric Prenowitz (London: University of Chicago Press, 1996), pp. 90, 18 and 19.
9. Charles A. Read (ed.), *The Cabinet of Irish Literature* (Dublin: Blackie, 1895). The other most notable effort at a comprehensive anthology of Irish writing at this period was Justin P. McCarthy (ed.), *Irish Literature*, 10 vols (New York: Bigelow, 1904).
10. David J. O'Donoghue, *The Poets of Ireland: A Biographical Dictionary with Bibliographical Particulars* (London: Paternoster Square Press, 1892).
11. Kelly and Domville (eds), *The Collected Letters of W.B. Yeats, Volume I*, p. 151.

12. See Chris Baldick, *Criticism and Literary Theory: 1890 to the Present* (London: Longman, 1996) on the forms of criticism which existed at the beginning of the twentieth century. In a further complication to the Irish picture, Baldick's description of the *belle lettrism* of English literature in the 1890s has Wilde, Shaw and Yeats as his first three examples (p. 59). To Baldick's credit he does acknowledge the obvious coincidence here.

13. Edgeworth's exceptionalism is ensured by Yeats calling her the 'one serious novelist coming from the upper classes in Ireland': Yeats (ed.), *Representative Irish Tales*, p. 27.

14. E. Owens Blackburne, *Illustrious Irishwomen* (London: Tinsley, 1877); Helen Zimmern, *Maria Edgeworth* (London: W. H. Allen, 1883); Emily Lawless, *Maria Edgeworth* (London: Macmillan, 1904); Constance Hill, *Maria Edgeworth and Her Circle in the Days of Buonaparte and Bourbon* (London: John Lane, 1910).

15. Yeats, 'The Celtic Element in Literature' in *Essays and Introductions*, p. 174.

16. Yeats, 'The Celtic Element in Literature', p. 180.

17. Yeats, 'The Celtic Element in Literature', p. 181.

18. Yeats, 'The Celtic Element in Literature', p. 182.

19. Yeats writes, for example: 'all ancient peoples, who, like the old Irish, had a nature more lyrical than dramatic, delight in wild and beautiful lamentations' (p. 182); the slightly cagey 'more lyrical than dramatic' avoids Arnoldian caricature by relying on the particularities of Yeats's version of non-history.

20. Yeats, 'The Celtic Element in Literature', p. 182.

21. On Celticism and Primitivism in Yeats see Sinéad Garrigan Mattar, 'Primitivism and the Writers of the Irish Dramatic Movement' (DPhil thesis, Oxford, 1997).

22. Thomas MacDonagh, *Literature in Ireland*, p. vii.

23. MacDonagh was famously supposed to have been working on the final drafts of the book while participating in the Easter Rising, but as Johann A. Norstedt points out we should be mindful of the book's long and erratic gestation over a number of years. See Johann A. Norstedt, *Thomas MacDonagh: A Critical Biography* (Charlottesville: University Press of Virginia, 1980).

24. MacDonagh, *Literature in Ireland*, p. 6.

25. On the relationship between MacDonagh's writing and the Rising see also William Irwin Thompson, *The Imagination of an Insurrection: Dublin, Easter 1916: A Study of an Ideological Moment* (New York: Oxford University Press, 1967), pp. 124–31.

26. The term 'aporetic' is derived here from its use in Jacques Derrida, *Aporias*, trans. Thomas Dutoit (Stanford, CA: Stanford University Press, 1993).

27. Ernest Boyd, *Ireland's Literary Renaissance* (London: Grant Richards, 1923).

28. William Kirkpatrick Magee ('John Eglinton'), *Anglo-Irish Essays* (New York: Books for Libraries Press, [1918] 1968); see also Stephen Gwynn, *Today and Tomorrow in Ireland* (Dublin: Hodges Figgis, 1903).

29. Daniel Corkery, *The Hidden Ireland: A Study of Gaelic Munster in the Eighteenth Century* (Dublin: Gill & Macmillan, [1924] 1989), p. 9.

30. Corkery is most specifically a Romantic when, echoing Wordworth's 'Preface' to *Lyrical Ballads*, he writes '. . . every Romantic movement is right in its intention: it seeks to grow out of living feeling, out of the here

and now, even when it finds its themes in its people's past . . . Dialect is the language of the common people', *The Hidden Ireland*, p. 14. For Corkery's view of rural England and Wordsworth see Patrick Maume, *'Life that is Exile': Daniel Corkery and the Search for Irish Ireland* (Belfast: Institute of Irish Studies, 1993), pp. 113–14 and 121.

31. Corkery, *The Hidden Ireland*, pp. 12 and 13.

32. Corkery, *The Hidden Ireland*, p. 13.

33. Corkery, *The Hidden Ireland*, p. 12. Terence Brown notes a different and more positive view of Europe in Corkery's idealisation of 'the mediaeval world of Catholic Europe', and in the connections to Europe (bypassing England) in Big House culture in the eighteenth century: see Terence Brown, 'Yeats, Joyce and the Irish Critical Debate', in *Ireland's Literature: Selected Essays* (Mullingar: Lilliput, 1988), p. 78.

34. For an excellent critique of Corkery on this basis see Louis M. Cullen, *The Hidden Ireland: Reassessment of a Concept* (Mullingar: Lilliput, 1988).

35. Corkery, *The Hidden Ireland*, pp. 21 and 23.

36. Corkery, *The Hidden Ireland*, p. 40.

37. Hugh Alexander Law, *Anglo-Irish Literature* (Dublin: Talbot Press, 1926), p. viii.

38. Law, *Anglo-Irish Literature*, p. ix.

39. Stephen Gwynn, *Irish Literature and Drama in the English Language: A Short History* (London: Thomas Nelson, 1936), p. 1.

40. Gwynn, *Irish Literature and Drama*, p. 1.

41. Gwynn, *Irish Literature and Drama*, p. 2 (emphasis added).

42. Gwynn, *Irish Literature and Drama*, p. 206.

43. Law, *Anglo-Irish Literature*, p. vii.

44. Gwynn, *Irish Literature and Drama*, p. 230.

45. On the rise of institutionalised literary study in Irish universities see, *passim*, Smyth, *Decolonisation and Criticism*, and Edna Longley, '"A foreign oasis"?: English Literature, Irish Studies and Queen's University Belfast', *The Irish Review*, 17/18 (Winter 1995), 26–39. On the professionalisation of literary study in the Anglo-American academy see Bruce Robbins, *Secular Vocations: Intellectuals, Professionalism, Culture* (London: Verso, 1993).

46. Richard Kearney, *Transitions: Narratives in Modern Irish Culture* (Manchester: Manchester University Press, 1988), p. 261.

47. Kearney, *Transitions*, p. 260.

48. Smyth, *Decolonisation and Criticism*, p. 118.

49. Seán Ó Faoláin, 'This is Your Magazine' in Sean McMahon (ed.), *The Best of the Bell: Great Irish Writing* (Dublin: O'Brien Press, 1978), p. 13.

50. Ó Faoláin, 'This is Your Magazine', p. 14.

51. Seán Ó Faoláin. 'Signing Off' in McMahon (ed.), *The Best of the Bell*, pp. 120–3.

52. Ó Faoláin, 'Signing Off', p. 123.

53. Ó Faoláin, 'Signing Off', pp. 123–4.

54. See Frank O'Connor's 'Introduction to the 1964 Edition' of Eric Cross, *The Tailor and Ansty* (Cork: Mercier, 1999), p. 12.

55. Terence Brown, *Ireland: A Social and Cultural History, 1922–1985* (London: Fontana, 1990), p. 199.

56. Ó Faoláin, 'This is Your Magazine', p. 13.

57. Denis Donoghue, 'Notes Towards a Critical Method: Language as Order',

Studies, 42 (1955), 181.

58. Donoghue warily notes that Catholic scholars are to the fore of New Criticism: he cites Fr William Lynch, William Wimsatt and Victor Hamm, while noting that they would not necessarily see themselves as Catholic critics.
59. Donoghue, 'Notes Towards a Critical Method: Language as Order', p. 200.
60. Donald Davie, 'Reflections of an English Writer in Ireland', *Studies*, 44 (1955), 442.
61. Davie, 'Reflections of an English Writer in Ireland', 440.
62. Davie certainly misreads Donoghue when he says: 'Mr Donoghue, one comes to see, was not so much arguing for the one and only true critical method, as for any critical method at all' (p. 440).
63. Vivian Mercier, 'An Irish School of Criticism?', *Studies*, 45 (1956), 84.
64. Mercier, 'An Irish School of Criticism?', pp. 84–5.
65. Mercier, 'An Irish School of Criticism?', p. 85.
66. Mercier, 'An Irish School of Criticism?', p. 86.
67. Mercier, 'An Irish School of Criticism?', p. 86.
68. Mercier, 'An Irish School of Criticism?', p. 87.
69. Richard Kirkland, *Literature and Culture in Northern Ireland Since 1965: Moments of Danger* (Harlow: Longman, 1996). For a discussion of the institution in Irish criticism see also Kirkland's 'Questioning the Frame: Hybridity, Ireland and the Institution', in Colin Graham and Richard Kirkland (eds), *Ireland and Cultural Theory: The Mechanics of Authenticity* (London: Macmillan, 1999), pp. 210–228. See also Claire Connolly's 'Introduction' to *Theorising Ireland* (London: Macmillan, forthcoming). My thanks to Claire Connolly for giving me access to her work during the writing of this chapter.
70. Declan Kiberd, *Inventing Ireland: The Literature of the Modern Nation* (London: Jonathan Cape, 1995); Seamus Deane, *Strange Country: Modernity and Nationhood in Irish Writing Since 1790* (Oxford: Clarendon, 1997); Terry Eagleton, *Crazy John and the Bishop and Other Essays on Irish Culture* (Cork: Cork University Press/Field Day, 1998).
71. Edna Longley, *Poetry in the Wars* (Newcastle upon Tyne: Bloodaxe, 1986) and *The Living Stream: Literature and Revisionism in Ireland* (Newcastle upon Tyne: Bloodaxe, 1994).
72. Longley, *Poetry in the Wars*, p. 185.
73. On the power of 'Irish studies' to preserve itself against the category of gender studies see Moynagh Sullivan, 'Feminism, Postmodernism and the Subjects of Irish and Women's Studies', in P. J. Mathews (ed.), *New Voices in Irish Criticism* (Dublin: Four Courts, 2000), pp. 243–51.
74. David Cairns and Shaun Richards, *Writing Ireland: Colonialism, Nationalism and Culture* (Manchester: Manchester University Press, 1988).
75. Collected as Seamus Deane (ed.), *Nationalism, Colonialism and Literature* (Minneapolis: Minneapolis University Press, 1990).
76. David Lloyd, *Anomalous States: Irish Writing and the Post-Colonial Moment* (Dublin: Lilliput, 1993).
77. David Lloyd, *Ireland After History* (Cork: Cork University Press/Field Day, 1999).
78. Lloyd, *Ireland After History*, p. 88 (emphasis added).
79. Lloyd, *Ireland After History*, p. 2.
80. Lloyd, *Ireland After History*, p. 2.

81. Neil Corcoran, *After Yeats and Joyce: Reading Modern Irish Literature* (Oxford: Oxford University Press, 1997).
82. Brown, 'Yeats, Joyce and the Irish Critical Debate', pp. 77–90.
83. Seamus Deane, *Heroic Styles: The Tradition of an Idea* (Derry: Field Day, 1986).
84. See note 5 above.
85. Marjorie Howes, *Yeats's Nations: Gender, Class, and Irishness* (Cambridge: Cambridge University Press, 1996); Elizabeth Butler Cullingford, *Gender and History in Yeats's Love Poetry* (Cambridge: Cambridge University Press, 1993); Vincent J. Cheng, *Joyce, Race and Empire* (Cambridge: Cambridge University Press, 1995); Suzette A. Henke, *James Joyce and the Politics of Desire* (London: Routledge, 1990).
86. W. J. McCormack, *From Burke to Beckett: Ascendancy, Tradition and Betrayal in Literary History* (Cork: Cork University Press, 1994), p. 9.
87. Denis Donoghue, *Yeats* (London: Fontana, 1971), p. 17.
88. Donoghue, *Yeats*, p. 16.
89. Denis Donoghue, 'Afterword', in *Ireland's Field Day*, ed. Field Day Theatre Company (London: Hutchinson, 1985), p. 120.
90. Derrida, *Archive Fever*, p. 4.
91. Derrida, *Archive Fever*, p. 11.

3

'A warmer memory':
Speaking of Ireland

The colonized considers those venerable scholars relics and thinks of them as sleepwalkers who are living in an old dream.[1] (Memmi)

. . . he says that in the course of his labours it would happen that inspiration failed him: he then would go downstairs and out of his house, and enter a public urinal whose odor was suffocating. He breathed deeply, and having thus 'approached as close as he could to the object of his horror', he returned to his work. I cannot help recalling the author's countenance, noble, emaciated, the nostrils quivering.[2] (Bataille on Michelet)

The role of the intellectual voice in the construction of radical identities has been central to the postcolonial critique of Ireland. Memmi's amusedly affectionate dismissal of 'venerable scholars' sleepwalking their way through a colonial history that is constantly passing them by is an appealing way to circumvent the interminable question 'Can the Subaltern Speak?', which shadows, *in potentia*, all pronouncements on the postcolonial subject and, by analogy, all acts of speaking of Ireland too. Spivak's question and its possible declensions essentially deny that an academic voice can be elevated to a point of enlightenment above the shadows of history and, since Spivak's essay, postcolonial theory has had a shorthand way in which to express its awareness of the potentially crippling vacuity at its centre. Yet, as the previous chapter sought to show, Irish criticism, postcolonial or otherwise (along with postcolonial criticism more generally) *has* gone on despite itself, with a Sisyphian doggedness, and continues to find a way of speaking 'of' Ireland. Memmi's analysis and Spivak's question pressurise intellectually radical discourse which avows to be from 'below', in two distinct ways. For Memmi, the conditions of colonialism and the postcolonial outstrip the capacities of the scholarly, so that the possibility of finding an adequate, conceptual and historical framework for the (post) colonial is always archaised and shut off by the place in which that framework must be articulated. For Spivak, the critical voice (or any voice which speaks 'about' the colonised) immediately suffers the distancing institutionality which fractures the 'object' of discourse from the voice which speaks it and which it attempts to make its own, simultaneous 'subject'.

In remembering the anecdote about Michelet, Bataille brings together these two problems in one 'embodied' moment. And Bataille thus ennobles the pathos of Michelet's solution – Michelet, constantly 'feeling' history as personal physiological trauma, tries to break through to 'the people', his object of study, by forcing himself through another physiological trauma which brings him face to face with the evidence of 'their' literal body politic. The quivering of Michelet's nostrils may be comically deflationary, in the first instance (like Memmi's intellectuals Michelet could be missing the substance of history, experiencing the nightmare of loss while dreaming delusions of grandeur), but his descent downstairs, his leaving of the sanctity of his own house and place of writing, and his self-degradation in primal excreta, function as a parable of the 'scholarly' when it lives off 'the people' as the basis of its existence. Michelet is alone, silent, inadequate, but ultimately valiant because he confronts and knows the abyss at the centre of his project. Above all, Michelet (in having this story known as well as enacting it) forces his writing about 'the people' to a crisis which involves the elemental nature of his self identity. In doing this Michelet certainly anticipates the gap between colonised people and postcolonial critique which has recently resurfaced; more profoundly he moves to the edge of that aporia, needing the object of his study to be the most sensate of realities, and insisting that it disturb his own calm. If Michelet cannot be *of* the people (and as we will see later he knew that he always failed to be), his sense of their corporeality as refracted through his own is as appropriately 'noble' and 'emaciated' as the dilemma which he lives out.

In his book *Michelet*, Roland Barthes allows Michelet to incant the indulgences of 'venerable scholars' who utter 'the people'. This chapter uses Barthes's Michelet to initiate a discussion of the strategies of writing about Ireland in relation to the critical 'self' which becomes implicated in that 'Ireland'. The chapter attempts to examine the role which the 'warmer memory' of 'the people' crucially undertakes in the processes of a criticism which takes to itself or asserts identity politics, and discusses the 'organic' necessities of the intellectual as they are reacted against and reconstructed in Joyce's Stephen Dedalus.

THE NEED FOR WARMTH

Michelet's view of history intrigues Barthes for many reasons (its critical sense of the bodily is only one example[3]). But above all it offers Barthes, pre-*Mythologies*, a challenge which Michelet also sets himself when he suggests that in history-writing 'words must be heard which were never spoken'.[4] In one way this is the purest of structuralist challenges; Barthes's Michelet is engaged in writing a history of France through a self-consciously doubled order of signs, in which historical events as signifiers act as a sign system in themselves, revealing history as other historians write and read it, but also point to a mythological second order of signs which delineates the words of an embedded and 'impossible language'. Michelet, as quoted by Barthes, writes:

I was born of the people, I have the people in my heart. The monuments of its olden days have been my delight . . . But the people's language, its language was inaccessible to me. I have not been able to make the people speak.[5]

Michelet's failure as historian hinges on his acceptance of what Spivak, through Said, constantly reminds us of in 'Can the Subaltern Speak?': 'the critic's institutional responsibility'.[6] And Michelet takes this 'responsibility' not in its meanest sense (that is, in being responsible to itself, to history, to objectivity, to disciplinary rigours), but in its weightiest connotation as predicatory foundation for the critical voice. Michelet's voice here is close to the 'baleful innocence'[7] which Spivak identifies when, in 'Can the Subaltern Speak?', she analyses Deleuze's conversation with Foucault. However, in the end, Michelet's balefulness, in its raw self-aware state, is entirely opposite to theirs. Contrast Michelet's abnegation in the urinal to Spivak's comment on Deleuze and Foucault:

The banality of leftist intellectuals' lists of self-knowing, politically canny subalterns stands revealed; representing them, the intellectuals represent themselves as transparent.[8]

Michelet, painfully, cannot believe himself transparent and yet cannot break out of the connective fabric of 'representation' which interweaves 'the choice of and need for "heroes"' with re-presentation in the 'scene of writing'.[9] Writing itself thus becomes for Michelet a bodily enterprise, just as the evidence of the history he lives off takes on a repulsive–attractive corporeal form; history for Michelet, as Barthes suggests, is to be 'consummated' and 'consumed'.[10] And yet Michelet's history, bound by the strictures of representation, is riven by the movement to the material and bodily, set against a realisation of the 'impossible language' needed to conceive history. Both the textuality and the mystically unsayable nature of this dilemma are embodied in Barthes's summary of Michelet's idea of the 'historian's duties': 'The historian is in fact a civil magistrate in charge of administering the estate of the dead'.[11] As civil *servant* (of the people), as 'the magus who receives from the dead their actions'[12] and who is duty-bound to voice words 'never spoken', Michelet's own corporeality and self-hood are continually questioned in this self-exiled existence between the paradoxically substantial ghosts which are 'the people' and the spectral realities which are historical facts.

The importance of Michelet's example lies in his ability (and in that of Barthes's prompting critique) to make 'the people' site and receptor of his energies while knowing their unbridgeable distance from himself. Michelet, through Barthes, turns on their heads the transparency of the subaltern and the self-knowing of the intellectual, so that 'the people', source of his very existence, are at best for him an 'it', and so veering towards being an Other, while the self 'Michelet' which writes is made strange and decayed to itself. Moving towards the people and towards him-self, Michelet vainly but heroically empties the heroism of history, questions his own heroism, and keeps 'the people' from the text. Michelet's example is no solution to the question of how the act of representing 'the people' can be made transparent; what he stands as, through Barthes, is a statement of the nature of the difficulties which Spivak sees postcolonial and poststructuralist radicalism constantly evading. Michelet frankly acknowledges the attraction of 'warmth' over 'light', light being a 'critical idea [which] implies culture and brightness', while warmth is 'a phenomenon of depth; it is the sign of the mass, of the innumerable, of the people, of the barbarian'.[13] And so it is that the 'voice of the people affords Michelet a warmer memory that is more "linked together" than all the writings of the legislators and witnesses'.[14] The bifurcation of 'light' and 'warmth' as poles of repulsion and attraction undoes that banality which Spivak bemoans and puts in process a deconstruction of 'the people' as intellectual piety.[15] The tension between the scholar and the people can be figured in these terms, as they are for Michelet when in self-contemplation, and as they are in Joyce's Ithacan meeting of Stephen Dedalus and Leopold Bloom, as I suggest later. 'Light' and 'warmth' are definitively not opposites for Michelet; their phenomenological interrelation and inter-reliance, and yet their inherent difference, give them a coexistence which conceptually is able to symbolise the tortured kind of self-sustenance which the intellectual voice finds itself reluctant, unable and unwilling to achieve. The 'warmth' of 'the people' for (Irish) criti-cism proves irresistible but may need to be forever unobtainable.

'The people' as Michelet always fails to find them are thus fetishised to some extent, and would be fully, if only he could find 'it', and so make 'it' into 'them'. 'The people' as 'it' plays hide and seek with Michelet so that he can never say for certain whether 'it' is now or will be soon a 'they'. All he has is the unrecapturable certainty of the past tense ('I was born of the people') and so he senses and remembers the 'warmth' of the people, but never regains 'its' heat in his writing. The impossible language of the subaltern people will always attract him, by choice and by necessity; more than this, 'it' (as entity and as language) demands the absolute atten-tion of his writing and in the end his whole self as intellectual. So Michelet's journey out of his house is the closest that he can come to the double representation which he desires. That journey makes foundational and yet absent 'the people' and the form of language they demand but which cannot be attained.

Irish critical voices, I would argue, find themselves in varieties of Michelet's structural predicament. The 'hidden' Ireland of Irish crit-icism (or more generally, writing about Ireland) is very obviously conceived in many ways by many writers, but that variety of politics and of interpretative modes need not be flattened out to a homo-geneity in order to see that the site of that 'warmth' which Michelet sought, whether 'found', disavowed or revised, is the 'impossible lan-guage' which underlies each statement of definition of what Ireland is or might be. Michelet's self-critical journey mirrors, for example, Daniel Corkery's journey into his 'Hidden Ireland', 'leaving the cities and towns behind', venturing 'among the bogs and hills, far into the mountains . . . [where] the native Irish . . . still lurked'.[16] But we need not take either the journey or the 'hiddenness' of Ireland so literally in order to see how Barthes's Michelet reveals the warmth which Irish criticism seeks by being Irish criticism. To extend the above example, we might ask what it is that leads Corkery, 'upbraided', as he terms it, at the end of *The Hidden Ireland*, to finish his book with these heartfelt words of his own inadequacies in the face of 'the people':

Here, then, my tribute, humble, halting, inept, unlearned, to a body of men who for long were almost entirely forgotten and who as yet are only clumsily apprehended – their lives, their works, their genius. Of all our forgotten dead, of whom these words following have been written, those poets, it seems to me, most terribly upbraid us: 'To them has been meted out the second death – the lot feared beyond all else by men of honour. They have been buried by the false hands of strangers in the deep pit of contempt, reproach and forgetfulness – an unmerited grave of silence and shame'.[17]

CRITICAL FUTURES

In speaking of Ireland, in any critical or metadiscursive context, the question of what the word 'Ireland' signifies is obviously semantically and politically fraught to the extent that it is tempting to suggest that Irish critical discourse, in its multiple manifestations, finds itself *de facto* always returned to exactly that defining activity. Giving 'Ireland' a meaning which fills out the term comfortably is seemingly the underwriting principle of Irish criticism's existence, with the aesthetic, the cultural, the generic and the 'minor' all given a presence within critical writing on Ireland by their contribution as slivers of 'Ireland', which are temporarily imagined as hived off from the undisrupted, unseeable whole. Each book and article on Joyce or on the Whiteboys, each individual account of Irish memoir, each reclamation of Irishness from the diaspora, then risks becoming subsumed in the perpetually deferred but always desired, Casaubon-like quest for the settling of 'the Irish question', a question which both begs a definition and a definitive answer; and that question transcends the politics of unionism or nationalism, the force of revisionist historiography, the regional and the local, and indeed the course of historical change itself, being always sure of its position as the reason for what is spoken about 'Ireland' and never in fear of alteration by these pronouncements. It needs to be made clear that this is not the same as saying that Ireland as a political entity has never changed; nor is it the same as saying that Irish nationalism has a fixed, archaic sense of what the Irish nation is. This underwriting 'Ireland' is constituted not primarily by politics and history *per se*, but by the structural necessities of (what is inadequately termed) 'identity' and by the predominance of proper noun and adjective, Ireland and Irish, as identifications of place, identity and, just as comprehensively, academic discipline and intellectual thought; this 'Ireland' inhabits a domain which is closer, as an analogy, to the inevitable ever-presence of historiography within the evidence of history than it is to historical 'facts' or interpretations themselves. It is always implied and implicated in criticism's voice rather than being given substance by any transparent relationship which criticism claims to have with its object. Hence to speak of Ireland is to project forward to a future project in which all facts, opinions and statements on Ireland find a home within the encompassment of what 'Ireland' is; this 'Ireland' is constituted through critical language as a 'transcendental signified' which 'would place a reassuring end to the reference from sign to sign'.[18] And so we should anticipate that the expectation of reassurance and resolution will pervade the Irish critical voice, its 'Ireland' always projected hopefully into a sense of an ending.

Such an 'end', however, would be far from reassuring, since this critically anticipated 'Ireland' also brings a danger. Its putative and ever-promised achievement carries with it the death of 'Ireland' as foundation; in its promise to 'place a reassuring end to the reference from sign to sign' it carries the fear of turning 'Ireland' into real 'presence'. Through its articulation 'Ireland' is *not* the effective end-point of a narrative, despite the constant futurity of a notional set of Irelands in the realm of the political. The transcendent 'Ireland' which accommodates all statements about Ireland slips out of time before it can be entrapped, and thus avoids collapsing the trope of narration. Indeed it could be argued (as I suggest below about Declan Kiberd and Emer Nolan in their critiques of Joyce) that narrative time is the way in which 'Ireland' escapes and puts off definition, ensuring its place as an absent presence now, and a promissory repletion later, when time itself is full and 'nostalgia' no longer has a role; in this, Irish criticism is caught in the excessive/aporetic play of the utopian, delayed 'Ireland' described in Chapter 1.

This notionally transcendent 'Ireland' is not, then, just another sign. No alternative transcendent lies in wait to take over; the possible alternatives (those which are foundational, for example, in liberal humanism *and* nationalism – the literary, the good, the just) have already been deployed in the perpetual process of definition and fixing, and so exist below the transcendent status of 'Ireland', having been in its service. Hence there must be a necessarily tremulous method of approaching 'Ireland' within Irish criticism, on the one hand seeking its definition as the key to all mythologies, as the *langue* of speaking about Ireland which binds together and explains the fact of speech in this discourse itself, on the other hand knowing that the act of defining 'Ireland' as *langue* begs a replacement which is unimaginable, given the exhaustion of resources deployed in order to get to that point of definition. For the critical voice, the 'self' which speaks in relation to 'Ireland' needs, expects and functions by, the anticipation of continual deferral; only its own collapse into a vacuum is imaginable beyond the ever held-off future moment of absolute fulfilment. Put simply, if 'Ireland' existed self-evidently, why would we need to examine it, contest it, invent it, state its anomalies or write it?

That this underwriting 'Ireland' is a deferred transcendent, and thus always a symbol of futurity, could of course be traced in a genealogical way to the history of its formation. In a Foucauldian scheme one might be able to untangle the epistemic moment(s) at which 'Ireland' became the invisible listener to and ultimate receptor of all statements about itself,[19] and this would undoubtedly be a result of the context of European nationalism and British colonialism in which the structural functions of Irish nationality are again and again thrust into teleologies of progress and change, so that future transcendence is the refuge for 'Ireland', clearing the way for political Irelands to manifest themselves. More clearly evident is that any postcolonial critique of Irish culture, for all its apparent and/or potential radicality, runs the danger of all postcolonialism in regard to its understanding of time itself. As Anne McClintock points out, through the term postcolonial theory the focus of critical analysis 'is ... shifted from the binary axis of *power* ... to the binary axis of *time*, an axis even less productive of political nuance ... [The] *singularity* of the term effects a re-centring of global history around the single rubric of European time. Colonialism returns at the moment of its disappearance'.[20] For Irish postcolonialism the effects of this narrativising of a theory, which has a supposed theoretical bent towards the synchronic examination of systems of colonialism, are doubly inflected through the particularities of the nation-narrative and its state of suspension post-Partition. Thus the paradoxical reintroduction of 'European time' lifts 'Ireland' as a form of address out of its sign system and propels it for its own preservation into a future which needs to be undetermined. The desire for a synchronous definition of what 'Ireland' is remains behind as trace evidence of this continual projection forward, while the linear temporality which enthrals radical politics means that the 'Ireland' of Irish criticism makes promises which perplexingly are never kept.

MOURNING AND CELEBRATION

The link between the twin strands I have been developing here can be established in another way by noting their shared trait of impossibility and their use of a necessary intractability; 'Ireland' as subject, and the critical voice which speaks of 'Ireland' both disappear into a place which lies beyond what can be known, so that the tantalising prospect of a new 'Bloomusalem' remains eternally fresh. Hence Michelet and his relationship with 'the people' is useful since it embodies both a subject and an academic voice which needs and constitutes this dependency as perpetually unfulfilled.

Barthes' Michelet represents a paragon of the academic quest for its national subject; raising that search to the level of trauma certainly clarifies that the 'culture' sought can function as much more than a material superstructure, and that it has a predicatory role for critical discourse which is projected into an ever-deferred future. The drama of Michelet's descent from his study is also personal, in the most fundamental of ways. It is Michelet who feels the need for 'the people' (to an extent it is Michelet who labels and identifies 'the people'), just as it is Michelet who is jarred by the 'impossible language' which keeps the people 'inaccessible';[21] Michelet 'sees himself as feeble, unhealthy',[22] and, in the urinal, his abjection is a dramatised ontological crisis in which Michelet's 'self' competes for priority with the idea of 'the people' which induces his crisis. In inculcating a pathos of the critical voice as disjunctive from yet seeking for its subject, Michelet acknowledges the risk of a bathetic self-engrossment which is its own end. We may not expect others to follow his extraordinary example, but keeping Michelet in mind helps in thinking about how the critical voice in its own right is constituted by its construction of 'Ireland', and how, as in Michelet, the primacy of 'the people', or 'Ireland', may fade into the critical voice's fascinated instabilities as it searches for the fantasy of teleological fulfilment.

Michelet's search for atonement in the urinal has an obvious counterpart in Irish writing in the 'Ithaca' chapter of *Ulysses*, when Stephen and Bloom urinate together (more on this below). Equally the Stephen of *Stephen Hero, A Portrait of the Artist as a Young Man* and *Ulysses* has in many ways become the archetype of a fledging Irish intellectual, the 'undergraduate artist-hero'[23] in dispute with himself on the subject of his relationship to 'the people'. In his diary entries at the end of *Portrait* Stephen famously and bitingly recounts Mulrennan's return from the West of Ireland where 'he met an old man there in a mountain cabin'.[24] Stephen's 'fear [of the peasant's] ... redrimmed horny eyes' and his anticipated 'struggle' to the death with the old man pass quickly into a reconsideration which is a form of distanciation: '. . . Till what? Till he yield to me? No. I mean him no harm'.[25] As David Cairns and Shaun Richards note, Joyce's attempt to achieve an unobtrusive concern for the peasant, to reassess and diminish the pressing claims of Stephen's connection with the peasant, is 'untypical' of the period,[26] and Len Platt points to the distinct way in which Joyce negotiates the ever-present demands of addressing a 'real' Ireland in opposition to Synge and Yeats, whose contact with the peasantry is too often unproblematically physical and has a 'reality [which] throbs with significance, which the text simply and humbly transcribes'.[27] Stephen's existence as character and as representation of the young intellectual is the initial act of distanciation which enables Joyce to escape the necessity for 'struggle' (which, arguably, Yeats and Synge escape differently, through a revivalist form of mythologisation). Stephen's passingly anticipated, chaotic confrontation with the peasant is a direct inversion of Michelet's panic at the loss of contact with the people, and reiterates 'the people' as a structural foundation before the revolution of a contingent forgetting of them.

As Declan Kiberd says of this part of Stephen's narrative, '[this] is not just a caustic parody of Synge's peasants, but a terrified recognition that Joyce's liberation from Ireland was more apparent than real'.[28] Kiberd sees here an anticipation of the 'guilty compromise' of 'postcolonial exile' which means, on the part of the writer, 'a refusal of a more direct engagement',[29] and this is certainly one way of expressing the dynamic of 'the people' for the postcolonial intellectual. Stephen's diary entry for 14 April is also part of a sequence which is illuminated further by looking at the preceding and successive days – the previous day's entry recounts the much discussed revelation that the word 'tundish' is 'English and good old blunt English too',[30] while on 15 April Stephen writes of his last meeting with EC, a meeting which, like that *imagined* the day before with the peasant, ends with an effort at achieved distance ('in fact . . . O, give it up, old chap! Sleep it off!'[31]). The three entries replay *encounters* of varying hostility (with the Dean of Studies and his Englishness, with the peasant and the acute version of Irishness which he represents, with EC and the tremor which her sexuality brings to Stephen) and are thus linked by the repulsion–attraction form of personalised contact, merging the physically abject with the politically righteous, which Michelet desires and which Stephen is, in all three cases, pulled towards before finding forms of rejection which are suitably temperate.

If, as is often the case, Stephen is elided into 'Joyce', then there is work to be done by the radical Irish critic in reclaiming through Joyce's work a voicing of either 'Ireland' or 'the people', and not only because, as Vincent Cheng, points out, Joyce's relation to Ireland has traditionally gone relatively unprivileged because the 'Academy... has chosen to construct a sanitized "Joyce" whose contributions are now to be measured only by the standards of canonical High Modernism'.[32] Stephen's rejection of something that is at least Dublin if not Ireland, followed by his (and Joyce's) return to that rejected entity in *Ulysses*, seems to offer a possibility of redemption for an Irish criticism of Joyce. Kiberd, for example, finds Ireland emerging triumphant in a form of orality which is a 'tradition' set in motion alongside the 'bookishness' also found in *Ulysses*, with the balance 'tilted finally towards the older tradition'.[33] Emer Nolan suggests of *Finnegans Wake* that

[when] ALP-as-river joins the sea, something specific is lost in an oceanic chaos. As with her, so with Ireland. Both have entered the devil's era of modernity, liberated into difference, lost to identity. This is not a simple transition. Joyce both celebrates and mourns it; his readers have so far tended only to join in the celebration.[34]

Taken together, the rising again of oral tradition out of 'bookishness' and the mourning of lost identity looks to be a tentative reinstatement, through Joyce, of the forms of nationalism he himself ironises.[35] Nolan and Kiberd, in their different ways, insist on Joyce's reintroduction and resolution of the postcolonial problematic of 'the people' as precept for intellectual speech. Seamus Deane's remark on a post-Burkean Irish trope which sees Ireland as having 'no narrative but the narrative of nostalgia' embodies, in charged forms, both Kiberd's 'tradition' 'renovated' (to use another of Deane's words) and Nolan's deeply ethical pleading for a 'mourning' of lost 'identity' and the realisation that incoherence is the price of the 'devil's era of modernity'.

Deane says, further, that '[nostalgia] was the dynamic that impelled the search for the future'.[36] Certainly critical futures are implied by Nolan and Kiberd; in Nolan's complaint that Joyce's 'readers have so far tended' to read his nationalism in one way, and in Kiberd's suggestion that *Ulysses* 'would only be given its full expression in the act of being read aloud'[37] (presumably also anticipating *Finnegans Wake*), both Nolan and Kiberd position their critiques as entailing future projects. These futures importantly cast Joyce's Ireland from an unsatisfactorily indeterminate present into a futurity which can allow for a resolution that can be decided upon then; and that future is dependent on a wash back to what is figured as a 'past', a 'tradition', a state before 'loss'. In other words, underwriting these complex critical repositionings of Joyce and Ireland is a state in which Joyce and Ireland are synchronous with each other, but only because history coincides with itself so that the organicism of the intellectual is transformed into transparency, and in which the past we've never known meets itself again in the future.

The lesson which Michelet so painfully learns is, however, a very different one, and might be borne in mind as we construct our future critical Irelands out of our putative Irish pasts. The 'lost' organicism of the intellectual is too swiftly conceptualised in temporal terms, which mutate easily into historical terms. Both Stephen and Michelet see their distance from 'the people' as an occurrence of biography; therefore a slippage to personal narrative, then to cultural narrative is an enticing mindset for imagining the 'recovery' of this loss. But as Anne McClintock (quoted earlier) reminds us, the postcolonial compels criticism, against its own better judgement, to see linear temporalities first and synchronous structures second. Stephen's biography in *Portrait*, along with his return to Ireland in *Ulysses*, tantalise with the elements necessary for Deane's nostalgic futures, but, I would argue, Michelet's example usefully reveals to us that the failure to meet 'the people' in the intellectual voice, the failure to make the subaltern speak, is not a temporally 'new' phenomenon at any stage, but is a consistent fate of the intellectual voice. Thus pasts are nostalgised and futures imagined, and mourning, celebration and prediction (or more grandly, prophecy) become compelling modes of academic speech.

TAKING THE PISS

Joyce as ever can be seen to anticipate this. Bloom is no 'redrimmed horny' eyed peasant, but in his Everyman role he becomes Stephen's counterpart and his substitute father. Stephen and Bloom are, archetypally in early Joyce criticism, 'two souls in search of the spiritual salvation that they can never find'.[38] As Anthony Burgess puts it, in 'Ithaca' even the act of making cocoa reminds us 'of the unconscious groping towards each other that Bloom and Stephen have, usually off their guard, in the margins of thought, exhibited all day'.[39] For Stephen, Bloom can be what Mulrennan's old man of the west cannot be. In 'Ithaca' the ordinariness of the corporeal becomes an act of celebration rather than abjection, constituting a response to Michelet's crisis and his privation.

In a critique of Fredric Jameson's account of *Ulysses*, Thomas Hofheinz lambasts Jameson's continual positioning of the collective as having primacy over the individual (Jameson's 'theoretical compulsion to subsume individual human lives within ideal collectivities'[40]), and while Jameson's position is somewhat caricatured as a result, the point is well made:

> Jameson's assertion that the cocoa-making [in 'Ithaca'] is 'inauthentic' because the kettle is mass-produced and somehow not an organic part of its user's 'destiny' depends upon a bizarre assumption that such domestically familiar objects are not meaningful to those individuals who cherish them.[41]

In an argument, moving on from Hofheinz's, I want to argue that in 'Ithaca' can be found a moment of ordinariness (among many possible others) which addresses the profound tension between the collective and the personal, the national and the 'human', the political and the everyday, and which also reveals Joyce's text to be returning to that fundamental notion of 'the people' as precept for the intellectual voice in a revising if open-ended (and eventually gendered) way. And in his defence of cocoa-making, Hofheinz is strangely correct, since it is in the ordinariness of the bodily, not in a 'struggle' with a cultural demon, that Stephen, the figure of the intellectual, finds himself as close as possible to 'the people' in a new way ('the people' having been redefined and so brought closer). Here also the self-excoriation which Michelet forces himself to endure is circumvented, as are the stringencies of grand narrative, and the pain and mourning of continual cultural deferral are turned to shadows.

Suzette A. Henke, in *James Joyce and the Politics of Desire*, writes: '"Ithaca" concludes the man's epic (his)story'.[42] My contention about the chapter is similar, in that the aspects of 'Ithaca' on which I focus show Joyce's text to be coincidental with the fundamentals of the Micheletian dilemma, in which history and an epic heroism are brought into contact with the voice which voices both. Bloom's and Stephen's rich duality (father–son, Everyman–intellectual) plays out the desire for 'contact' which Stephen retracts from in three different ways in the diary entries towards the end of *Portrait* because the crises which result are self-perpetuating. 'Ithaca' reveals these '(his)stories' to be imbued with a masculine fear of 'contact' which is simultaneously a fear of being washed over by 'history' ('history' demanding the presence of the people and so functioning as the reminder that the intellectual self should efface itself to the point of transparency and to the end of alterity). Hence I am suggesting that reading 'Ithaca' provides some of kind release from the bonds which Michelet confronts, by particularising, parodying and accepting the structural deficiencies of the intellectual voice.

Stepping outside 7 Eccles Street, Stephen Dedalus and Leopold Bloom contemplate the stars, their wonder continually compromised by the 'catechismal' (or impersonal) technique of the Ithacan narrative.[43] Bloom's meditations 'of evolution increasingly vaster' (17: 1043)[44] lead him through the celestial and the mathematical and the contemplation of alien life 'Martian, Mercurial, Veneral, Jovian, Saturnian, Neptunian or Uranian' (17: 1095), and eventually to a typical Bloomian recognition that

an apogean humanity of beings created in varying forms ... would probably there as here remain inalterably and inalienably attached to vanities, to vanities of vanities and to all that is vanity. (17: 1096–100)

Bloom's often touchingly instinctive inclusivity here reaches an 'apogee' in that it extends even beyond the human to the literally 'alien', the ultimate of alterities, and collapses all into the humility of 'vanity'. Bloom then considers the stars, as a 'logical conclusion' (the term which the catechismal questioning voice uses at this point), a 'Utopia', 'a mobility of illusory forms immobilised in space, remobilised in air' (17: 1137–44), and ends his 'logical' contemplation by acknowledging that the heavenly bodies are

a past which possibly had ceased to exist as a present before its probable spectators had entered actual present existence. (17: 1144–5)

Bloom is, in other words, able to analytically recognise the 'present' as always viewing the past, recapturing it as itself, and, I would suggest, it is this (as a capacity for such realisation and in the particular analysis of 'time') which allows the relationship between Stephen and Bloom to move on to a reorganisation of the recurrent trope of the intellectual's distance from *his* subject and his own (male) subjectivity. Bloom has, to put it a different way, an ability to understand time as past, present and (Utopian) future, but not necessarily to need them placed in that order, and in this his potential liberation from the absolutes of linearity allow his sense of the 'moment' and of synchronicity a freedom which Stephen is still 'struggling' for.

Bloom's passage from the rationalised discourse of astronomy, inter-laced with his contemplation of humanity's 'vanity' and inability to place even the night sky in a telos, is the bridge which facilitates the bringing together of Stephen and Molly (which has been signalled earlier, for example, in the cabman's shelter, when Bloom shows Stephen a mildly erotic photograph of Molly (16: 1425)). This is effected firstly through the 'esthetic value' which poets have attached to the heavens (a reminder of Stephen's pretensions), and then through the 'science' of 'selenographical charts', since this in turn allows for a question asking about the 'special affinities . . . between the moon and woman' (17: 1146–58). Stephen and Bloom now both gaze up at Molly's window, and Bloom having elucidated 'the mys-tery of an invisible attractive person, his wife Marion (Molly) Bloom', Stephen and Bloom are left silently to contemplate each other. This moment of contact is described thus:

Both then were silent?

Silent, each contemplating the other in both mirrors of the reciprocal flesh of theirhisnothis fellowfaces. (17: 1182–4)

Thinking of Molly turns both *men* to a contemplation of each other and of what Emmanuel Levinas calls 'the face of the Other as . . . the original site of the sensible'.[45] After an undefined period of inactivity in which Michelet's 'light' and 'warmth' are integrated in Stephen and Bloom's joint illumination by the feminised moon/Molly's lamp, the 'sensible' 'flesh' of this masculinised moment of silence is turned to the most publicly phallic of endings when Stephen and Bloom, at 'Stephen's suggestion, at Bloom's instigation' (17: 1186), piss together.

Clearly, in terms of my argument, this incidental moment in 'Ithaca' can be set beside Michelet as a replaying and a revision of that desire for intellectual self-abjection. Stephen, unlike Michelet, has Bloom by his side and an absoluteness of isolation is no longer possible. The suspended looking into 'theirhisnothis fellowfaces' is not only for Stephen (and Bloom) a form of companionship, and, despite the gendered nature of the events, it is not solely a male bonding exercise. As Levinas suggests:

The Other becomes my neighbour precisely through the way his face sum-mons me, calls for me, begs for me, and in doing so recalls my responsibility, and calls me into question.[46]

The 'fellowfaces' are defined at this point by each other alone,[47] and the ethical charge which they create in seeing each other's faces is, as Levinas suggests, both the end of an enclosed sense of self and a recall of responsibility which is forced to 'face' the Other, not just imagine it distantly. The alterity found in the 'face to face' calls Stephen to a responsibility for the Other which he (if we take 'Stephen' as a continuous character in Joyce's fiction) has not been able to find previously within the Dean's paternalistic colonialism, within the peasant's challenge of essential Irishness, within EC's romance. And in a sense we have moved here beyond Michelet's trauma of the loss of 'the people' as subject. As Levinas suggests: 'It is as if the other established a relationship or a relationship were established whose whole intensity consists in not presupposing the idea of community'.[48] Stephen and Bloom have, in other words, fleetingly surpassed that sometimes stifling foundational need to speak to the future nation, seeing in the difference of each other a 'deeper', and so 'warmer', version of ethical responsibility than even that 'depth' which the 'the people' gives. As Richard Kearney says, Joyce 'preferred to deconstruct rather than reconstruct the myth of a Unity of Culture'; and we can go further than Kearney, since when Joyce finds 'where *I* becomes *other*' it is not only that he overturns 'the classic myth of narrative as a one-dimensional communication of some fixed prede-termined meaning'; the I becoming other is the point at which Joyce gets underneath the 'Unity of Culture', showing its attested status as only-possible-first-principle to be a self-perpetuating sense of its own 'destiny' which has an alternative and an alterity.[49] What Paul Ricoeur calls 'the aporia of anchoring', the central trauma of the self, is deployed by Joyce as an antidote to the 'identification with heroic figures [which] clearly displays . . . otherness assumed as one's own'; for Stephen and Bloom the time which is described as 'theirhisnothis' turns a captured otherness into a confronted alterity and dissipates the trait of 'loyalty' to 'causes' which results from the *idem* and *ipse* natures of the self being made to 'overlap', to 'accord with one another'. Of this process, which conflates sameness and selfhood, Ricouer writes: '[an] element of loyalty is thus incorporated into character and makes it turn toward fidelity, hence toward maintaining the self'. Joyce's Stephen struggles with the necessity of 'loyalty' as part of the maintenance of the self, and in 'Ithaca', in a qualified, gendered, almost comic way, he glimpses in the face of Bloom a form of other-ness which demands no outside 'loyalty' but fulfils his desire and lost hope for responsibility.[50]

It is thus in the paring away of '(his)story', in the recognition of 'vanity', and despite the incessant demands of logical and temporal linearity, that Stephen finds literal bodily relief following ethical contact. The fraught distance which is necessarily embedded in the intellectual's idea of 'the people' is temporarily forgotten. This, of course, must end. The time has already ended, once the pissing begins, and as they piss, Bloom and Stephen are reasserted in their difference – Bloom's thoughts remain bodily (he contemplates, among other things, 'tumescence', 'irritability', 'sanitariness' (17: 1201–2)) and Stephen is reclaimed by the intellectual and by history (he is parodied as his thoughts wander to the sanctity of Christ's foreskin (though in this he is still arguably contemplating Bloom, 17: 1203)). However, just before this, staring at each other, Bloom and Stephen have found themselves not 'presupposing the idea of community' and the idea of 'the people', but under the thrall of an 'anarchic responsibility, which summons me from a nowhere into a present time',[51] much as the light from the stars which Bloom observes arrives in the present from an unimaginable time and distance.

To summarise this incident, and this chapter, it is necessary to go back to my beginning. Michelet sets out for us, through Barthes' reading of him, how 'the people' troubles academic discourse on culture and how it becomes a foundational pretext for speaking about that culture at all. My suggestion is that in the Irish context, and partly in relation to the particular forms of political and historical factors which have been in play, Ireland has become an always 'putative', future 'Ireland' demanding a double form of deference: a bowing down to as sacred, while at the same time pressing itself into a continual futurity which can never facilitate full definition. Corkery's feeling of being 'upbraided' by the Ireland he tries to describe replicates Michelet's disappointed desire to meet, touch and ventriloquise 'the people' without the self-consciousness of knowing that such articulation is happening. The example of Stephen in Joyce's works shows that, firstly, in *Portrait*, Stephen is unwilling to accept the duty to 'the people' which Michelet berates himself with. Then, in 'Ithaca', Stephen, face to face with Bloom, replaces that rejection of 'the people' with a form of alterity which questions his ontology at a level beyond Michelet's intellectual dilemma. For Stephen, Bloom is 'the face of the Other' which demands 'the right to be'[52] and which in doing so questions Stephen's own justification for being. All this is why Barthes' Michelet constitutes so important a model; he both reveals the barrier to be surpassed, and at the same time his insistence on the ethics which throw the intellectual self into doubt is a lesson in how move on. 'Ireland' calls that Irish critical voice home beguilingly and encompassingly. If we want to change this destiny for our critique, which may be fated to fall forever into unsatisfied forms of definition, and become servile to the idea of 'the people',[53] we need to know its existence, its power to turn us into Memmi's 'sleepwalkers', and that, despite placing itself as a presupposition, it is not the only place in which the ethics of the critical voice can find their justification.

Notes

1. Albert Memmi, *The Colonizer and the Colonized* (London: Earthscan, 1990), p. 172.
2. Bataille from 'Preface to *La sorcière*', quoted in Roland Barthes, *Michelet*, trans. by Richard Howard (Oxford: Basil Blackwell, 1987 [1954]), p. 221.
3. Michael Moriarty notes that the 'phenomenological stress on the lived experience of a physical individual in contact with the material world is central to Barthes's . . . *Michelet* of 1954': Michael Moriarty, *Roland Barthes* (Oxford: Polity Press, 1991), p. 187.
4. Michelet quoted in Barthes, *Michelet*, p. 102.
5. Barthes, *Michelet*, p. 199.
6. Gayatri Chakravorty Spivak, 'Can the Subaltern Speak?', in Patrick Williams and Laura Chrisman (eds), *Colonial Discourse and Post-Colonial Theory: A Reader* (London: Harvester Wheatsheaf, 1994), p. 75. For Said's discussion of intellectual responsibility see Edward W. Said, *The World, the Text and the Critic* (London: Vintage, 1991).
7. Discussing Deleuze's 'genuflection' to 'the worker's struggle' Spivak writes: 'The invocation of *the* worker's struggle is baleful in its very innocence': 'Can the Subaltern Speak?', p. 67.
8. Spivak, 'Can the Subaltern Speak?', p. 70.
9. See Spivak's discussion of *Vertretung* and *Darstellung* in 'Can the Subaltern Speak?', p. 74 and *passim*.
10. Barthes, *Michelet*, p. 25.
11. Barthes, *Michelet*, p. 82.
12. Barthes, *Michelet*, p. 82.
13. Barthes, *Michelet*, p. 184.
14. Barthes, *Michelet*, p. 82.
15. Spivak writes: 'The subaltern cannot speak. There is no virtue in global laundry lists with "woman" as a pious item': 'Can the Subaltern Speak?', p. 104.
16. Daniel Corkery, *The Hidden Ireland: A Study of Gaelic Munster in the Eighteenth Century* (Dublin: Gill & Macmillan, 1989 [1924]), pp. 19–20.
17. Corkery, *The Hidden Ireland*, p. 285. The quotation which Corkery ends with is from Alice Stopford Green, *The Making of Ireland and Its Undoing*.
18. Jacques Derrida, *Of Grammatology*, trans. Gayatri Chakravorty Spivak (London: Johns Hopkins University Press, 1976), p. 49.
19. Exemplary in this regard would be Joep Leerssen, *Mere Irish and Fíor Gael: Studies in the Idea of Nationality, its Development and Literary Expression Prior to the Nineteenth Century* (Cork: Cork University

Press/Field Day, 1996) and *Remembrance and Imagination: Patterns in the Historical and Literary Representation of Ireland in the Nineteenth Century* (Cork: Cork University Press/Field Day, 1996).

20. Anne McClintock, 'The Angel of Progress: Pitfalls of the Term "Post-colonialism"', in Williams and Chrisman (eds), *Colonial Discourse and post-colonial Theory: A Reader*, pp. 292–3. Emphasis in original.
21. Barthes, *Michelet*, p. 188.
22. Moriarty, *Roland Barthes*, p. 187.
23. Seamus Deane, 'Joyce the Irishman', in Derek Attridge (ed.), *The Cambridge Companion to James Joyce* (Cambridge: Cambridge University Press, 1990), p. 31.
24. James Joyce, *A Portrait of the Artist as a Young Man*, ed. Seamus Deane (Harmondsworth: Penguin, 1992), p. 274.
25. Joyce, *A Portrait of the Artist as a Young Man*, p. 274.
26. David Cairns and Shaun Richards, *Writing Ireland: Colonialism, Nationalism and Culture* (Manchester: Manchester University Press, 1988), p. 85.
27. Len Platt, *Joyce and the Anglo-Irish: A Study of Joyce and the Literary Revival* (Rodopi: Amsterdam, 1998), p. 199.
28. Declan Kiberd, *Inventing Ireland: The Literature of the Modern Nation* (London: Jonathan Cape, 1995), p. 333.
29. Kiberd, *Inventing Ireland*, p. 333.
30. Joyce, *A Portrait of the Artist as a Young Man*, p. 274.
31. Joyce, *A Portrait of the Artist as a Young Man*, p. 275.
32. Vincent J. Cheng, *Joyce, Race and Empire* (Cambridge: Cambridge University Press, 1995), p. 3.
33. Kiberd, *Inventing Ireland*, p. 355.
34. Emer Nolan, *James Joyce and Nationalism* (London: Routledge, 1995), p. 181.
35. This has certainly been the most centrally contentious of issues in the Irish reclamation of Joyce in recent years, and Nolan's *James Joyce and Nationalism* is one of the most sustained and clear advocations of the argument. Cheng, in *Joyce, Race and Empire*, for all that he submits to L. P. Curtis's scheme of *Punch*-inspired and evidenced racism, in the end argues for a Joyce set against 'the pitfalls and limits of certain very alluring but limited nationalist visions . . . [by which] one is doomed to failure by reproducing the same binary hierarchies inherited from one's oppressors': Cheng, *Joyce, Race and Empire*, p. 218. On this topic see also Willy Maley, 'Postcolonial Joyce?', in Alan Marshall and Neil Sammells (eds), *Irish Encounters: Poetry, Politics and Prose Since 1880* (Bath: Sulis Press, 1998), pp. 59–69.
36. Seamus Deane, *Strange Country: Modernity and Nationhood in Irish Writing Since 1790* (Oxford: Oxford University Press, 1997), p. 2. I am indebted here to Claire Connolly's discussion of Deane's *Strange Country* in Claire Connolly, '*Reflections* on the Act of Union', in John Whale (ed.), *Edmund Burke's 'Reflections on the Revolution in France': New Interdisciplinary Essays* (Manchester: Manchester University Press, 2000), pp.168–92.
37. Kiberd, *Inventing Ireland*, p. 355.
38. John H. Roberts, 'James Joyce: from Religion to Art', in Robert H. Denning (ed.), *James Joyce: The Critical Heritage*, Vol. 2 1928–1941 (London: Routledge & Kegan Paul, 1970), p. 612.
39. Anthony Burgess, *Here Comes Everybody* (London: Arena, 1982), p. 171.

40. Thomas Hofheinz, *Joyce and the Invention of Irish History: 'Finnegans Wake' in Context* (Cambridge: Cambridge University Press, 1995), p. 15. Hofheinz is writing specifically of Jameson's essay '*Ulysses* in History', in W. J. McCormack and Alistair Stead (eds), *James Joyce and Modern Literature* (London: Routledge & Kegan Paul, 1982), pp. 126–41 and more generally of Jameson's *The Political Unconscious: Narrative as Socially Symbolic Act* (Ithaca, NY: Cornell University Press, 1982).

41. Hofheinz, *Joyce and the Invention of Irish History*, p. 14.

42. Suzette A. Henke, *James Joyce and the Politics of Desire* (London: Routledge, 1990), p. 122.

43. As the technique is standardly described in Joyce criticism. See, for example, Don Gifford, with Robert J. Seidman, *'Ulysses' Annotated: Notes for James Joyce's 'Ulysses'* (London: University of California Press, 1989), p. 566.

44. James Joyce, *Ulysses: The Corrected Text*, ed. Hans Walter Gabler (London: Bodley Head, 1989). All subsequent references to *Ulysses* are to this edition and are cited in parantheses.

45. Seán Hand (ed.), *The Levinas Reader* (Oxford: Blackwell, 1996), p. 82.

46. *The Levinas Reader*, p. 83.

47. Though see Vicki Mahaffey's reading of the same incident which suggests that this pragmatic joining of Stephen and Bloom is symbolised as 'waste' through their urination. Mahaffey does, however, note that an 'example of mutual recognition through difference is the moment when Bloom and Stephen regard each other as both familiar and strange, when they see in other the outlines of the "unheimlich"': Vicki Mahaffey, 'Sidereal Writing: Male Refraction and Malefactions in "Ithaca"', in Kimberley J. Devlin and Marilyn Reizbaum (eds), *'Ulysses' – Engendered Perspectives: Eighteen New Essays on the Episodes* (Columbia: University of South Carolina Press, 1999), pp. 259 and 264.

48. *The Levinas Reader*, pp. 83–4.

49. Richard Kearney, *Transitions: Narratives in Modern Irish Culture* (Manchester: Manchester University Press, 1988), pp. 32 and 34. Kearney's analysis sees Joyce's project as one revolving, in a double sense, on the word.

50. Paul Ricoeur, *Oneself as Another*, trans. Kathleen Blamey (London: University of Chicago Press, 1994), pp. 52 and 121.

51. *The Levinas Reader*, p. 84.

52. *The Levinas Reader*, p. 86.

53. The 'servility' of the intellectual to Irish nationalism is famously summarised by Patrick Pearse: 'Patriotism is at once a faith and a service . . . and it is not sufficient to say "I believe" unless one can also say "I serve"'. Pearse's words here are quoted (with slight variation) concerning Joyce's views of nationalism by Seamus Deane in the 'Joyce and Nationalism' chapter of *Celtic Revivals: Essays in Modern Irish Literature, 1880–1980* (Winston-Salem, NC: Wake Forest University Press, 1987), pp. 94–5, and in Kearney, *Transitions*, p. 32.

4

Liminal Spaces: Postcolonialism and Post-nationalism

'Ireland's putatively "post-colonial" culture'[1]

The phrase which ends David Lloyd's *Anomalous States* in many ways belies what precedes it. The certainty and complexity of Lloyd's postcolonial assumptions could be seen to render spurious the 'putative' in his closure. However, the 'moment' of methodological questioning might, in its apparent uncertainty, seem to catch the stabilised and contained form of insecurity which typifies Irish criticism. Lloyd is surely recognising here at least two problematic areas for a postcolonial theorisation of Irish culture: firstly, the unsystematic, *ad hoc* and tendentious ways in which the theories of postcolonial criticism have been applied to Ireland; and secondly, the need for any postcolonial reading to take account of the 'atypicality' of Ireland's (post)colonial cultural configurations. This latter involves a tangle of theorisations in which Ireland becomes either particular of or, more often, exceptional within colonialism, as first and/or last colony, and in which the force of postcolonial theory itself is stymied when met by the repetitious patterns of Irish criticism discussed in Chapter 2.

In recent years it can hardly be said that postcolonial theories, of a sort, have not been applied in readings of Irish culture and literature. During the process there has been a relative standarisation of this application, mainly seeing the 'national' as the primary (and often only) level at which the postcolonial is relevant to Ireland. While this is an obvious and important context for the 'colonial' 'meeting' Ireland, it largely reflects an identity politics on the national/cultural level which was already apparent in Irish criticism 'before' postcolonial theory. With this being the case, postcolonial readings of Ireland remain 'putative' and almost mutative. What follows in the first part of this chapter is a survey of the ways in which two apparently contending critiques from within what can loosely be called Irish studies, Field Day and historical revisionism, have less than deliberately embodied some of the problems which are met with at the edges of this relatively comfortable reassertion of old agendas. The aim here is to take this discomfort in academic ways of seeing Irish culture and use it to examine the sense of critique which is inherent in the Field Day project, in revisionism and indeed in postcolonial theory.

THE POSTCOLONIAL

An essential component of postcolonial criticism has been its evolution as an ethical criticism. In that it is diagnostic of a political and historical situation, postcolonialism makes the crucial identification of who is the coloniser and who the colonised – it also morally evaluates this colonial relationship as one of fundamental inequality, in which a wrong is done to the colonised, whose integrity, space and identity is taken over and controlled against his/her will. This crucial ethical consideration has caused problems which have been unexamined as postcolonial criticism has evolved new ways of thinking on other subjects, and it is a problem particularly relevant to a discussion aimed at rethinking postcoloniality in the contemporary Irish critical context, in which the national has been the predominant formation of the present and future critical word and in which the nation has become the grammar through which all forms of colonial contact and lack of contact have found their explanation. But to allow the nation to monopolise the postcolonial field is to withhold the Irish case from a more radical interrogation by the difficult ethics of the colonial encounter, a process of Othering which is not only 'unethical' but also a series of moments constituted by the Levinasian 'face-to-face', and by a cultural process built on dependence and interdependence.

In the Irish context, postcolonial criticism appears to be tied to a narrative which celebrates the entity of the nation as the logical and correct outcome of the process of anti-colonial struggle. One of postcolonialism's earliest and still most useful texts, Frantz Fanon's *The Wretched of the Earth*, describes this procession towards the nation thus:

The immobility to which the native is condemned can only be called into question if the native decides to put an end to the history of colonization – the history of pillage – and to bring into existence the history of the nation – the history of decolonisation.[2]

The progression here is obvious: colonisation → resurgence → nationalism → liberation → the nation. This narrative has continued to underpin much postcolonial critical thinking from Fanon onward, being continually drawn into defending the anti- and postcolonial nation as an ethically and politically proper readjustment of the wrong of colonisation.

However, in recent years the teleology of nationality which seemed so crucial to postcolonialism has been challenged by a building critique of the ideology and praxis of nationality in the postcolonial world. And while ideological wariness of the nation is already apparent in Fanon (in what is quoted above from *The Wretched of the Earth* the nation has an indeterminate status in 'the history of decolonisation' which Fanon goes on to explore in 'The Pitfalls of National Consciousness'[3]), this critique of nationalism has found its most succinct and effective expression in the Subaltern Studies Group in India, publishing under the editorial auspices of Ranajit Guha, in which Guha describes postcolonial India as a 'historic failure of the nation to come into its own'.[4]

The Subaltern Studies' critique of postcolonial nationalism has two important aspects. Firstly, as the Gramscian term 'subaltern' suggests, it aligns itself with social groups which it sees as excluded, dominated, elided and oppressed by the state (effectively peasants, the working classes and latterly women and other minority and marginalised ethnic and social groups). Subaltern Studies sets out to write what Gramsci famously described as the 'fragmented and episodic' histories of subaltern social groups,[5] and what Guha refers to as the 'politics of the people',[6] which he suggests have been previously omitted from Indian history. To effect this Subaltern Studies utilise the historical methodology laid out in Gramsci's six-point plan in 'Notes on Italian History'.[7] Secondly, and as something of a necessary by-product of this mission, Subaltern Studies allows for an understanding of the postcolonial nation in a new way – no longer need the nation be regarded as the glorious achievement and fruition of the labours of an oppressed people; the postcolonial nation can now be figured as 'the ideological product of British rule in India',[8] repeating and aping the colonial structures which it displaced. Indeed it is now arguable, though this is not a notion always specifically ascribed to by Subaltern Studies, that the very idea of nationality which was used by decolonising peoples to coalesce themselves into a coherent political force was itself transferred to the colonies by imperialist ideology.[9] In other words, imperialism justified itself by an ideology of hegemonic nationalism in which the national people think of themselves, in Derrida's words, as 'the best representatives of mankind',[10] thus being burdened with a 'duty' to civilise. This ideology was adopted and turned back upon the coloniser by the colonised in order to conceptually justify their own anti-colonial struggle. The result is a postcolonial world of nation states which structurally and practically imitate western nations. This is a powerful, though as yet not fully explored view – however, research into Indian education systems and uses of nationality in postcolonial African states provide substantial contextual evidence.[11]

Broadly speaking, the Subaltern Studies (perhaps implicit) critique of the ideology of nationalism, as a restrictive and totalising political force, has gained a relatively widespread currency in postcolonial studies. However, the strength of the ethically-embedded anti-colonial nation-narrative, and the security of origin, identity and affiliation it offers, have meant that the postcolonial nation remains an entity continually reverted to, even in those who explicitly recognise the ideology of nationalism to be a replaying of imperialist structures. The nation as an object of sentimental attachment, cultural pride and communal fixity combines with the ethics of postcoloniality, referred to earlier, to maintain the teleological aura which the idea of the nation can glean from postcolonialism. Nationalism has, as suggested above, been the ideological level on which the political, cultural and material repercussions of colonialism and anti-colonialism have fought their ideological and moral battles so that, in Ireland as elsewhere, the definition of the 'nation' (as narrative) became the focus for identity politics, and the primary social level on which the troublesome nature of the Same/Other ethics of colonialism has been played out. The postcolonial nation as a moral and political triumph is thus often ruefully given up, while its sense of its own destiny and inevitability conspires to produce images of moral void, political vacuum, and a sense of the loss of all that has been gained, should the 'nation' be even contemplatively relinquished; such an end to the futurology offered by the nation would leave no obvious alternative direction for the trajectory of the Irish critical word, since that word is directed at its own future role, being 'Irish' and explaining 'Ireland'. In a parallel context Edward Said's *Culture and Imperialism*[12] both criticises the nation in a pseudo-Subaltern Studies way, and yet reads colonial literature and texts of resistance with a continually celebratory tone when referring to the nation (his writing on Yeats, whom he

calls 'Ireland's national poet',[13] is one example). For Said the dilemma
is at least compounded by, if it does not have its origins in, his advocacy of Palestinian nationalism. I will argue later that writings by
Seamus Deane on the postcolonial status of Ireland evince the same
dilemma: recognising the paucity of nationalism while lacking a
substantial position to replace the certainties nationalism offers.

The postcolonial critique of nationalism, which sees the nation as
an entity derived from and imitative of the imperial centre, leads to
another aspect of current postcolonial theorising which has liberated
the discipline from a moribund reliance on what Said refers to as
'the binary oppositions dear to the nationalist and imperialist enterprise'.[14] Postcolonial criticism, including that addressing itself to
Irish culture, has increasingly turned its attention to areas of colonial
discourse where the apparently monolithic, stifling and dis-articulat-
ing presence of the coloniser is refuted by evidence of the colonised
speaking back, by imperialist ideology being figured as neurotic and
uncertain rather than bombastic and unshakeable, and by focusing on
cross-cultural movements rather than on any simple cultural dichotomy made of the colonial situation. This critical turn to a more
synchronic view of the power dynamics of the colonial allows for a
shift away from the process of historical analogy which dogs Irish
debates, often mired in the question of the 'relevance' of the postcolonial as a way of reading Ireland.[15]

Whether Ireland has a story to tell which is 'like' that of Algeria or
a history which precedes (and is a model for) India's becomes less
immediately the burden on which the 'proof' of the validity of the
colonial rests. The conditions of a series of cultural 'moments', in
which one culture seeks its own coalescence of definition 'against'
another which it dominates, are in themselves the reasons why the
figurations of postcolonial criticism can be effective in the context
of Irish cultural production. The structures of colonial (dis)empow-
erment, not the contours of historical development, are what make
Ireland once colonial and, at least 'putatively', postcolonial.

These types of long-standing changes in postcolonial criticism have,
ironically enough, come about partly as a reaction to that founding
moment of postcolonial studies, Edward Said's *Orientalism*.[16] Said
was immediately, and has been continually, criticised because his
scheme of East–West cultural construction seemed to perpetuate that
which he diagnosed.[17] Nowhere in Said's construction of the notion
of Orientalism could the East effectively speak to the West, nor could
it subvert the notions of the East which the West was in the continuous process of forming, and such ideological deadlock frustrated those

who saw the colonised as more active agents in the colonial process.
The result has been a diverse but nevertheless identifiable movement
into what might be called the 'liminal spaces' of colonial discourse,
marginal areas, where the ultimate opposition of coloniser and
colonised breaks down through irony, imitation and subversion. The
term 'liminal' (of the threshold) is used by Said in *Culture and
Imperialism*[18] in his analysis of Kipling's *Kim*, in which Kim's social
and racial position allows him to move with relative, almost arbitrary
freedom between coloniser and colonised, British and Indian, tra-
versing and deploying the network of spying and intrigue which is
layered over Kipling's India. Kim's Irish yet military parentage offers
itself as explanation for this capacity to act as nomad within the
regulating framework of the colonial system.[19]

Perhaps the most eminent example of the examination of these
liminal spaces comes in the work of Homi K. Bhabha whose notions
of colonial mimicry, imitation and agency prise a gap in the Saidian
colonial configuration through which the colonised can begin to be
seen working against colonial ideology. Benita Parry describes
Bhabha's work as a contestation of the notion which Bhabha

considers to be implicit in Said's Orientalism, that 'power and discourse
[are] possessed entirely by the coloniser' . . . [Because Bhabha] maintains
that relations of power and knowledge function ambivalently, he argues
that a discursive system split in enunciation, constitutes a dispersed and
variously positioned native who by (mis)appropriating the terms of the
dominant ideology, is able to intercede against and resist this mode of
construction.[20]

Parry's is a sceptical summary, but it does describe accurately the
places which Bhabha's critique has sought to inhabit and, by extension, indicates the stratified sets of debates which Irish postcolonial
theory has run into. The direct refutation of Ireland's postcolonial
status by historians is perhaps the least productive example of such
arguments (though I will suggest later that certain strands of revisionism have a deconstructive germ contained within them).[21] Bhabha's
'ambivalence' has, equally, been stabilised in Irish criticism into a
notional 'hybridity' which understands the enunciative split as a
replay of the binary divide of colonialism itself and therefore dead-
ens its impact on either side of that divide; Declan Kiberd's image of
the 'quilt of many patches and colours, all beautiful, all distinct, yet
all connected', wrapped around the shoulders of Cathleen ní Houlihan,
is one striking example of how the hybrid can be reconfigured into
old totalities.[22] Equally David Lloyd's notion of Ireland as anomalous

has suffered by being interpreted as a contradiction (both/neither) which can be rendered meaninglessly the same as before that anomaly was articulated.[23]

'ULTIMATE FAILURE'

Given the strong tendency in postcoloniality to celebrate and uphold resurgent nationalism, it might be thought that in the Irish context postcoloniality would appeal to those who wish to restate Irish nationalism in contemporary, radical terminologies. What has been said above about postcolonial criticism, as it currently exists, should show that contemporary postcoloniality has the potential to shatter the self-image of nationalism as much as it might function to radicalise it. The Subaltern Studies' political and historical questioning of the postcolonial Indian nation can to an extent be a model for an Irish cultural criticism which seeks to go beyond the circular return to the sanctity of the nation. But that model (whether it be called post-national or anti-national) already partially exists in two separate (and sometimes opposing) intellectual phenomena in contemporary Ireland – Field Day (in its specifically postcolonial moments) and revisionist historiography. A Subaltern Studies and postcolonial critique of these two formations will take us a considerable distance towards delineating the position which postcolonial criticism can occupy in Irish cultural debate.

At first glance it is Field Day, especially through Seamus Deane, which has come closer than revisionism to allowing a postcolonial critique of Ireland of the type towards which I am attempting to move. Deane's partial embracing of postcoloniality can be most succinctly understood in his 'Introduction' to the collected edition of the *Nationalism, Colonialism and Literature* Field Day pamphlets by Eagleton, Jameson and Said. Here Deane says very simply: 'Field Day's analysis of the situation derives from the conviction that it is, above all, a colonial crisis'.[24] Deane describes a realisation that certain aspects of Field Day's thinking accord with developments in post-colonial criticism, most significantly the turn against nations and nationalism as repressive, ideological reproductions of the colonial regime. Compare Ranajit Guha in Subaltern Studies, who says that the postcolonial Indian nation is 'the ideological product of British rule in India',[25] to Deane, who says that 'Irish nationalism is, in its foundational moments, a derivative of its British counterpart'.[26] Guha talks of the 'historic failure' of the Indian nation;[27] Deane talks of the 'ultimate failure' of the project of Irish cultural nationalism.[28] Guha's critique of Indian history leads him to follow Gramsci's six-point plan for restoring the history of the subaltern, reversing the nation's exclusion of minority groups. Deane says:

Almost all nationalist movements have been derided as provincial, actually or potentially racist, given to exclusivist and doctrinaire positions and rhetoric.[29]

However, comparison of the Gramscian Subaltern Studies critique of nationalism with Deane's is even more revealing when they part company than when they appear to be in parallel.

Where what could broadly be described as the postcolonial Subaltern Studies position is able to ideologically reject nationalism and replace it with a neo-Marxist commitment to groups oppressed by the workings of nationalism, Deane, however, falters at the conceptual leap from the nation into whatever comes next. His 'Introduction' to *Nationalism, Colonialism and Literature*, even while it sets out this postcolonial agenda of 'anti-nationalism' (at least anti-state-oriented Irish nationalism), is simultaneously drawn back to the formation of the nation in apparent disbelief that it can ever be intellectually jettisoned. What he attempts to salvage from the nation-narrative can only then take the form of an aestheticisation of national achievement (a strategy for dealing with intellectual aporia which we will see repeated later in post-nationalism):

Ireland produced, in the first three decades of this century, a remarkable literature in which the attempt to overcome and replace the colonial experience by something other, something that would be 'native' and yet not provincial, was a dynamic and central energy. The ultimate failure of that attempt to imagine a truly liberating cultural alternative is as well known as the brilliance of the initial effort.[30]

Falling back here on the quality of national literature rather than its ability to be culturally national, Deane reveals that the necessary postcolonial denigration of the nation as a political ideology is intensely problematic for him – the solution is complex in its interpolation of the aesthetic with the failed nation, and finds its comfort in the disintegration of history itself. Deane's analysis, as it initially appears, is a literary judgement on the quality of cultural achievement under strained circumstances. Yet that relies on a breach in history which leads back to the most unsatisfactory of all resolutions of the post-national postcolonial dilemma – a re-indulgence in the ethics of the colonial dichotomy – in this case blaming the British, while for

Ireland there is a by now familiar cyclically apocalyptic ring to 'ultimate failure' and brilliant effort. Deane points out that all nationalisms can be understood as repressive in formation and practice, and goes on:

These descriptions fit British nationalism perfectly, as the commentaries of any of its exponents on Ireland – Edmund Spenser, Sir John Davies, Sir William Temple, Coleridge, Carlyle, Arnold, Enoch Powell, Ian Paisley – will prove. The point about Irish nationalism, the features within it that have prevented it from being a movement toward liberation, is that it is, *mutatis mutandis*, a copy of that by which it felt itself to be oppressed.[31]

While Subaltern Studies are able to produce a critique of postcolonial nationalism as an imitative, repressive entity and to focus on those groups within society for whom nationalism has been a continuity of oppression, Deane rebounds postcolonial dissent against nationalism so that it is forced to return to the ethical origins of postcolonialism. 'British nationalism', because Irish nationalism copied it (could only copy it), is to blame. The silent implication is that Irish nationalism, without the pernicious influence of Britain, would have been liberating (though of course paradoxically unnecessary). Deane balances uneasily on the apex of the conceptual progression out of reliance upon the nation as the essential unit of culture – when he wavers it is to save what baggage he can from the crisis, to retain nationality as a liberating aspiration rather than fully concede nationalism to be a monolithic elision of ineluctable multiplicity. So Deane identifies the blockage in the telos which is the moment of casting adrift, but his analysis rattles up points within the confines of the national pinball game which had its limits set by the imperialism preceding it. Thus Deane reaches an ethical dilemma which postcolonial theory inevitably tends to, when the process of understanding and subsequently conceptually dismantling the ideologies of empire leads to a suspicion of ideology, and points awkwardly to the unforeseen consequences of the critical distrust of ideologies (including anticolonial nationalism) produced by the colonial situation.

Deane's hesitancy at the point where the 'nation' becomes restrictive rather than glorious or even aspirational allows us to turn to Irish historical revisionism, which has been based on a long goodbye to the sanctified centrality of the nation. That revisionism is relatively unblinking in its loosening of the grip of the nation on the intellectual parameters of thought in and about Ireland initially seems to afford the final step Deane was unable to take. Revisionism would presumably agree with Fanon's statement: 'The makers of the future nation's history trample unconcernedly over small local disputes' (the point also made, of course, by Subaltern Studies).[32]

Revisionism's critique of Irish history is well known and the extent of its disagreement with the kind of cultural critique which Field Day represent is now so settled as to make the comparison of the two seem nearly perverse.[33] Revisionist methodology is interestingly expressed, for present purposes, in an essay by R. V. Comerford which illustrates forcefully how revisionism has approached the dominant, hagiographical, national history of Ireland: 'The teleological myth tends to bestow the status of finality on contemporary arrangements and in particular on the nation state'.[34] This accords to a large degree with the implicit criticism postcolonialism has made of itself, disrupting its own complacent reliance on the teleology of anti-colonial nationalism, and as such Comerford here raises interesting possibilities of concurrence and interchange across revisionism and postcolonialism. But, very obviously, from this point revisionism and postcolonialism diverge (sometimes into forms of unrecognised similarity). To continue with Comerford as an example, in the piece quoted from above he goes on to say:

The understanding of national identity as a platonic essence, transcendent and indefeasible, now enjoys a much reduced currency among Irish historians, but some practitioners of other humanist disciplines who venture into the field of Irish history come with a preconceived ideal of Irishness that belongs to the realm of well-worn myth.[35]

Inherent in this piece is the disagreement which revisionism will have with a cultural criticism derived from postcolonialism. Revisionism shares with Subaltern Studies a recognition that the 'nation' has become a restricting force, and was so in the midst of its liberatory powers. But their emphases immediately differ in diagnosing the nature of this restriction. For revisionism the nation-narrative had become *the* macro-narrative, denying the plurality and complication of history – this is essentially a historiographic, intellectual turn away from the nation – any political implications tend to follow on from this rather than inspire it (though critics of revisionism would tend to disagree with this analysis). Subaltern Studies have a specifically political critique of the 'nation', and put this into effect by using historiography. Comerford encapsulates the ways in which this potential disagreement will be played out in an Irish context when he says that 'practitioners' from other disciplines remain in the sway of these now-refuted myths. At the centre of this historiographical disagreement is the nature of historical agency – revisionism reimagines the historical agent as everything but the national myth, so history is at times accidental, contingent, at the behest of the motivation of the powerful individual – leading to back to an old Joycean chestnut that 'history, it seems, is to blame', and History is therefore its own subject.

In *The Irish Review* Liam Kennedy's article 'Modern Ireland: Post-Colonial Society or Post-Colonial Pretensions?' set out to refute the use of the postcolonial model for Ireland.[36] This article was aimed by Kennedy specifically at literary and cultural critics rather than at fellow economic historians – indeed the tenor of the article suggests that economic historians would never be duped by postcolonialism. Kennedy's conclusion when he examines the statistical evidence for Ireland's postcolonial status is simply that the theory does not hold. This forces him to speculate on why, if the theory is so obviously irrelevant, it is used by what he refers to as '*homo academicus* on the make'.[37] Some of his suggestions accord with ground already covered above – postcolonial theory can, in Kennedy's view, be used to 'modernise' the 'threadbare quality of traditional [ultra-nationalist] rhetoric';[38] it can also, Kennedy asserts, justify Anglophobia and, concomitantly, anti-Unionism. However, Kennedy's reading of Field Day's forays into postcolonialism as 'emotional satisfaction, even inspiration, in the exploitation of loose images and metaphors'[39] underestimates Field Day's, and Seamus Deane's, serious and troubled relationship with postcolonialism, even while it catches on the centrality of the agency of the academic voice within the postcolonial.

In his 'Introduction' to *Paddy and Mr Punch* R. F. Foster writes about the sort of theoretical disagreement between cultural criticism and revisionism which has been outlined above. Foster, incidentally, replicates Kennedy's dig at *homo academicus* when he deflates the 'fashionable':

It is significant that some of these denunciations [of revisionism] come from literary critics, because the effect of critical theory on historical discourse is worth noting – in Ireland as in America, in the age of Hayden White and Paul Ricoeur. Some accompanying concepts have added much enlightenment to Irish history, notably the analysis of colonial collusions elsewhere in the Empire. But the recently fashionable idea that the historian/writer is in corrupt and unconscious collusion with the text, and that reference to an ascertainable body of fact is a delusion of the late bourgeois world, leads quickly to the useful position that all history is suspect and all readings questionable. By an elision, this sanctions a turning back to the old verities and the old, atavistic antipathies.[40]

As an act of polemic self-defence Foster's dismissal of cultural criticism is boldly all or nothing. History or no History is the only choice
available; no History means no future in the backward turn to the past.
History as subject and discipline (objectively-tending, non-ideological)
is defended by Foster before history as progress or history as past
resurrected, since 'the old' is something to be healthily allergic to. But
Foster is like-minded with many of the other ways in which the
postcolonial has interacted with existent models of Irish studies. The
supply of analogies is seen as possible (here in the illumination of
'colonial collusion') where they will readily confirm or unthreaten-
ingly adapt what we already know to be the case; analogies which
threaten the framework rather than the detail are quickly dispelled
through overcharacterisation.

It is possible at this stage to begin to move towards a view of how
these connections between the radical drives which underlie both
Field Day and revisionism (and the central dilemma of the 'nation'
which they both face up to) might be made to coalesce to produce a
critique of Ireland in postcolonial terms which embodies the energy
of both, while refuting to some extent their mutual problematics,
embedded in being reluctantly beholden to the nation post-nationally,
and after the nation has been able to set itself as the agenda.

Postcolonialism will inevitably read Irish culture through its
inherited theoretical dichotomy of coloniser and colonised, identifying competitive cultural formations held within an empowering and
disempowering system. But the Subaltern Studies' critique of postcolonial nationalism allows postcolonialism to sidestep a persistent
positioning with the colonised against the coloniser. Instead, postcolonial criticism is increasingly able to discuss the ideological
restrictions which a culture imposes upon itself by fetishising its
'other' – and this without a necessary privileging of the colonised,
but with a retention of the knowledge that empowered discourses
constitute the colonial situation.

In identifying ideological, monolithic blocks, postcolonialism is
also able to undermine the rhetorical strategies of those ideologies as
they seek approval within the power structures of colonialism. An
Irish postcolonial critique can thus follow revisionism in its disdain
for the impositions of ideology – but it would see a continual turn
away from ideology as a process which would set up a new teleology
in which the disintegration of ideological thought would become
supposedly inevitable and in which an indecisive defence of the 'late
bourgeois world', as Foster calls it, is the only possible response. A
postcolonial Irish cultural criticism can deconstruct the ideologies

arising from colonialism and postcolonialism while moving beyond only understanding its subject as the meeting of uncomprehending cultural affiliations. Postcolonialism's movement into the 'liminal spaces' of colonial discourse needs to be superimposed over the model which sees colonial structures purely in terms of division. It is this newly developed ability to identify transcultural[41] movements and interactions which makes postcolonial theory a necessary intervention in understanding Irish culture. Because the ideological blocks of colonialism are less easily pinned down and dichotomised in the Irish situation than in other postcolonial societies, the interchange which takes place within the conceptual restrictions of colonial discourse is both extensive and potentially amorphous. Rethinking concepts such as irony, hybridity, mimicry, the 'contact zone' and transculturation in the Irish context will produce readings of Irish culture which arise out of a recognition of the claustrophobic intensity of the relationship between Ireland and Britain. It can also allow for the fractured range of complex cross-colonial affiliations which have existed within the British/Irish cultural axis by acknowledging and adapting the critical methodologies which postcolonialism has employed to disintegrate and fragment the monologism of cultural affiliation.

It is these abilities to read culture as ideological, while criticising the homogeneity of ideology, and to prioritise cultural interchange within a colonial structure, which makes postcolonial theory an essential critical tool for understanding Irish culture. Edna Longley has said, regarding the intervention of critical, and particularly postcolonial, theory into Irish culture:

Our impulse should be not only to decolonise, to criticise English canons and English ideologies of Ireland, but to subvert indigenous canons and ideologies. Actually, unionism and nationalism afford opportunities for mutual deconstruction unrivalled in any other country.[42]

Postcolonial criticism, as it currently exists, has the capacity to undertake exactly this critical project – to produce readings of Irish culture which stress its dependency on 'Englishness', on rhetorical formations, on defining its 'other', and which will simultaneously comprehend the ironies of cultural interchange in a theoretical framework which is both rigorous and precise.

A reading of Irish culture in the framework of the colonial with an acknowledged tension between the synchronic and the diachronic withdraws to an extent from affiliation to the national as the conceptual entity validating the radicalism of critique. It could then be argued that this leaves an ethical void at the heart of criticism, a traumatic repetition of Michelet's search for 'the people'. Derrida vividly summarises such a dilemma:

Does this 'disorder of identity' favor or inhibit anamnesia? Does it heighten the desire of memory, or does it drive the genealogical fantasy to despair? Does it suppress, repress, or liberate? All of these at the same time, no doubt.[43]

The liminal status of Ireland means that the 'disorder' that is already written into 'Ireland' colonially makes inevitable a volatility in theorising 'Ireland'. If the colonial brings certainty, it rubs against that liminality (in a hollow way it confirms the nation-narrative, while the analogies it sets up are emptied of their meaning). If postcolonial theories bring further disorder then, as Derrida predicts, fantasy is highlighted and edges into despair. Allowing for the anteriority of the sign 'Ireland' as both colonially resonating and ideologically disruptive is a process which continually, often surprisingly, is already underway in writing about Ireland, but is then stopped dead by 'memories' and 'genealogies' of various kinds, the necessary fantasies by which 'Ireland' is kept at the status of 'superstructural predicate floating on the surface of experience'.[44]

POST-NATIONALISM

The rethinking, repositioning and revising of nationalism which have become the central preoccupations of intellectual movements in Irish culture have been paralleled in the political realm by the arrival of the notion of 'post-nationalism', a term with a blurred provenance in Irish political and cultural debate. In concluding this chapter, I want to focus my discussion of post-nationalism as a concept quite selectively through two individuals who have exercised great influence in Irish culture and politics in recent years – John Hume and Richard Kearney – and then to briefly set post-nationalism against the possibilities offered by the version of postcolonial criticism tentatively moved towards above.

John Hume's enthusiastic deployment of the notion of post-nationalism is well documented to the point of cliché in Ireland; however, it retains an interest because of the continually disingenuous prospect it creates – the leader of a nationalist party arguing the concept of the nation out of currency. The logic for Hume's post-nationalism lies, of course, in the political and economic formations of the European Community (Hume's simultaneous status of MP/MEP is inherent to this double play).

Kearney's advocacy of post-nationalism in the European context arises primarily out of intellectual and cultural commitments, but his support for Hume's notion of a Europe of the Regions as opposed to a Europe of Nation States illustrates their broadly concurrent thinking. To make the anatomy of post-nationalism clearer I want to look briefly at how Hume and Kearney set out their arguments, noting the movement and slippage in each from analysis to diagnosis to cure.

The separate but paralleled post-nationalism advocated by Hume and Kearney can be seen in Kearney's edited collection of essays *Across the Frontiers: Ireland in the 1990s.* In this context, it is worth drawing attention both to the arguments that Hume and Kearney present and noting the concurrent rhetorical constructions of their agendas. Hume's contribution to *Across the Frontiers*, 'Europe of the Regions', sets out his now familiar attempt to argue for a decentralised European community which dissolves the boundaries of nation-states and replaces them with a concept of regionality (part of the impetus for this argument is that the dissolution of Ireland and Britain as nation-state members of the European Union will make the Northern Ireland conflict pointless and therefore, presumably, bring it to a close[45]). Hume's piece begins:

Given our island setting, our history of colonisation and our wounds of division it is understandable that so much of our political thought and approach should hinge on the nation state.[46]

These words must be reassuring for members of the SDLP – though as members of a constitutional nationalist party they might wonder at the perceived need to make an apologia for the idea of the nation (Hume has always taken a carefully managed line between nationalism and internationalism, and in turn the priority of democratic socialism within negotiating the two). Hume's argument winds carefully through the various advantages of the (then) EC, continually emphasising the benefits of decentralising policies already in existence (the encouragement of minority languages, for example). This leads to his main argument:

We are moving into a post-industrial or more aptly the 'Post Fordist' era and this poses questions for social and political processes. The kaleidoscope is shaking, patterns will be changing, we must plan accordingly.[47]

Analysis ('Post Fordist') and diagnosis (the 'kaleidoscope is shaking') are compressed here – the cure is only hinted at as yet (in 'we must plan accordingly'). Hume later furthers this movement from diagnosis to cure when he says that the 'macro-context of these ['Post Fordist'] trends means that this task cannot be tackled practically in the nation-state context'.[48] The true parameters of the solution to the 'Post Fordist' disease come at the end of his piece:

It depends on our political vision and will whether we want to make of the single Europe simply a dilution of national sovereignty or a dilation of democracy. The peoples of smaller countries like Ireland, because of the common interests and identification with regions across Europe and within the larger Nation States, will wield a much greater influence in shaping that Europe and in developing their own distinctiveness in a Europe of the Regions rather than in a Europe of the Nation States.[49]

There are two important aspects of Hume's argument which can be rhetorically focused, and which will pan out into a wider critique of post-nationalism as he uses it. The first is the structuring of post-nationalism around the teleology described above as analysis→ diagnosis→cure. This framework may allude to the relative comfort of a medicinal discourse, but it contains within it unrecognised problems. Hume's need to find a solution to the Irish national problem is the significant spur to his post-nationalism. His analysis, which suggests that post-Fordism, postmodernism, technological change and reshapings in the labour market are the 'symptoms',[50] constitutes a plausible but recognisable attempt to find a disease to fit the cure. The fascination of this version of 'post-nationalism' is whether the nation as concept can survive being treated for an illness which is integral to the life expectancy of its metaphoric body politic.

Kearney follows a similar path in his 'Introduction' to Across the Frontiers, though he begins with a more strident comment than Hume's apology:

Ireland can no longer be contained within the frontiers of an island. Since the signing of the Anglo-Irish Agreement and the Single European Act, we find ourselves committed to a new 'totality of relationships' extending well beyond the limits of the Nation State.[51]

Like Hume, Kearney is quick to collapse analysis into diagnosis. 'Our present state of affairs is, by most accounts, bleak', he says, going on to note symbols of decline in population, employment and welfare.[52] (Notably the collective 'our' or 'we' in Kearney and in Hume refers to

'Irish' – Europe is still an eavesdropper on this post-national Irish debate which does not dissolve the assumed constituent national audience until 'European' contributors are called in.) Kearney's argument for a pluralised European identity then rests like Hume's on a critique of the present state of things and a belief in a Europe 'which may enable us to overcome the traditional antagonism between Nation States and redefine our cultural identity positively rather than negatively'.[53] As with Hume, Kearney's qualified utopia needs a dystopia to emerge from.

This in turn necessarily leads to the exposure of a more fundamentally undermining conceptual crutch in the reinterpretive future visions Hume and Kearney espouse. Again the rhetorical constructions of their prose are significant. Hume's need to acknowledge the nation as a basic and understandable political concept in Ireland is only part of the discomfort he experiences in reworking his political vision in European terms (and should be taken in conjunction with his nationalist domestic policies, bound up in phraseologies which define the (Northern) Irish problem as one in which the people – becoming singular – of one island – already singular – need to learn to 'share' it). Kearney similarly negotiates with the national, wishing to preserve it in a pluralised atmosphere:

Do our writers not show us how indigenous material from Irish myth and history can be successfully conjoined with the most innovative forms of international literature? Do our artists and musicians not show us how to proclaim Irish origins while transcending national barriers and communicating with the citizens of other European and world cultures? . . . Perhaps it was in anticipation of such feats that Joyce recommended the cultural project of 'hibernicizing Europe and Europeanizing Ireland'.[54]

Like Deane's kick against the colonial end of history discussed earlier, Kearney's plea here settles for origins (Deane has 'native') and a simultaneous transcending of Ireland (though Deane has the more cagey 'not provincial'). 'Innovative' (Kearney) and 'brilliant' (Deane), Irish culture has a similar trajectory and telos in the postcolonial and post-national paradigms, and at times seems only distinguishable in each by the addition of optimism or pessimism about the effects of/on 'Ireland' when in contact with anything beyond itself. Whichever path is chosen, the 'origins' of 'Ireland' are secure, while its future is uncertain.

The particular point here about Hume and Kearney is that, in the analysis→diagnosis→cure which leads to Europe and post-nationalism, it is not nationalism itself which is the problem to which a solution needs to be found – rather nationalism is placed in a 'natural' politico-cultural teleology which is poised to move into a new post-national phase. Nationalism is being left behind with a reluctance and a nostalgia – indeed for Kearney the national is still the defining site of cultural indigeneity and authenticity: *our* writers and *our* singers (*our* culture) will allow *us* to retain a grasp on a real cultural base while addressing ourselves to the post-nationalist, European situation.

The disabling conceptual course of post-nationalism means that, firstly, its analysis and diagnosis are projected from a prearranged point in a teleology which has not yet quite played itself out. Secondly, that teleology is actually one which confirms the value (and hence ideology) of the nation rather than critiquing it, since the teleology, by its nature, implies inevitability – indeed the residue of the nation in post-nationalist thought becomes as glossed with optimism as the path ahead – the nation is nostalgically transcended, while the threads it can offer in the construction of a pluralist identity politics are salvaged and cherished.[55] (If this is a postmodern version of the nation it sits within the postmodernism of architectural nostalgia and neoclassicism, its referentiality devoid of irony). Post-nationalism evolves from rather than rejects the nation; but its dependency on the maintenance of the conceptual value of the nation goes unrecognised. In this, post-nationalism philosophically dilutes postmodernism and uncomfortably straddles national and European polities. Most importantly, post-nationalism refuses the ability to conceptually reject and comprehend the ideological constructions and restrictions of the nation, and hopes instead to be able to preserve and move beyond them simultaneously.

So while post-nationalism can only fade into the problematics of Europeanisation and the troublesome negotiations of cultural iden-tities which it decides can be 'left over' from nationalisms, a post-colonial critique of Irish culture, following Subaltern Studies, might be able to disrupt the dominance of the discourse of nationality in Ireland, reinvigorating the dissidences of gender and subalternity, undermining the complacencies of historiography, and moving towards a notion of Irish culture which views the dialogic hybridity of 'Irishness' in empowered ways. The next chapter, through a discus-sion of gender as subaltern in Irish postcolonial theory, attempts to examine the wider connotations of a belief that Ireland's postcolo-niality is 'a mode of duality rather than a contradiction in terms'.[56]

Notes

1. David Lloyd, *Anomalous States: Irish Writing and the Post-Colonial Moment* (Dublin: Lilliput, 1993), p. 155.
2. Frantz Fanon, *The Wretched of the Earth* (Harmondsworth: Penguin, 1990), p. 40.
3. Fanon, *The Wretched of the Earth*, pp. 119–65.
4. Ranajit Guha, 'On Some Aspects of the Historiography of Colonial India', in Ranajit Guha (ed.), *Subaltern Studies: Writings on South Asian History and Society*, vol. I (Delhi: Oxford University Press, 1982), p. 7.
5. Antonio Gramsci, *Selections from the Prison Notebooks*, eds and trans. Quintin Hoare and Geoffrey Nowell Smith (London: Lawrence & Wishart, 1971), p. 55.
6. Guha, 'On Some Aspects of the Historiography of Colonial India', p. 4.
7. Gramsci, *Prison Notebooks*, p. 52.
8. Guha, 'On Some Aspects of the Historiography of Colonial India', p. 1.
9. For an alternative reading of the Subaltern Studies' critique of nationalism see Aijaz Ahmad, *In Theory: Classes, Nations, Literatures* (London: Verso, 1992), who says that, as a result of the postcolonial and Subaltern Studies attack on nationalism: 'Colonialism is now responsible not only for its own cruelties but, conveniently enough, for ours [in the post-colonial world] too' (pp. 196–7).
10. Jacques Derrida in conversation with Alan Montefiore in Derek Jones and Rod Stoneman (eds), *Talking Liberties* (London: Channel Four/BSS, 1992), p. 8.
11. See Gauri Viswanathan, *Masks of Conquest: Literary Study and British Rule in India* (London: Faber & Faber, 1990) and Basil Davidson, *The Black Man's Burden: Africa and the Curse of the Nation State* (London: James Curry, 1993).
12. Edward W. Said, *Culture and Imperialism* (London: Chatto & Windus, 1993).
13. Said, *Culture and Imperialism*, p. 281.
14. Said, *Culture and Imperialism*, p. xxvii.
15. For example, such questions debilitate Stephen Howe's assessment of Irish postcolonial criticism and historiography in *Ireland and Empire: Colonial Legacies in Irish History and Culture* (Oxford: Oxford University Press, 2000).
16. Edward W. Said, *Orientalism: Western Conceptions of the Orient* (London: Penguin, 1991).
17. See, for example, Dennis Porter, 'Orientalism and Its Problems' in Francis Barker (ed.), *The Politics of Theory* (Colchester: University of Essex, 1983), pp. 179–83.
18. Said, *Culture and Imperialism*, pp. 159–96.
19. For a discussion of *Kim* and the context of colonial networks of knowledge see Thomas Richards, *The Imperial Archive: Knowledge and the Fantasy of Empire* (London: Verso, 1993). The connections between the colonial military and the Irish postcolonial condition are imaginatively explored by Ronan Sheehan in *Foley's Asia* (Dublin: Lilliput, 1999).
20. Benita Parry, 'Problems in Current Theories of Colonial Discourse', *Oxford Literary Review*, 9:1–2 (1987), 40.

21. An example of historiographical failure to engage with the substance of the theoretical elements of postcolonialism in Irish studies is found in Brian Walker, 'Ireland's Historical Position – "Colonial" or "European"', *Irish Review*, 9 (1990), 36–40. One of the more thoughtful examples of historiographical reflection on the subject is James Livesey and Stuart Murray, 'Post-colonial Theory and Modern Irish Culture', *Irish Historical Studies*, 30:119 (1997), 452–61.

22. Declan Kiberd, *Inventing Ireland: The Literature of the Modern Nation* (London: Jonathan Cape, 1995), p. 653.

23. The difference between Lloyd's *Anomalous States* and his later *Ireland After Theory* (Cork: Cork University Press/Field Day, 1999) might be regarded in this way also, with Lloyd reining in the possibilities of his own concept (see discussion of Lloyd in Chapter 2 above). On the use of the term hybridity and its relevance to Irish debates on colonialism see Gerry Smyth, 'The Location of Criticism: Ireland and Hybridity', *Journal of Victorian Culture*, 2:1 (1997), 129–38, which is a response to Robert Young's *Colonial Desire: Hybridity in Theory, Culture and Race* (London: Routledge, 1995). In reply see Young's 'Response', *Journal of Victorian Culture*, 2:1 (1997), 138–51. Young interestingly insists on a basic mode of historical judgement: 'Whatever Ireland has suffered and been subjected to in the past, that history does not place it outside Western culture', p. 141.

24. Seamus Deane, 'Introduction', in Terry Eagleton, Fredric Jameson and Edward W. Said, *Nationalism, Colonialism and Literature* (Minneapolis: University of Minnesota, 1990), p. 6.

25. Guha, 'On Some Aspects of Historiography in Colonial India', p. 1.

26. Deane, 'Introduction', p. 7.

27. Guha, 'On Some Aspects of Historiography in Colonial India', p. 17.

28. Deane, 'Introduction', p. 3.

29. Deane, 'Introduction', pp. 7–8.

30. Deane, 'Introduction', pp. 3–4.

31. Deane, 'Introduction', p. 8.

32. Fanon, *The Wretched of the Earth*, p. 90.

33. See Deane's discussion of revisionism in 'Wherever Green is Read', in Máirín ní Dhonnchadha and Theo Dorgan (eds), *Revising the Rising* (Derry: Field Day, 1991), pp. 91–105.

34. R. V. Comerford, 'Political Myths in Ireland', in The Princess Grace Irish Library (ed.), *Irishness in a Changing Society* (Gerrards Cross: Colin Smythe, 1988), p. 7.

35. Comerford, 'Political Myths in Ireland', p. 11.

36. Kennedy's article is also discussed in Lloyd, *Ireland After History*, pp. 5–12; Howe, *Ireland and Empire*, pp. 151–3; and Conor McCarthy, *Modernisation, Crisis and Culture in Ireland 1969–1992* (Dublin: Four Courts, 2000), pp. 25–6.

37. Liam Kennedy, 'Modern Ireland: Post-Colonial Society or Post-Colonial Pretensions?', *Irish Review*, 13 (1992/93), 119.

38. Kennedy, 'Modern Ireland', p. 118.

39. Kennedy, 'Modern Ireland', p. 118.

40. R. F. Foster, *Paddy and Mr Punch: Connections in Irish and English History* (Harmondsworth: Allen Lane, 1993), p. xv.

41. 'Transculturation' is a process of colonial interaction described specifically in Mary Louise Pratt, *Imperial Eyes: Travel Writing and Transculturation* (London: Routledge, 1992).

42. Edna Longley, 'Writing, Revisionism and Grass Seed: Literary Mythologies in Ireland', in Jean Lundy and Aodán Mac Póilin (eds), *Styles of Belonging: The Cultural Identities of Ulster* (Belfast: Lagan Press, 1992), p. 21.

43. Jacques Derrida, *Monolingualism of the Other; or, the Prosthesis of Origin*, trans. Patrick Mensah (Stanford, CA: Stanford University Press, 1998), pp. 17–18.

44. Derrida, *Monolingualism of the Other*, p. 15.

45. Hume has more explicitly described the EU 'as the greatest example of conflict resolution in the history of the world'. Quoted in Paul Routledge, *John Hume: A Biography* (London: HarperCollins, 1997), p. 7.

46. John Hume, 'Europe of the Regions', in Richard Kearney (ed.), *Across the Frontiers: Ireland in the 1990s* (Dublin: Wolfhound, 1988), p. 45.

47. Hume, 'Europe of the Regions', p. 53.

48. Hume, 'Europe of the Regions', p. 53.

49. Hume, 'Europe of the Regions', p. 57.

50. Hume, 'Europe of the Regions', p. 53.

51. Kearney, 'Introduction: Thinking Otherwise' in *Across the Frontiers*, p. 7.

52. Kearney, 'Introduction: Thinking Otherwise', p. 7.

53. Kearney, 'Introduction: Thinking Otherwise', p. 22.

54. Kearney, 'Introduction: Thinking Otherwise', p. 25.

55. This view of the nation's past is expanded on in Kearney's *Postnationalist Ireland: Politics, Culture, Philosophy* (London: Routledge, 1997).

56. Sheehan, *Foley's Asia*, p. 5.

5

'Staged Quaintness': Subalternity, Gender and Popular Identity

Floozy, Skivvy, Whore is my name and symbol of my identity.
> Which brings me in passing to the
> question of Irish women's place
> within but without culture and
> identity
> Transparent floating capacious signifier,
> from what place can I speak?
> Confined 'by the waters of Babalong'
> in sink, sewer, bidet, jacuzzi, in a
> flowing babel of other-determined
> myths, symbols, images, can I speak
> myself at all?[1]

What Ailbhe Smyth calls 'the question of Irish women's place / within but without culture and / identity' certainly constitutes a 'running sore on the body politic of Ireland';[2] the position of women in Irish society, bound to constitutional, institutional and religious issues of abortion, contraception and divorce, has invoked serious examination of how gender and femininity relate to the notion of an Irish identity. And, as Smyth suggests, it has been the specifics of the category of 'Irish' which has necessitated a debate, envisaging alternative placings 'within but without culture and identity' in an Irish context – Irishness, variously understood, may encapsulate or expunge the female, denying or seeking to define and legitimise what the 'Irish woman' may be. To this extent even the constitutional issues which most publicly resonate with gender politics and policies in both Irish states tend to occlude the economics of gender equality and issues of women's participation in the workplace and in policy making, while the constitutional issues which have arguably been the most serious of challenges to the nation's sense of itself as embodied in the state have, in highlighting constitutionality itself, in some ways reinforced the notion that gender debates in an Irish context *must* refer back to the concept of the nation for their meaning.

Given the power inherent in the public sphere's ability to turn even the terms of its own questioning into a reinforcement of its ideological priorities, it is important that developments in understanding, argument and resistance, unfolding from the domain of constitutional and activist politics, are given parallel expression in reading cultural texts which both absorb and deny the changes in how gender is understood in Ireland. As Smyth suggests, the 'change' is still very much a flux, a debate without resolution, in which the relationship between gender issues and the potential solidities of 'Irishness' have yet to settle. Equally, previous chapters have attempted to suggest that Irish criticism, in keeping with its subject, 'Ireland', is capable of forms of detour and delegation which become its own structural necessities; so writing on the politics of gender in Irish cultural texts may find itself a hostage to 'change'. This chapter scrutinises the difficulties and potentialities of the socio-cultural and postcolonial category of the 'subaltern' in Irish cultural criticism, focusing in particular on how ideas of subalternity can be applied to gender issues in the Irish context. The aim here is to move towards an understanding of the subaltern which can be specific to the constitutive fabric of Irish cultures, which can retain a theoretical rigour and radicalism, and which can place 'gender' within a framework capable of accounting for alterations in the prioritisation and submergence of gender issues within Irish societies. As will be apparent by now, the place of the intellectual/critical voice is central to the movements from authenticity to dispersal/excess/aporia which this book seeks to trace. In criticism which attempts to account for the difference which 'Ireland' must accept or reject through the inflection or disruption of gender, that critical voice is perhaps initially in the same 'doubly oppressed' circumstances as its subject. If our understanding of that subject changes to a more complex form of overdetermination, in which 'gender' plays at least a dual role in terms of postcolonial models, then the responsibility for speaking which the critical voice takes upon itself becomes altered and prismatic. The prospect is that the 'Ireland' of Irish criticism, because it is expectant of its own fulfilment, will make 'gender' a perpetual resident in its waiting room.

GRAMSCI'S SUBALTERN

The 'subaltern' in contemporary critical theorisation usually functions as a description of 'oppressed groups within society', though the term has transformed from its original Gramscian definition to its more recent provenance in postcolonial criticism; this, in turn, offers a variety of competing ways in which the subaltern could be and has been used in relation to gender and Irish culture. Out of the problems and debates of this discussion I attempt, in this chapter, the beginnings of an alternative construction of the gendered subaltern suitable to the complexities of the Irish postcolonial situation. In order to contextualise these debates around the issues of power, cultural positioning and gender in Ireland I discuss Gerry Adams' short story 'The Rebel', which includes Irish women in the politicisation of the subaltern and thus appears to envisage the deletion of the category at some future point. That said, 'The Rebel' arguably replicates more complexly the inefficacy of subaltern affiliation in the name of power, while 'power' often finds the affiliation of the subaltern a comfortable conjunction. In contrast to Adams' political fiction is set the less engaged popular fiction of Frank Delaney's novel *Telling the Pictures*, in which the role of popular culture itself is interwoven into the everyday lives of Northern women and Northern politics, so that disjunction is accepted, though a homogeneous subaltern 'rebellion' is never feasible.

The category of the subaltern within contemporary cultural theory has two important sources. The origins of the term as a means to understanding the position and possible coherence of oppressed groups are found in the writings of the Italian Marxist thinker Antonio Gramsci, especially the 'Notes on Italian History' in his *Prison Notebooks*. For Gramsci, the subalterns are a diverse collection of social groups subject to the rule of dominant classes and the state. Gramsci's main concerns in the 'Notes on Italian History' were the methodological processes involved in writing the history of these groups: he set out a six-point plan in which he stressed that the subaltern has a 'fragmented and episodic'[3] history, that the subaltern groups are disunited and that, despite their definition as subaltern, they are *affiliated* to 'dominant political formations'.[4] Importantly, Gramsci notes that the subaltern groups 'cannot unite until they are able to become a "State"';[5] an unlikely prospect in Gramscian analysis given the nature of the dominance of the ruling classes, but nevertheless an essential defining feature of these groups – they aim for 'integral autonomy', unity and dominance.[6] The subaltern classes, then, in a Gramscian critique, will be counter-hegemonic, seeking not only to destabilise the dominant ideology but to take over its position. This is a crucial distinction between subversity from below which seeks only to subvert, and that which seeks to topple and replace 'the dominant'. Gramsci's notion of the subaltern as a collection of groups with a shared oppression is then vitally underlain by the knowledge that the subalterns are not willing participants in their social and political position – they seek to 'rise' out of their status, and they do so, as Gramsci says, by 'active or passive affiliation' to dominant formations in order 'to influence the programmes of these formations [and] . . . to press claims of their own'.[7] This Gramscian definition is central to, and yet significantly distorted by, the second source of the usage of the term 'subaltern' in contemporary vocabularies which derives, broadly speaking, from postcolonial criticism and most specifically from the work of the Subaltern Studies group of historians in India, discussed in the previous chapter, which takes the methodological challenge of Gramsci's project as a literal historiographical challenge to write the 'politics of the people'.[8]

The Subaltern Studies project has had two important effects on thinking concerning the category of the subaltern which need to be understood in order to read the subaltern into an Irish context. Firstly, and almost despite themselves, they have expanded the remit of the term 'subaltern' beyond the confines of a solely class-based Marxist critique. While the initial volumes of *Subaltern Studies* concentrate almost entirely on peasant insurgency, trade unionism and the working classes, there is a perceptible widening of focus in the later volumes, which is perhaps traceable to the intervention in Volume IV of the feminist cultural critic Gayatri Chakravorty Spivak. Spivak's deliberate reading 'against the grain of [Subaltern Studies'] theoretical self-representation' is remarkable in itself, but in tactical terms it seems to have opened the project to allow the inclusion of, for example, feminist and ethnic critiques of the 'dominant', and thus by implication to have expanded the idea of the subaltern beyond a class/peasantry base to include oppressed and marginal groups of many other formations. This expansion of the term has been increased by the concentration in postcolonial cultural and literary criticism on the conflux of discourses of gender, nationalism, colonialism and post-colonialism, in which the subalternity of women is reassessed, revised and often complexly affirmed.[9] The second major effect of the Subaltern Studies project arises in its originary moments and from its frustration with the historical narrative and political formation of the Indian nation, referred to in the previous chapter. This sees nationalism after the moment of postcolonial liberation as a continuum of oppression for subaltern groups. In this the historical and political credentials of anti-colonial nationalism are, at the very least, severely interrogated for their elisions and power structures, and for their strength and pattern of 'affiliation' to the previously dominant colonial ideology.

It is important to note at this point the distinction between Gramsci's understanding of the subaltern and that of Subaltern Studies and a vast body of postcolonial criticism. Gramsci stresses that the subaltern is linked, 'actively or passively', to the dominant structures which seek to maintain the subaltern *as subaltern* – for Gramsci, the subaltern seeks to become part of the dominant structures, to gain power, to form a 'State' – thus the subaltern, while defined by its subordinate relationship to the dominant, is not 'innocent' of the processes of domination. In Subaltern Studies, and particularly in postcolonial criticism, there is tendency to read into the category of the 'subaltern' an ethics of oppression, which can be seen to be doubly justified by an ethics of a postcolonialism which purports to speak for victims – the subaltern thus becomes made subaltern by colonialism and by post-colonial nationalism. The result is often a cultural criticism which makes the subaltern a theoretical site of disempowered purity – social groupings apparently so subsumed by colonialism, capitalism and nationalist ideology and practice that their oppression leaves them unsullied by these dominances. In other words, the subaltern can become prioritised, even utopianised, in critical discourses, functioning eventually as a refuge for cultural and political authenticity. This necessarily reads against Gramsci's notion of 'affiliation' between subaltern groups and their dominants which sets up a more complex, almost complicit, system of socio-political stratification – Gramsci effectively denies the ideological sanctity of the 'subaltern' which is apparent in later rereadings.

IRISH SUBALTERNS

Bearing these distinctions and tendencies in mind, how will the contemporary conceptual bases of the subaltern read when they are then translated into Irish cultural and gender criticism? From the context of the notion of the 'subaltern' in contemporary cultural criticism it is clear that the term brings with it a particular type of postcolonial thinking – one which is aware of the failure of nationalism in the postcolonial world, and one which highlights the hierarchical nature of social, cultural and gender relations. Additionally, it is obvious that the questions which are raised by the use of subalternity as a critique will concern the relationships between nationalism and feminism, nation and gender, questions which have been confronted in recent years in Ireland.

A broad consensual view can be discerned among critics and writers who deal with feminism, gender and nationalist (and indeed unionist) ideology in Ireland, suggesting that nationalism and unionism encompass gender in their theoretical constructions and social workings in patriarchal, controlling ways, creating metaphors and cultural discourses which Gerardine Meaney says exhibit 'for Irishwomen the sign of their invisibility'.[10] Recognition of the enforced silence of women and their simultaneous importance as a representational category integral to a dominant discourse is unsurprisingly common to both Irish and postcolonial feminist thinking. For example, in 'Identity and Its Discontents: Women and the Nation', Deniz Kandiyoti sees the concept of nation, indeed the whole discourse of cultural difference, as an assertion of 'control over women'.[11] Nationalism, says Kandiyoti, '[exerts] pressure on women to articulate their gender interests within the terms of reference set by nationalist discourse'.[12] Gender then becomes subaltern to dominant nationalism, being forced, in Gramsci's configuration, into 'affiliation' in order to press its claims. The subaltern/dominant relationship of gender/nation is further described by R. Radhakrishnan, who notes that:

The politics of nationalism become the binding and overarching umbrella that subsumes other and different political temporalities . . . [The] ideology of nationalist politics . . . acts as the normative mode of *the political as such* . . . Consequently, the woman's question (. . . or the subaltern question . . .) is constrained to take on a nationalist expression as a prerequisite for being considered 'political'.[13]

The resonances of such critiques hardly need to be laboured in the Irish context, where the liberative doctrine of nationalism became the nation-state's constitutional discrimination and where, in the Republic, the woman as revolutionary transmuted into what Eamon de Valera sanctified in his St Patrick's Day broadcast of 1943 as the 'laughter of comely maidens', an image ironically appropriate for its linguistically silenced subject.[14] Nationalism (or the nation-state), in this configuration, is complicit in assuming and enforcing the subaltern status of women and other marginalised groups.

Recently, however, the turn against the 'overarching umbrella' of Irish nationalism and its end-product state has been challenged in ways which directly impinge upon reading the category of the (gendered-)subaltern into Irish culture. Both David Lloyd and Carol Coulter have dissented from what Lloyd describes as the 'anti-nationalist prejudice', which they see as a critical 'distaste' for nationalism, pervasive in Ireland and beyond. Lloyd and Coulter both imply that this turn against nationalism, promoted by the liberal West, deliberately detaches nationalism from any radical forces or histories it might claim – and Lloyd and Coulter seek to counter this by reinscribing nationalism as a subversive force in cultural theory, stressing its anti-colonial energies as resources still available for radicalism.

For Lloyd anti-nationalism is a modern trait, what he has called a 'traditional metropolitan antagonism towards anti-colonial movements',[15] a convenient liberalised veneer under which resides a continuing Eurocentric disabling of peripheral politicisation. Lloyd thus prioritises the anti-colonial nature of nationalism and insists that solidarity within oppressed societies reveals what he suggests is a common experience of domination among those oppressed. This describes a particular kind of subaltern position – one which has changed from the Gramscian 'fragmented and episodic' to a more coherent collective experience initiating and describing collective action (bringing feminists and socialists into common bonds with nationalists – thus Countess Markievicz, Sinn Féiner and first woman to win a seat in Westminster, becomes a useful and important figure for Lloyd). In his article 'Nationalisms Against the State: Towards a Critique of the Anti-Nationalist Prejudice', Lloyd interestingly turns away from Gramsci, extending his reading of 'Gramsci's portrayal of the subaltern group's history against itself' which is already apparent in Anomalous States.[16]

The collective, rather than dispersed, experience of subalternity which arises from Lloyd's critique is not merely a conglomeration of feminism, socialism and nationalism – rather nationalism is acknowledged as the ideological gel of these subaltern movements (a notion which ironically already recognises the fact that nationalism later enacts a transformation into the oppressive constitutional state). Lloyd's version of nationalism as subaltern thus relies upon a de-hyphenation of the nation-state. Nationalism cannot be continually thought of as teleologically intended for statehood; rather it is preserved as an insurgent force – nationalism, in Lloyd's terms, has an 'excess' over the nation, containing groups, notions and individuals which deny the nation's push to homogeneity. In theoretical terms the effect of this 'excess' is to some extent to provide an arena outside the purview of state hegemony, but also to maintain the link with an identitarian essence which forms the nation (and whatever its relation to the postcolonial state might be). Hence, even though the nation's subalternity is in excess of the nation-state, when its own ideological substance flows out over its edges the challenge it poses is to its mode of containment, not its elemental properties.[17]

It becomes increasingly obvious why Lloyd must reject Gramsci, since, as pointed out above, Gramsci's version of the subaltern is defined by its desire to form the state. Lloyd's attempted subalternisation of nationalism is reliant upon understanding nationalism as *always insurgent* but never hegemonous, a notion with intensely problematic connotations to which I will return in a moment.

Lloyd's reassessment of the subaltern nature of nationalism may well have had an influence on (since it is cited in) Carol Coulter's contribution to the 'Undercurrents' series, *The Hidden Tradition: Feminism, Women and Nationalism in Ireland* (1993). Coulter follows Lloyd's initial reaction against the 'commonplace [notion] in modern debate in Ireland [. . .] that nationalism and feminism are opposites',[18] and partially echoes Lloyd in identifying this binarism as a metropolitan construction acting as a cover for another agenda.[19] Coulter argues that there is a 'tradition of women's involvement in nationalist struggle',[20] and that this calls for a revaluation of the relationship between nationalism and feminism. Like Lloyd's, Coulter's critical rhetoric relies on a crucial distinction between, rather than a Gramscian mergence of, the nation and the state – thus it is, for Coulter, the 'patriarchal state' and not nationalism which 'closed off'[21] the political activity of women in Ireland (though Coulter interestingly goes on to argue for a constant level of such activity despite the state).

Lloyd's use of nationalism as an ideologically active site for the meeting of various subalternities translates into Coulter's idea of nationalism as a 'unifying ideology [. . .] subversive of all authority'.[22] Nationalism is then prioritised as always subaltern, always insurgent, and thus inherently compatible with the claims of women within the state and of subaltern groups in general. There are various problems with reassessments of the putatively subaltern status of nationalism such as Lloyd's and Coulter's, and it is in discussing these that I hope to move towards an alternatively positioned use of subalternity and gender in the Irish context.

Firstly, there is the assumption that nationalism can be viewed as orientated only towards subversion and not towards power and homogeneity. While this can explain the inclusion of feminists in insurgent nationalist movements, it contorts the ideology of nationalism by separating it from and fetishising the concept of the state, and ignores Gramsci's implicit insistence that a subaltern force such as anti-colonial nationalism was always aimed at becoming the state. Indeed Gramsci's belief that subaltern groups 'affiliate' themselves to dominant groups can be adapted to suggest that nationalism succeeded precisely because it imitated so exactly the state which preceded it and that, beyond the process of 'imitation', anti-colonial nationalism, like its 'host' oppressor, became caught in a cycle of hegemony–affiliation. The ground here is that awkward and uncharted area between Field Day's insistence that Irish nationalism was corrupted by its imitation of British imperialism and Lloyd's 'excess', which remains always and forever 'outside history'.

The prioritisation of nationalism and subalternity as always insurgent leads to a second problem. If nationalism is subaltern only when it is unsuccessful (still insurgent, rather than in the process of forming the state), then there is a serious intellectual danger of celebrating the subalternity of subaltern groups. Ethically endowing the position of the subaltern can lead to a revelling in the insurgency of nationalism or feminism which easily slides into a continuous and necessary restatement of their oppressed position. Indeed it forms an academic subject which would be lost were it to progress, and in this it bears a familiarity to the rainbow-chasing of the perpetuating utopian trope of 'Ireland' discussed in Chapter 1. When the unsettled trauma of the intellectual Irish critical voice is added to this relentless futurity the pressure to prophecy (to predict what utopia will look like, yet to deny its ready fulfilment) manifests itself in manifestos.

In such a scenario, where the subaltern becomes the object of study because it is always in unsuccessful revolution, the subaltern becomes the site of cultural integrity and authenticity, filled with an ethically charged identity which paradoxically relies on what Spivak calls the 'monolithic and anonymous [subject]-in-revolution'.[23] Subalternity, decried as a politically unjust status by those who speak about it, will simultaneously function as an invocation of an unspoilt consciousness, pure because disempowered. Spivak notes the danger, in talking of the subaltern, of 'a nostalgia for lost origins [which] can be detrimental to the exploration of social realities within the critique of imperialism'.[24] Lloyd's reading of street ballads, his notion of the people as 'excess'[25] over the nation (so that any denigration of nationalism leaves the 'people' untouched) and Coulter's emphasis on 'tradition' as a historical and conceptual link between women and the nation, all seem to be perilously close to such a nostalgic purification of the subaltern as a political residue, reducing the 'popular' to the monolith of 'tradition' and reinforcing this process through acceptance of the dichotomisation of cultural production and cultural history along state/subaltern, high/low, modern/traditional faultlines.[26]

Reinventing nationalism as subaltern has a third problem which directly concerns how gender can be read into the subaltern category. In Lloyd's and Coulter's works there is an implicit acknowledgement of the fact that nationalism, even when it was subversive and subaltern, still ordered and dominated women's movements – that feminism became an exigent aspect of nationalist subversion. This ensures that 'women' will always remain submerged by nationalism no matter how much gender plays a part in nationalism, and that this will be the case even when nationalism is frozen in its pre-statehood embodiment. The 'commonality' of oppression which Lloyd sees as the means of coalescing subaltern groups in fact works as a hegemonic stratification within the whole collection of subaltern groups – women's movements are subsumed within nationalist movements and resetting nationalism as an always-subaltern force condemns the 'woman-as-subaltern' to a perpetual existence under the 'overarching umbrella' of nationalism. As Spivak points out, the notion of the subaltern already runs the risk of being a 'global laundry list with "woman" as a pious term' – and she criticises the *Subaltern Studies* historians for 'emptying' women of meaning. Insisting on nationalism as always-subaltern seems to flirt with confirming this discrimination and repeating such a semiotic disappearance.

RENAMING THE SUBALTERN

How, then, as a result of this critique of the reassessment of nationalism and subalternity, can we posit an alternatively configured concept of the subaltern? How can we read gender as subaltern in the Irish context without allowing the 'nation' to dictate our discourse?

Spivak points out that the 'colonized subaltern subject is always irretrievably heterogeneous'.[27] In the heterogeneity which Spivak identifies lies the need to allow discourses within the subaltern category to collide as well as collude, to be in conflict with each other, and thus to be closer to Gramsci's original definition of the subaltern. Spivak criticises the Subaltern Studies historians for 'renaming' sexual difference as class or caste solidarity:[28] in the Irish context such transmutations of gender in the name of nationalism can be submerged in the wake which the unfinished teleology of the nation creates behind it, thus making it more difficult to allow gender an existence within, outside and in opposition to the state *and* the nation.

Spivak's most important comments on the subaltern are in relation to the construction of the subaltern as a site of subversive 'consciousness'. Spivak writes that 'the subaltern's view, will, presence, can be no more than a theoretical fiction to entitle the project of reading'.[29] This is intended partly to warn the academic against privileging a notion of the subaltern as a coherent site of insurgency called into theory by a need to find a place pure and free of political corruption. Lloyd's use of a notional 'experience' in his idea of 'a common *experience* of domination' seems liable to fall into this 'fiction', positing the intellectual as what Spivak ironically describes as 'the absent non-representer who lets the oppressed speak for themselves'.[30] Spivak's comments point to a specific danger in an Irish context: a complex, contorted intellectual nativism, rehearsing the idioms and rejuvenating the discourses of an essentialist Irishness which is always oppressed, and yet is itself oppressive of the heterogeneity with which it is confronted. The subaltern can, in other words, be both a replay of the utopianism of 'Ireland', gratifyingly never brought to fruition, and simultaneously a solution to the Micheletean dilemma of the historiography of 'the people'.

Spivak's alternative methodology is summarised in the following, challenging remark: 'What I find useful is the sustained and developing work on the *mechanics* of the constitution of the Other; we can use it to much greater analytic and interventionist advantage than invocations of the *authenticity* of the Other'.[31] Emphasising the mechanics of the ordering of subaltern/dominant relations rather than searching for an authentic site of pure insurgency is the starting point of reading the gendered-subaltern.

The analysis of the subaltern and its relationship with gender in both postcolonial and more specifically Irish critical contexts which I have so far undertaken implies a way of reading Ireland and Irish culture which recognises that gender interests will exist 'inside' and 'against' the nation, but which will deny the necessity of the domination or absolute stratification of 'woman' by nation as replicated in the theoretical models used to understand Irish gender issues. In the bluntest sense this is an attempt to accept the potential conflict as well as compatibility which comes from adding 'Irish' to 'gender' or 'women'. In order to make more specific the power relations involved in the notion of the gendered-subaltern in Irish postcolonial terms, I wish now to examine a text in which the relationship between the politics of gender and nation in Ireland is specifically contemplated and to suggest that in order to maintain the theoretical ideal that subalternities are best seen to be complexly affiliative rather than commonly oppressed, we must be aware that even where nation acknowledges 'woman' as subaltern such recognitions will retrace themselves into hierarchised relationships.

'THE REBEL'

Gerry Adams' *The Street and Other Stories* aims, in the author's words, 'to be a celebration of the people I have tried to build my stories around',[32] in this case the people of West Belfast whom he regards as having had 'a common experience of the trials and tribulations and pleasures of living against the backdrop of the Troubles'.[33] In these comments, and in his *Falls Memories*,[34] Adams draws together an experience of oppression into a commonality which begins to define those oppressed in terms approaching homogeneity – this functions then in the same way as Lloyd's 'common experience of domination' binding a variety of groups under a dominant political discourse. But *The Street* does not only imply a 'common experience' of oppression; in this collection Adams attempts to describe what Spivak calls the 'mechanics' of this common experience.

In 'The Rebel' (from *The Street*) Adams plays out his wish, stated to James McAleavy, 'to do something to celebrate this community and to project women in a way which doesn't happen that often'.[35] In 'The Rebel' Margaret transforms from being politically dormant (both in terms of Republican and gender politics) to becoming an activist in her community. Her *dual* politicisation is important for Adams – the humour of the piece is supposedly at the expense of her husband and his complacent patriarchal views; the serious message of the story traces the coming together of a community under an oppressive regime. The very title of the story, 'The Rebel', suggests a revision of Republican ideology (which celebrates and renews the rebels of Easter 1916) to *include* a celebration of the-woman-in-rebellion. The story begins:

Margaret became a rebel when she was fifty-three years old. She remembers exactly when it happened. It was 2 July 1970 at about half-past two in the afternoon.[36]

Thus this story's defining moment is the instigation of a consciousness of subalternity:

It can be hard to be a rebel with so many mouths to feed and so many bodies to clothe. That was Margaret's preoccupation . . . and ironically that's what led indirectly to her becoming a rebel.[37]

What leads directly to Margaret's politicisation is the arrest and imprisonment of her son Tommy. After his first court appearance

Margaret is told by a RUC officer "'Missus . . . you have no fucking rights'"; when Tommy is imprisoned, Margaret's political education takes place in the ITL bookshop where she is primarily obtaining books for her son to read in prison. A 'woman of her own age called Mary' persuades Margaret that she too should be reading and her gendered-political education begins in earnest.[38]

Throughout this story, then, Adams seeks to interweave the politics of national struggle and gender liberation in the way that the punning title of the story suggests; 'The Rebel' includes a moment of deflation for an old and dormant rebel, Margaret's husband, when she asks him not to call her 'mother' again – this presumably having a resonance for the 'old' republican/nationalist ideological image of 'Mother Ireland' (though to assume the rejection of this persistent model either in contemporary Republicanism or this particular story, as I suggest below, is dubious[39]). At this moment one of Margaret's daughters says 'proudly' "'Our Ma's just become a woman's libber'".[40] This ironic if gentle attack on patriarchal views culminates with the conclusion of the story:

She got slowly to her feet. 'And now I suppose we better get back to our oul' lads. Mine's only started getting used to being married to me. And,' she looked at Mrs Sharpe with a smile in her eyes, 'he ain't seen nothing yet.'
    They laughed together as they locked up the school for the night. Outside, people were gathered at barricades and street corners. They all greeted Margaret and Mrs Sharpe as they passed. At Mrs Sharpe's house the two women parted and Margaret walked slowly up the street. She was tired, middle-aged and cheerful as she made her way home to liberate her husband.[41]

Here the story might even be seen to prioritise, over national struggle, the need for revolution in the gendered nature of everyday life, down to the level of domestic forms of language. Yet this would be to take the narrative's ending too much on its own terms. What is at stake here is not the old Republican ideology which Margaret's husband represents, but the new radicalism of those who defend the barricades looming over the story's conclusion. It is they who 'greet' Margaret, and it is they she is in solidarity with. The story implies that this renewed politicisation (beginning when the story is set, at the start of the 'Troubles') includes both Republican and gender politics. At best the story seems to argue that both necessarily coexist, that the barricades are simultaneously physical, political and gendered. Yet what kind of subalternity does this narrative give to the Irish, now Republican, woman? In 'The Rebel' the supposed irony of the title turns on the change from an old patriarchal republicanism to a new gender-aware community radicalism; but 'The Rebel', despite its attempt to include and in places elevate the subalternity of women, still pulls gender under the 'umbrella' of nation – it is the politics of national struggle which are most savagely forced into revision in this story (the target for Margaret's rebellion, her dormant-old-style-rebel husband, has in this sense already been 'softened' by the radicalism in which her politicisation becomes enveloped). Margaret's politicisation takes place *because* of her son's predicament (replicating her situation as a 'Mother Ireland'), hence her political birth is the moment of his arrest; her activism is centred on the community, which itself is spurred by the 'national' rather than any gender struggle; and the ending, which seems to bring the issue of Irish gender to the fore, replicates the gendered division of labour inherent in nationalism (neither Margaret nor Mrs Sharpe even contemplate 'manning' the barricades) – the immediacy and physicality of national struggle is in danger of making hollow the humour of 'domestic' struggle. For all its encompassing of a recognition that Irish republicanism should attend to gender as an issue both within Ireland and within its own ideology, and for all that 'The Rebel' allows the subaltern position of women to be stated within a 'national' discourse, the story continues to hierarchise 'subaltern' groups, restating a narrative in which nation precedes gender – in this it unwittingly reverts to the Gramscian model which acknowledges that subalternity is a series of political struggles in which the desired end in each case is to replace the dominant rather than to retain a continuity of subversion. For Gramsci the 'subaltern' is in one sense the germ of the practicalities of utopian thought, attempting to produce its own future in material and ideological terms; for Lloyd, the subaltern is very much more typical of the Irish utopian strands of excess and its twin, aporia. When the subaltern is in excess of the nation, yet by definition devoid of the politics of power conferred by statehood, its existence is found in a place which cannot be critically rendered, unless by impossible paradigm shifts, and it is thus paradoxically reified in its radicality.

So how do we progress to a notion of subalternity which views the subaltern as a cross-hatched collection of discourses in which the subcategories of the subaltern are not given a fixed or over-determined status? Ailbhe Smyth's 'The Floozie in the Jacuzzi', an extraordinary and multifarious examination of the meeting points of 'Irishness' and femininity, offers a series of contemplations on the subject:

The ex-colonised oppressors colonise. (Habit of centuries) They don't listen.
Theirs is the Republic, the Power and the Discourse.[42]

Dual struggle with the imprint of colonially-induced dependence and
patriarchally-imposed otherness struggling to extricate ourselves from the
simultaneous web that binds us into the pattern of non-entity . . . The
    problem
is *not* how to negotiate entry *inside*, into a tradition, culture, discourse
    which
designates the Other as necessary alien, necessarily *outside*.[43]

Smyth acknowledges the potential dual history of oppression in
subaltern groups in Ireland – 'woman' and 'Irish' implies a 'dual
struggle'. What Smyth lucidly denies is the necessity, plausibility and
wisdom of combining these struggles, since to struggle to be Irish is,
for Irish women, to risk attempting acceptance where 'she' can only
ever be 'Other', and to fall back into the belief in dual subalternities
working harmoniously in their perpetual subalternity.

The extent to which the subaltern can 'contain' gender, in an Irish
and a wider postcolonial context, only becomes clear when gender and
nation are both seen as potentially subversive *and* affiliative, existing
variously in the subaltern matrix of empowerment, disempowerment,
confrontation and hierarchisation. Such a model may then be able
to explain the contradictions of gender, its roles in and outside
nationalism, without resort to the ethics of authenticity and without
surrendering a critique of nationalism's homogeneity.

TELLING THE PICTURES

Fictional accounts of Northern Ireland have become dominated in
recent years by the thriller, to the extent that 'literary' and 'popular'
narratives have at times generically blurred into each other; so 'literary' novels such as Bernard McLaverty's *Cal* and Brian Moore's *Lies
of Silence* bear formal and thematic comparison to Peter Leslie's *The
Extremists* or Tom Clancy's *Patriot Games*.[44] At either side of this
merging tendency have been attempts to break out of the stereotypes
(these are many and include analysing the conflict as one of tribal
atavism and a recurrent obsession with the 'mindless' and/or beautiful
terrorist).[45] The new 'literary' fiction of Glenn Patterson and Robert
McLiam Wilson, and the satiric grotesque of Colin Bateman's novels,
are in some ways attempts to rewrite the North and save it from its
narrators. With a different sense of audience and purpose, Gerry

Adams' fiction, like his *Falls Memories*, deploys '[anecdote] and an artificially respirated sense of folk-memory . . . [to] bear witness to the truth of oppression'[46] and in this sense is a critical attempt to describe a structure of feeling 'as a collective, imaginative response to the relations between what is inherited and what seems contemporary'.[47]

Frank Delany's novel *Telling the Pictures* is not notable for its ambition in undermining Northern Irish stereotypes; it has hard-working, deeply sectarian, dour Protestants and fundamentally decent, observant but not pious, quietly nationalistic, live-and-let-live Catholics. And then it is capable of reversing these attributes in its minor characters to reveal that they are only partially true after all, and that Northern society as a whole is tricked into its sectarian division by Protestant bosses who 'control everything by pretending your people are better than mine',[48] as the central male (Catholic) character tells the tragic female (Protestant) heroine. The novel is packaged and sold in the classic 'producerly' way recommended by John Fiske as the critical marker of the 'popular text', inviting an 'essentially passive, receptive, disciplined reader who tends to accept its meanings as already made'.[49] In its sense of what Northern culture and society is, *Telling the Pictures* narratively and thematically not only expects the 'already made' to stay 'made' in its reader, but in Northern culture too. Its story, for all its social and personal trauma, re-establishes equilibrium, with the Northern unionist hegemony reasserted, largely unruffled, but shown up in its moral corruption.

However, there is an element of 'difference' introduced into *Telling the Pictures* which makes it useful in the context of the question of the subaltern status of gender, and in examining the productive modes of culture which define Irishness in the postcolonial world. Like many popular texts, *Telling the Pictures* shows an *awareness* of its own 'producerly' status, and generically sets itself in a 'hetero-geneity in which specific voices compete and become mutually exclusive'[50] – that exclusion begins in the novel's recognition of its own non-'literary' status (as we will see it aligns itself with Margaret Mitchell's *Gone With the Wind*) and extends to the realms of gender and 'national'/sectarian politics.

The novel's main character is Belle MacKnight, a worker in a Belfast linen mill. Belle achieves local fame by 'telling the pictures'; each morning she re-enacts movies for her co-workers, giving them access to the world of Hollywood and romance which they otherwise find it difficult to afford (they collectively pay for Belle's cinema tickets). The plot is disrupted by the entrance of Eugene (Gene) Comerford. Gene is a 'southerner' who had worked for a Protestant firm in rural Ulster and has been moved to the Blackwood's linen mill in Belfast because he refused the sexual advances of his employer Lady Cruiseman (this subplot deploys a Lady Chatterley narrative, given a very standard Big-House-in-decay twist – the predatory Lady Cruiseman has a club foot and her husband appears to be impotent). Belle and Gene fall in love and meet secretly, but their 'love across the barricades' romance is disapproved of and colluded against by the Protestant workforce and their bosses. Gene, having been an unwitting attendant at an IRA meeting, handled a gun which was later used in a murder, and he is arrested, convicted and eventually sentenced to death. Belle, having been persuaded by her Protestant colleagues that Noreen, a Catholic girl, has wooed Gene away from her, murders Noreen in full view of her colleagues (her rage is compounded because Noreen has begun 'telling the pictures' in Belle's absence). There are two trials: Gene is found guilty and hung for a crime which he did not commit; Belle is found not guilty of murder, there is no charge of manslaughter and she is freed.

Telling the Pictures has a female central character; it is set in a time of sectarian conflict (1942 – the Second World War context is secondary); it examines the place of women 'inside' a society which is tightly regulated and hegemonised along the lines of 'national' politics, while having an awareness of radical alternatives (Gene is avowedly a socialist before he is a nationalist); the novel has the obligatory good cop/bad cop model transferred to the RUC/prison service. In all these ways *Telling the Pictures* coincides with 'The Rebel' – it is in terms of cultural and individual agency that they diverge. *Telling the Pictures*, in its producerliness, falls outside the cultural possibilities of subaltern studies as they currently exist in Irish criticism, largely because to read such a 'producerly' text is to forgo the 'agency' necessary for the justification of subalternity as always-outside hegemonic structures. Where 'The Rebel' promotes (while politically controlling) an activism subversive of the state, *Telling the Pictures* has a fatalism about its narrative which arises because of the liberal-political and romance plot. Yet the focus on romance and drama is re-presented, at a distance, through a self-consciousness about popular narration which then opens gaps in the representation of politics at the same time as showing an awareness of the politics of representation.

Telling the Pictures runs its own narrative in parallel to the film version of *Gone with the Wind*. Belle 'tells' the narrative of *Gone with the Wind* in daily, serialised parts on the factory floor. Her modes of explanation and the expectations of her audience continually pull the cinematic narrative ('a four-hour Irish mystery play incorporating every ancestral trope of Irish fiction'[51]) into analogies with Northern Irish society (the American Civil War) and the romance plot (Scarlett O'Hara and Ashley Wilkes equated with Belle and Gene). The analogies are reinforced by Belle's colloquial 'telling':

Of course Scarlett flounces off and she's only livid on account of fancying Ashley Wilkes, and she scoots away from your two lads[52]

and her audience's local interpretation:

Belle knew their timing and her own, and she waited.
  'And this plantation is owned by a man called O'Hara.'
  Another interruption brought louder laughter: 'Oh, a Catholic. A Papist! A real Taig!' Ann Hamill, married at twenty-two, lost her first husband on the Somme in 1916; remarried a man ten years younger and now, at forty-eight, was awaiting news from France or anywhere, she did not know where he was, no letter for nine weeks.[53]

As the above extract suggests, Belle has an ability to tell and retell cinematic narratives as an act of cultural translation in which romance is a universal mode and cultural specificity is partly diluted by its ability to be analogous. The tentative 'Irish' link with *Gone with the Wind* is played on in various ways throughout the novel, but the cinema itself, as cultural phenomenon, is seen as a place of feminine fancy by the society in which Belle lives. Called as a witness in Gene's trial (the only witness who can acquit him) Belle is persuaded by the prosecuting counsel to tell *Gone with the Wind* to the court. Gene, from the dock, tries to stop her but the Crown is able to label Belle a 'fantasist', who like 'all women' likes 'romantic little scenes' and whose alibi for Gene is the work of a 'practised storyteller'.[54] The court's will to truth is compromised both by its masculinity and its role in maintaining the political structures of the state; this is not unusual, and is made clear by the machinations of the mill-owning classes in the novel. But more revealing and interesting is the denigration of 'fantasy' as a cultural form and its association with the cinema.

The history of Irish cinema is increasingly well documented, as are the roles of censorship and state sponsorship of the industry throughout the twentieth century.[55] In mid-twentieth-century Ireland there were still voices advocating a cultural purity which was perceived as being defiled by the fact that a 'cinema industry mainly controlled by aliens imposes our entertainment on our young people', suggesting to its audiences 'ways of life that are lacking in social sense and moral responsibility' and dangerously indulging in 'the repetition and glorification of false patterns of life'.[56] Belle's court-room experiences obviously find themselves held hostage to this wariness of difference and 'fantasy', and their testing against the legal standards of truth, guilt and proof objectifies the kinds of restrictive, almost anti-narrative stance, taken by the state apparatus.

While Belle's removal of herself into 'fantasy' (along with the very act of storytelling) is degraded within the legal system, her whimsicality is made serious by the novel's awareness of its own reliance on the very elements of 'fantasy' which constitute Belle's sense of self. *Telling the Pictures* relies on *Gone With the Wind* (and, silently, *Odd Man Out*), and proliferates with the ephemera of movie-going (Belle's detailed knowledge of Hollywood stars' lives and fashions, her reading of film magazines). The 'popular' has its own importance inscribed into its plot, and in the 'analogy' of *Gone with the Wind* finds a political resonance which is 'Irish' yet not entirely politicised along Irish lines; therefore, *Telling the Pictures*, by making the popular a dissident form of access to romance which is tempered with 'Ireland' in a removed, Irish American way (yet turning that back on Belfast), finds a place where the popular text can exist on the margins of, and reflect on, the orthodox polity. The questions which *Telling the Pictures* asks of the political establishment it caricatures are not profound or new (they are the product of a post-Civil Rights nationalism) and are asked weakly if seen as a direct challenge to the hegemonic class ideology of the North. But the novel does, perhaps inadvertently, place the 'popular' in a gendered relationship with the state, symbolised by the way in which the 'fantasist' is suppressed in the courtroom. Very obviously, *Telling the Pictures* offers no liberatory programme or discourse for women – as a popular, male-authored text it is unlikely ever to do so. But it does point to the places where the 'popular' and the subaltern co-mingle in direct and potentially uncontrollable accessibility. Brigid Redmond suggested in 1952 that children watch films only half-attentively; believing all that they see on screen, they 'deceive adults into think-ing that they follow the film as a whole'.[57] Belle's innocence in the cinema (she will never watch movies with guns) is touchingly and excruciatingly naive given her later story, her society and the global conflict going on around her. Yet her cinema-going and her story-telling dramatise that fear which Redmond expresses – that fantasy, storytelling, interpretation and their popular marginal forms represent a field which the hegemony believes it can saturate but can never be sure that it has done so. Counsel Larkwood tries to reduce Belle to the status of liar after her courtroom performance of *Gone with the Wind* but fails in the eyes of the public, since he is caught in the space between the hegemony and its subaltern in which the articulation of that incessant difference needs to be as silent as possible.

At the end of his essay 'Outside History', David Lloyd, having made a case for a new critical and historiographic agenda in Irish subaltern studies, writes:

The *performativity* that I seek to draw from this currently fluid and by no means integrated body of researches involves the attempt to produce and theorize dialectically out of such materials the possibility that social and cultural forms which are necessarily relegated to residual status by dominant historiography might generate forms for emergent practices, even where their apparent content may be in some views conservative.[58]

Telling the Pictures may not be the 'form' Lloyd had in mind here, and Belle's performativity within that form may be more second-hand than Lloyd would imagine, but as elements of a *description* of Irish subaltern status and its relation to 'high' political activity, *Telling the Pictures* catches both the affiliative and the subversive aspects of the subaltern, while pursuing more radically, if accidentally, the space where the 'fantasy' of the popular can escape producerliness and become indeterminate. As Homi Bhabha suggests, writing on 'contingency as the time of counter-hegemonic strategies':

Such 'indeterminism' is the mark of the conflictual yet productive spaces in which the arbitrariness of the sign of cultural signification emerges within the regulated boundaries of social discourse.[59]

For Bhabha these 'productive spaces' are still 'restricted' yet abundant. In searching for them, and for the strategies by which the subaltern may be known, we should remember the affiliative properties of the subaltern (submerging the subaltern further into silence), the subaltern's relation to subsets of 'regulated boundaries' and the need to see the performative aspects of the subaltern emerge wherever the arbitrariness of the sign can be prised into a gap which offers indeterminacy, catching the hegemony off guard and complacent. In this, the 'popular' text will play a key role.

'THE PUBLIC EYE'

Suffragettes always before the public eye need to dress well![60]

This striking piece of advertising, reproduced in Rosemary Cullen Owens' history of the Irish women's suffrage movement, intensely summarises the kinds of contradictions and difficulties which beset the political and cultural 'resistances' offered by both feminism and postcolonialism. The ironies of a discourse which is undoubtedly radical being subsumed into a discourse of the utmost gentility are important, and while such ironies have their own humour, charm and arguably their own disruptive power, this disjunction also usefully raises vital issues about the 'public' nature of such radicalisms in contemporary terms. The kinds of intellectual discussions in Irish studies in which postcolonial critiques, or feminism, or gender studies now reside are compelled to address the need to appear before a 'public eye', since their very basis is often perceived as their 'connectedness' to a radicalism which attests its importance for Irishness in a 'lived' world. Where the writer of Gleeson & Co.'s advertising could afford, rather daringly (and with at least an appearance of unselfconsciousness), to cash in on the possibility of a suffrage market, the writer of gendered or postcolonial Irish criticism takes on the assumption of speaking directly to a radicalised audience less confidently, but with an even greater sense of urgency.

If a model is employed in which 'gender' or the 'colonised' have their critical positions as markers of oppression reread through their attempts at and existences as affiliative strategies, a major ethical problem for cultural theory is raised. For certain areas of cultural theory what Edward Said calls the intellectual 'problem of loyalty'[61] is central to their discourse. Speaking of and for a cultural grouping (whether it be a gender, class, race or nation), in a state of commitment, traditionally employs and conceptually relies on the foundational stability of the grouping itself (at the very least in future-utopian terms – achieving their nascent coherence is the goal of critique), and the binding of the individual to that group. Thus the currency of terms of collectivity is preserved in imminence and the relationship of the individual subject to that group maintained. When cultural/critical theory allows a challenge to the subject position the artifice of those collective discourses as pure constructions made from the (democracy) of its individual subjects (what Bhabha calls the 'uncanny sameness-in-difference'[62]) is shaken. The difficulty, differently put, is this: how can we talk of and for an oppressed 'Irishness', or femininity, or gendered marginality, when those categories are reliant and contingent in unacknowledged ways on metadiscourses which paradoxically need the subject to justify their existence? 'Irishness' needs an Irish subject; an Irish 'subject' is made by its Irishness. Most obviously, in terms of cultural theory, what can crudely be seen as the ends of the notion of identity brought about by poststructuralist/deconstructive practice rubs against the constructions of identities and of subalterni-ties undertaken by equally political and often partly poststructuralist criticism. While postcolonialism and feminism have both at times been used to build subjectivities alternative to the dominant, 'decon-struction' (to use the term without adequate care) has tended to push on aspects of poststructuralism by acknowledging the textual construction of identity and pointing to its arbitrariness and vulner-ability. This crude analysis is sharpened by Spivak, who usefully summarises the impact of deconstruction on identity politics:

Deconstruction does not say there is no subject, there is no truth, there is no history. It simply questions the privileging of identity so that someone is believed to have the truth. It is not the exposure of error. It is constantly and persistently looking into how truths are produced.[63]

Spivak's insistence here is a recognition of the fine line which 'deconstruction' can hardly maintain within a discourse of critical radicalism; 'questions' often read like assertions when aimed at accepted and 'privileged concepts'.

Along with its undermining of identities privileged as truths, 'deconstruction' has also forced an analysis of 'the political and institutional structures that make possible and govern our practices, our competencies, our performances'.[64] The tendency of the (largely) unspoken confrontation between a 'deconstruction' of the subject and 'radical', affiliated theory is for political critiques to move reassur-ingly, though often momentarily, into the 'nostalgias' which Spivak warns against. At the very least they must post significant reminders of what it's all for. Luke Gibbons' discussion of the postcolonial notion of hybridity, for example, worries itself over the possible exclusion of Ireland from a postcolonial canonicity.[65] Where hybridity might describe a complexity of colonial/postcolonial interchange in which sanctified binaries are disrupted (opening the 'uncanny sameness-in-difference' paradox), Gibbons rhetorically neutralises hybridity by throwing it against 'obsolete ideas of history, nation or indigenous culture';[66] of course we are intended to share with Gibbons the heavy and knowing irony that these ideas are far from obsolete in Ireland, but this says more about what 'needs' to be salvaged and protected by the Irish intellectual than it does about hybridity itself. The necessity for and the constitution of an Irish subalternity are made clear by Gibbons; not only this, but here they are importantly opposed to 'one influential strand in contemporary cultural theory'.[67] That this clear demarcation of the ethical definitives of Gibbons' work relies on history, nation and indigeneity, and an opposition to 'theory' in the amorphous and alienating way it is described here, is indicative of the centrality of the dilemma posed by the possibility of questioned identities and intellectual responsibilities. The debilitation of the 'deconstructive' critique of political/critical binarisms (a critique for which the 'influential' notion of 'hybridity' is made to stand in Gibbons) ensures the survival of 'rootedness' as a 'fact' of Irish culture and as a constitutive aspect of the Irish intellectual. Richard Kirkland summarises the outcomes of this process (the retention of the subaltern as an ethically charged critical entity) in Irish studies thus:

The danger remains that in evoking the subaltern within Irish cultural studies we merely buttress the prevailing discourse against its other by restricting the play of the hybrid to a containing metaphor.[68]

The 'strategic' essentialism demanded by 'committed', affiliated theory is the partial drive behind this regrouping effect. A combination of revulsion and retention is the outcome of the meeting of questioned subjectivity with 'radical' Irish theory. The *examination* of the potential confrontation between the 'radical' and a notional 'deconstruction' in terms of Ireland and gender may be as far we can currently proceed. But this is useful in itself, since it demonstrates the desperate tenacity of subjecthood in critical discourse.

Ailbhe Smyth summarises the dilemma at the intersection of 'discredited' identity with the chasm of non-identity. Smyth says:

Identity *is* an issue for those who have never had it or who are struggling to emerge from a (straight) jacket that most definitely does not fit, even while it shapes and moulds and stifles . . . I am ambivalent about identity: wary of its limits and constraints, yet unwilling to abandon it entirely in favour of – what?[69]

Smyth offers no firm solutions but her conclusion is interestingly similar to Lloyd's. Where Lloyd has 'inflection' as a description of the process by which gendered subalternity affects national identity,[70] Smyth has 'declining', in the sense of diminishing but also, as she quotes from the *Shorter Oxford Dictionary*, 'to inflect or recite in order the cases'.[71] Both Smyth and Lloyd, negotiating between identity and its constructedness, speaking the 'radical' and 'doing' theory, offer models of change which maintain the subject through the observance of/desire for changes in the subjectifier. They both hope that 'gender' will be an agent which will 'decline' or 'inflect' the Irish 'nation', altering its state if not its status. Lloyd's 'excess' beyond the nation is Smyth's 'space' at its borders.[72] If a confrontation between gender and nation, identity politics and the ends of identity has taken place in a critical Irish context, then these notions, of contested borders and 'space' beyond and almost imperceptibly at the edges of national identity, are the formulations which seek to allow for subalternity and agency to remain integral to intellectual discourse; yet, for all their radicalism and subtle foresight, and for all that they downplay their note of prophecy, their groundedness in geographical metaphors reinforces the perception that they sit precipitously at the edge of the whirlpool of the future tending 'Ireland' which has always before pulled these alternative identities into itself.

A POSTCARD FROM IRELAND

Lloyd and Smyth, in their different ways and with different objectives in mind, both find themselves confronted with the possibility of what Bhabha memorably calls the 'postmodern agent without a cause'.[73] Part of Bhabha's proposed solution to this dilemma is to continually 'invoke' '*contingency*' at the moments when the subject attempts to move towards a 'moment of conclusion and control'.[74] In different ways Lloyd and Smyth implement this idea; their 'solutions' are a mixture of the examination of 'contingency' with a re-avowal of intellectual agency. At times it is this continuation of intellectual/academic 'speaking' which seems slightly at odds with their critiques; but then, both 'inflection' and 'declining', 'excess' and 'borders' need to be marked, identified and articulated by someone.

In Smyth's 'Declining identities (lit. and fig.)' there is, characteristically in her writing, the interspersion of Irish women's poetry as a commentary on Smyth's own prose; in one sense the poetry, as with the various other art forms referred to, functions as a bulletin from the world outside the academic. The congruence of poetic voice with critical voice offers a more complete and perhaps 'justified' critique.

Lloyd's cultural contexts (from Markievicz to the Irish Cultural Center in San Francisco[75]) similarly form a site of justification for the 'excess' which is possible beyond the nation. Lloyd places his faith, most importantly, in the 'popular': 'Popular culture continues its hybrid and partially self-transforming, partially subordinated existence in the shadow of the state'.[76] Generically, Lloyd's sense of the 'popular' equates with the use of (Irish women's) poetic texts by Smyth since both forms exhibit the subalternity which exists in opposition to hegemony, where perhaps the subaltern can be found and quantified.

There is a potentiality and also a danger here for Irish (gendered) criticism. Reading the popular as a site of subalternity points to a fundamental review of what is effectively a curriculum of Irish studies; but if the popular becomes the subaltern, it can also quickly become the 'authentic' and thus undergo the same intellectual reading processes pointed to several times above; its subalternity will become the seal for its indigeneity, its purity, fixing it forever as a fiction of movement. At the same time the popular, defined as that which is outside the control of the state, retains a degree of agency and marginality which is at odds with some versions of the popular in which its apparently banal 'producerliness' is the cover for its ways of 'inflecting' the dominant ideology into contortions from *inside* itself.

In Myrtle Hill and Vivien Pollock's book *Image and Experience: Photographs of Irishwomen*, there is a reproduction of a photograph of two women in 'traditional dress' at the Wishing Chair, the Giant's Causeway, around 1895. As Hill and Pollock suggest, this is an exhibition of 'staged quaintness';[77] the women stare at the camera with a look of experienced blankness. The same two women, plus one other, also appear at the same site in an aquatint postcard (sent in 1907[78] – Figure 3). The sea behind them is a garish blue, the stones of the Causeway have been tinted with luminescently green 'algae', and the three women display the wares they sell to tourists. Like any such image, like any popular text, this is at once potentially replete with meaning and potentially entirely ephemeral. It is certainly an encapsulation of 'identity', marketed and distributed. Sent from Ireland to England, it circulates an image of gendered Irishness which is at once fixed and hopelessly passing. The 'exploitation' of these women, as Hill and Pollock see it, is also a fleeting colonial act of subjectification, undercut by the economic exchange which it implies. Buying a gendered 'Irishness', this postcard desires a narrative continuity (tradition and contemporaneity together; these women were always and will always be like this, and will always be available to be seen like this). But the proof of this continuity is only instantaneous; its staged nature is willingly ignored by all involved (photographed, photographer, sender, receiver), yet is essential to its production. This postcard functions like Derrida's: 'so modest, anonymous,

FIGURE 3 'Wishing Chair Giant's Causeway', postcard by W. Lawrence, Dublin, sent 1907.

offered, stereotyped, "retro" – and absolutely indecipherable'.[79] It is only by ignoring the underlying act of dressing up to be authentic that the sender and receiver of this postcard can give it the meaning they desire it to have. For them it evidences, fixes and illustrates gendered Ireland. Replacing the colonial gaze with the subaltern voice is a complex interchange, and not entirely a parallel reversal; but contemporary critical readings of gendered Ireland, are, as this chapter has tried to suggest, understandably struggling to resist the temptation to re-place the sign of 'Irish woman' under their own 'postal' gaze.

Notes

1. Ailbhe Smyth, 'The Floozie in the Jacuzzi', *The Irish Review*, 6 (1989), p. 7.
2. Margaret Kelly, 'Women in the North', in Thérèse Caherty, Andy Storey, Mary Gavin, Máire Molloy and Caitríona Ruane (eds), *Is Ireland a Third World Country?* (Belfast: Beyond the Pale, 1992), p. 53.
3. Antonio Gramsci, *Selections from the Prison Notebooks* (London: Lawrence

& Wishart, 1971), p. 55.

4. Gramsci, *Prison Notebooks*, p. 52.
5. Gramsci, *Prison Notebooks*, p. 52.
6. Gramsci, *Prison Notebooks*, p. 52.
7. Gramsci, *Prison Notebooks*, p. 52.
8. Ranajit Guha, 'On Some Aspects of the Historiography of Colonial India', in Ranajit Guha (ed.), *Subaltern Studies*, vol. I (Delhi: Oxford University Press, 1982), p. 7.
9. See, for example, Gayatri Chakravorty Spivak, *In Other Worlds: Essays in Cultural Politics* (London: Routledge, 1988) and *Outside in the Teaching Machine* (London: Routledge, 1993); Laura E. Donaldson, *Decolonizing Feminisms: Race, Gender and Empire-Building* (London: Routledge, 1992); Rajeswari Sunder Rajan, *Real and Imagined Women: Gender, Culture and Postcolonialism* (London: Routledge, 1993).
10. Gerardine Meaney, *Sex and Nation: Women in Irish Culture and Politics* (Dublin: Attic, 1991), p. 17. Similar assumptions about the relationship of nationalism and gender in Ireland can be found in Edna Longley, *From Cathleen to Anorexia: The Breakdown of Irelands* (Dublin: Attic, 1990); Margaret Ward, *The Missing Sex: Putting Women Into Irish History* (Dublin: Attic, 1991); Smyth, 'The Floozie in the Jacuzzi'; and Clair Wills, *Improprieties: Politics and Sexuality in Northern Irish Poetry* (Oxford: Clarendon, 1993); however, all of these writers tend to disagree beyond this basic notion of incompatiblity.
11. Deniz Kandiyoti, 'Identity and its Discontents: Women and the Nation', in Laura Chrisman and Patrick Williams (eds), *Colonial Discourse and Post-Colonial Theory: A Reader* (Hemel Hempstead: Harvester, 1994), p. 376.
12. Kandiyoti, 'Identity and its Discontents', p. 380.
13. R. Radhakrishnan, 'Nationalism, Gender, and the Narrative of Identity', in Andrew Parker, Mary Russo, Doris Sommer and Patricia Yaegar (eds), *Nationalisms and Sexualities* (London: Routledge, 1992), p. 78.
14. Quoted in Terence Brown, *Ireland: A Social and Cultural History, 1922–1985* (London: Fontana, 1990), p. 146.
15. David Lloyd, 'Nationalisms Against the State: Towards a Critique of the Anti-Nationalist Prejudice', in T. P. Foley, Lionel Pilkington, Sean Ryder and Elizabeth Tilley (eds), *Gender and Colonialism* (Galway: Galway University Press, 1995), p. 257.
16. David Lloyd, *Anomalous States: Irish Writing and the Post-Colonial Moment* (Dublin: Lilliput, 1993), p. 127.
17. More recently Lloyd has refined this idea of 'excess' to a description of 'performativity', and in the chapter 'Outside History' (which mirrors in many ways Spivak's questions to historiography in 'Subaltern Studies') this follows a discussion of the marginalisation of feminism and Marxism by the Irish nation-state. See David Lloyd, *Ireland After History* (Cork: Cork University Press/Field Day, 1999), pp. 87–8.
18. Carol Coulter, *The Hidden Tradition: Feminism, Women and Nationalism in Ireland* (Cork: Cork University Press, 1993), p. 2.
19. Coulter sees this division as part of the denationalisation of Irish debate, 'emancipating Ireland from the shackles of its obsessions with the past and [allowing] it to take its place among the nations of the new Europe': Coulter, *The Hidden Tradition*, p. 2.
20. Coulter, *The Hidden Tradition*, p. 3.

21. Coulter, *The Hidden Tradition*, p. 3.
22. Coulter, *The Hidden Tradition*, p. 54.
23. Gayatri Charavorty Spivak, 'Can the Subaltern Speak?', in Patrick Williams and Laura Chrisman (eds), *Colonial Discourse and Post-Colonial Theory: A Reader*, p. 69.
24. Spivak, 'Can the Subaltern Speak?', p. 87.
25. See Lloyd, *Anomalous States*, pp. 89–100 and 'Nationalisms Against the State', p. 276.
26. The exception here would seem to be Lloyd's description of Ireland's 'non-modernity' in *Ireland After History*.
27. Spivak, 'Can the Subaltern Speak?', p. 79.
28. Spivak, 'Subaltern Studies: Deconstructing Historiography', in Ranajit Guha (ed.), *Subaltern Studies*, vol. IV (Delhi: Oxford University Press, 1985), p. 358.
29. Spivak, 'Subaltern Studies: Deconstructing Historiography', p. 340.
30. Spivak, 'Can the Subaltern Speak?', p. 87.
31. Spivak, 'Can the Subaltern Speak?', p. 90. Emphasis in original.
32. Gerry Adams quoted in James McAleavy, 'The Imagination of Contemporary Republicanism' (MA Dissertation, University of Dublin, 1993), p. 36. My thanks to Jim McAleavy for lending me a copy of his dissertation.
33. Adams quoted in McAleavy, 'The Imagination of Contemporary Republicanism', p. 38.
34. Gerry Adams, *Falls Memories* (Dingle: Brandon, 1982).
35. Adams quoted in McAleavy, 'The Imagination of Contemporary Republicanism', p. 39.
36. Gerry Adams, *The Street and Other Stories* (Dingle: Brandon, 1992), p. 37.
37. Adams, *The Street*, p. 37.
38. Adams, *The Street*, p. 43.
39. See Longley, *From Cathleen to Anorexia*.
40. Adams, *The Street*, p. 44.
41. Adams, *The Street*, p. 46.
42. Smyth, 'The Floozie in the Jacuzzi', p. 16.
43. Smyth, 'The Floozie in the Jacuzzi', pp. 20–1.
44. Bernard McLaverty, *Cal* (London: Jonanthan Cape, 1983); Brian Moore, *Lies of Silence* (London: Bloomsbury, 1990); Peter Leslie, *The Extremists* (London: New English Library, 1970); Tom Clancy, *Patriot Games* (London: Collins, 1987). Leslie's *The Extremists* is one of the first of the genre and is discussed in Aaron Kelly, '"A Sense of Stasis, Fear and Hatred": The Politics of Form in Representations of Northern Ireland Produced by the "Troubles" Thriller' in P. J. Mathews (ed.), *New Voices in Irish Criticism* (Dublin: Four Courts, 2000), pp. 109–15. See also Joe Cleary, '"Fork-Tongued on the Border Bit": Partition and the Politics of Form in Contemporary Narratives of the Northern Irish Conflict', *South Atlantic Quarterly*, 95:1 (1996), 227–76.
45. See Jayne Steel, 'Vampira: Representations of the Irish Female Terrorist', *Irish Studies Review*, 6:3 (1998), 273–84.
46. Richard Kirkland, *Literature and Culture in Northern Ireland Since 1965: Moments of Danger* (London: Longman, 1996), p. 40.
47. Michael Pickering, *History, Experience and Cultural Studies* (London: Macmillan, 1997), p. 34.
48. Frank Delaney, *Telling the Pictures* (London: HarperCollins, 1994), p. 480.

49. John Fiske, *Understanding Popular Culture* (London: Routledge, 1994), p. 103.
50. Jim Collins, *Uncommon Cultures: Popular Culture and Post-Modernism* (London: Routledge, 1989), p. 71.
51. Harlan Kennedy, 'Shamrocks and Shillelaghs: Idyll and Ideology in Irish Cinema', in James MacKillop (ed.), *Contemporary Irish Cinema: From 'The Quiet Man' to 'Dancing at Lughnasa'* (Syracuse, NY: Syracuse University Press, 1999), p. 6.
52. Delaney, *Telling the Pictures*, p. 40.
53. Delaney, *Telling the Pictures*, p. 38.
54. Delaney, *Telling the Pictures*, pp. 422 and 424.
55. See particularly Kevin Rockett, John Hill and Luke Gibbons, *Cinema and Ireland* (London: Routledge, 1988) and Lance Pettitt, *Screening Ireland: Film and Television Representation* (Manchester: Manchester University Press, 2000).
56. Brigid Redmond, 'Films and Children', *Studies*, 45 (1956), 232 and 227.
57. Redmond, 'Films and Children', 229.
58. Lloyd, *Ireland After History*, p. 88.
59. Homi K. Bhabha, *The Location of Culture* (London: Routledge, 1994), p. 172.
60. Advertisement reproduced in Rosemary Cullen Owens, *Smashing Times: A History of the Irish Women's Suffrage Movement 1889–1922* (Dublin: Attic, 1984), p. 94.
61. Edward W. Said, *Representations of the Intellectual: The 1993 Reith Lectures* (London: Vintage, 1994), p. 30.
62. Bhabha, *The Location of Culture*, p. 54.
63. Gayatri Chakravorty Spivak, *The Spivak Reader*, eds Donna Landry and Gerald MacLean (London: Routledge, 1996), p. 27.
64. Derrida quoted in Jonathan Culler, *On Deconstruction: Theory and Criticism After Structuralism* (London: Routledge & Kegan Paul, 1983), p. 156.
65. Gibbons notes Ireland's omission from Bill Ashcroft, Gareth Griffiths and Helen Tiffin, *The Empire Writes Back: Theory and Practice in Post-colonial Literatures* (London: Routledge, 1989), a book which Gibbons identifies as implying that Ireland was coloniser rather than colonised.
66. Luke Gibbons, *Transformations in Irish Culture* (Cork: Cork University Press/Field Day, 1996), p. 172.
67. Gibbons, *Transformations in Irish Culture*, p. 172.
68. Richard Kirkland, 'Questioning the Frame: Hybridity, Ireland and the Institution', in Colin Graham and Richard Kirkland (eds), *Ireland and Cultural Theory* (London: Macmillan, 1999), p. 220.
69. Ailbhe Smyth, 'Declining Identities (lit. and fig.)', *Critical Survey*, 8:2 (1996), 152.
70. Lloyd, 'Nationalisms Against the State', p. 266.
71. Smyth, 'Declining Identities (lit. and fig.)', p. 146.
72. Smyth, 'Declining Identities (lit. and fig.)', p. 156.
73. Bhabha, *The Location of Culture*, p. 186.
74. Bhabha, *The Location of Culture*, p. 186.
75. See Lloyd's chapter 'The Recovery of Kitsch', in *Ireland After History*, pp. 89–100.
76. Lloyd, 'Nationalisms Against the State', p. 272.
77. Myrtle Hill and Vivien Pollock, *Image and Experience: Photographs of Irishwomen* (Belfast: Blackstaff, 1993), p. 66.

78. Postcard in the possession of the author. Sent on 18 September 1907, with a Larne postmark, to an address in Leeds, England.

79. Jacques Derrida, *The Post Card: From Socrates to Freud and Beyond*, intro. and trans. Alan Bass (London: University of Chicago Press, 1987), p. 47.

===== 6 =====

'... maybe that's just Blarney': Authenticity in Irish Culture

On the side of the colonizer, it is the inauthenticity of the colonized culture, its falling short of the concept of the human, that legitimates the colonial project. (David Lloyd)[1]

The Story of Ireland's heritage is a new reason for visiting Ireland. It is told in a modern but authentic style and mirrors European culture preserved in an island which makes it possible to visit centres from neolithic to 19th Century, even on a short visit. (Heritage Ireland, marketing brochure)[2]

INTRODUCTION

Somewhere between colonisation and postcolonialism, domination and independence, the in/authenticity of the colonised is overturned. The role of authenticity alters from being a signifier of the colonised's cultural incapacities to being a marketable sign of value. If authenticity is not only a product of colonialism but central to its ethics, then we need a clearer grasp of its definitions, of the means by which it comes to be elevated to the status of an evaluative ethic and of how it contorts with changes in the colonial situation. And as David Lloyd and 'Heritage Island' seem to suggest, authenticity may have both a typical and particular function in the context of Irish culture and the chronologies embedded in it.

'Blame it on Maureen O'Hara'[3] is one suggestive way in which to understand the recurrence of authenticity in the construction of material Irelands. Mary Flaherty, a designer, 'has created an "authentic reproduction" of the Galway shawl. The idea arose when she was talking to the star [Maureen O'Hara] who played opposite John Wayne in *The Quiet Man*'.[4] The very phrase 'authentic reproduction', by its apparently oxymoronic nature, begs its own questions, though in the

Irish case authenticity is only ever reproduced, filtered and reconstituted through a process of authentication and recognition of status (thus creating a further eddy of paradoxes).

To see colonialism as the destroyer of authenticity is tempting:

Ms O'Hara recalled how the wardrobe department working on the film had offered £25 to Galway people who were prepared to part with their shawls and so dress the cast on the production. She bemoaned the fact that the shawl had become almost 'extinct' after hundreds were taken back to the US by the Hollywood cast and crew.[5]

Yet the fact that the resurfacing of the 'authentically produced' shawl has its origins in that technicolor glorification of Irishness, *The Quiet Man*, alerts us to the capacity which the authentic has to find its own beginnings in the unlikeliest of places which are themselves attempts at the authentic.

Mary Flaherty's shawl is typical of what this chapter suggests is the inexhaustibility and centrality of the authentic in Irish culture: it is also an exemplary double-faced phenomenon, looking back to Hollywood (with O'Hara in a sense disowning the product she was part of) and the shawl as a nineteenth-century icon of Irishness, while at the same time being unashamedly and ephemerally in the marketplace of the present. Mary Flaherty's shawl ('intricately woven with symbols of the heart and hands, harp intertwined with shamrock . . ., bordered by Celtic knotwork depicting interlocking birds') is, of course, a limited edition since it spectrally replaces, two-thousand fold, the 'hundreds' which were lost; the Irish government 'bought a consignment to present as millennium gifts to visitors', so authorising its authenticity, while those lucky enough to own a shawl have its provenance clarified by 'an explanatory booklet'. The authentic, as will become apparent, is never obvious and is forever in need of the supplement of commentary.

This chapter explores various dynamics of authenticity in the context of Irish culture, arguing that the definition of the authentically Irish is central to claims for value. If the coloniser denies authenticity, then for Irish culture it becomes crucial that the 'birth of authenticity is rooted in revolution'.[6] Authenticity and claims to authenticity underlie the conceptual and cultural denial of dominance. The nation's very reason for being, its logic of existence, is its claim to an undeniable essence as a pure expression of the 'real', the obvious, the natural – it is partly out of the need for replication of that essence that authenticity arises as a way of facilitating yet controlling the replication of a singular essence, spreading it synchronically and diachronically to the boundaries (and no further) of the essence's framing ideological name. As will be clear by now, this book suggests that such a process of semiotic control is likely to find itself over-stretched and internally riven.

In the Irish context, claims for authenticity move from the 'revolu-tionary' (in all its aspects) to the dominant, following the path of the nation to the nation-state. And just as the nation in Ireland becomes questioned and ironised, so too the 'jargon of authenticity'[7] becomes critiqued as jargon. This chapter follows that process in Irish culture to its conclusion in a popular, advertising postmodernism which can be seen to make its own claims to authenticity through ironic rereadings of established versions of authentic Irishness. This leaves unanswered the question of the history of authenticity in Irish culture, which will always be inseparable from the history of the reproduction and circulation of the objects and materials of 'Ireland', and which begins to imply that to chase the authentic is to trace the origins of something that will always let us know that is has another origin further back.

This account of authenticity begins with an examination of the concept as it is discussed in writings by Jacob Golomb and Theodor Adorno, stressing how authenticity attempts to defy definition through its ambiguous stresses on origins and teleologies of completeness fused with continual change. Gareth Griffiths suggests that the autho-risation of authenticity can still be undertaken by the coloniser after decolonisation as a hierarchising form of control in the postcolonial period. This possibility needs to be addressed in the Irish context before going on to look at the categories of Irish authenticity which I have provisionally entitled Old Authenticities, New Authenticities and Ironic Authenticities. These distinctions are based not on the colonial/postcolonial chronology, but on the point at which an 'authentic' Ireland becomes more or less available apparently outside or in defiance of colonial dominance; thus the 'Old Authenticity' discussed is found in Yeats, the New Authenticity in the marketing of 'Heritage Island', and the Ironic Authenticity in a television advertisement for Smithwick's beer. My intention here is to begin a reassessment of the role of postcolonial cultural theories in Ireland by using 'authenticity' as a marker of the effects of the progress of colonialism in Irish culture – but a marker which unsettles certain of the teleologies of postcolonialism by virtue of its changeability and capacity for self-preservation. Authenticity is claimed and disclaimed in Irish culture, functioning as a standard of worth and a cultural core value. The origins of this cultural necessity may indeed lie in what David Lloyd (above) sees as the labelling of Irish culture as 'inauthentic' by the coloniser. But authenticity has not simply rolled along behind 'Irishness' in history; authenticity has affected the basic discourses of Irish culture in its prevalence, which has given it a status near to that of a shared currency; a focus on authenticity takes us to the verge of seeing Irish material history as an unravelling backwards in time, detecting signs which plough against the linearities we know from political history. In this sense authenticity is the paradoxically reversed trace of an Irish future trying to wipe its fingerprints from the scene of the crime.

THEORISING AUTHENTICITY

All agree in principle that any positive definition of authenticity would be self-nullifying.[8]

Jacob Golomb's *In Search of Authenticity* constitutes a major attempt to read authenticity as an integral part of western philosophical, humanistic traditions and to place the 'search' for the authentic, if not the thing itself, at the centre of humanistic energies directed against the undermining of our 'true' selves by the vagaries of the postmodern. Golomb concludes his crusading revival of the need for authenticity with the words: 'Only the return to our authentic pathos can prevent the betrayal of what is dearest to each of us: our own selfhood'.[9] Against this is set 'the decline of the ethic of subjectivity in the postmodern era, and the suppression of individuality encouraged by the mass media and multinational markets'.[10]

Authenticity is thus at least partially lost in postmodernity, in the contemporary. And humanistic strategies are flagrantly at work here; the 'selfhood' which protests its own benignity and logicality can only be defined by what it is 'other' than. Here the '*mass* media and *multinational* markets' deny the full existence of selfhood, drowning its self-expression, not through public discourse or capitalism, the market or the media, but through their postmodern reconfiguration into 'mass' events which stretch beyond the boundaries of class and nationality in which the notion of selfhood was fostered. Golomb is appropriately applying a nostalgia to a version of authenticity which itself relies on nostalgias for its definition – indeed by the end of

Golomb's book, and through the poetics of authenticity he describes, it is possible to see such 'pathos' expressed about the fate of the authentic as in fact a simple *restatement of the authentic*, retreading the paths of decline and difficulty on which authenticity depends.

Golomb's notion that authenticity is disintegrated by postmodernity needs some thought – as I have already suggested, this may be merely a strategy of authenticity rather than an analysis of its fate. In order to understand the ways in which authenticities are challenged, rewritten or recharged in Irish culture it is necessary to turn to Golomb's notion that 'multinational markets' are at odds with the authentic, since this not only allows us to see why authenticity may need to 'return' in the face of the postmodern (an 'authentic reproduction' of a 'nineteenth-century' shawl uses the actress from a 1952 film as its initiating point of validation), but offers a possibility in beginning to politicise Golomb's definition of authenticity.

Since the authentic, in Golomb's analysis, in articulated in the philosophies of Kierkegaard, Nietzsche, Heidegger, Sartre and Camus, it seems unlikely that when 'multinational markets' deface authenticity they do so because of their ideology of the market – if authenticity can arise in philosophical discourse during the times when these philosophers wrote then, whatever authenticity's relationship with capital, it can hardly be thought to be suppressed by the existence of capitalism. It is presumably then the 'multinational' that is stifling authenticity or that is perhaps itself 'inauthentic'. This is a vital recognition, since it allows Golomb's text to be read against itself, uncovering an alternative genealogy for authenticity to the one Golomb himself sets up. In the Irish context, and in the broader philosophical imaginings discussed by Golomb, it becomes clear that authenticity overlaps with nationalism's self-projections in crucial ways. Golomb may seek to avoid an explicit politics of authenticity, but the uses of authenticity in Irish culture reveal it to be a profoundly political pretext for evaluation. Authenticity may be traditionally reliant on the existence of the nation as the basis for political thought to the extent that it cannot, in some of its formats, be re-imagined beyond nationalism – alternatively, reviving a form of authenticity validated by the nation may be a way of resisting multinationalism, post-nationalism and any other contortion or disruption to the centrality of the nation as a political unit.

Authenticity, Golomb notes, is bound to notions of authority, and in Heidegger's version of authenticity the authority underpinning the authentic changes from an 'authoritative God' to 'the historical dimension of the people in which one is rooted':

One is historically authentic when one creates one's own history by utilizing and recreating one's past and the past of one's people, projecting them with anticipatory resoluteness towards one's future . . . [Authenticity] is the loyalty of one's self to its own past, heritage and ethos.[11]

Authenticity here, to employ Golomb's vocabulary, becomes rooted in 'the people' and the bond between the self and the group; and additionally, authenticity relies on the ability to 'utilize' and culturally employ such 'loyalty' – authenticity is thus constantly a cultural, textual phenomenon, defining, recreating and projecting. Authenticity may resist definition, but its materiality in textuality is undeniable. In this it shares with imaginings of nationalism an important reliance on its various media: what Benedict Anderson calls 'the technical means for "re-presenting" the *kind* of imagined community that is the nation'.[12]

Yet it is not just in its textually pervasive characteristics, or its espousal of connectedness with the past and a 'people', that authenticity overlaps with nationalism. Like nationalism, authenticity has an ambiguous relationship with 'origins': reliant upon their antiquity *as* authenticity, yet disparaging of teleologies which destroy the mystique of authenticity through their rationalisation of history. Golomb, early in *In Search of Authenticity*, argues that authenticity 'calls for no particular contents or consequences, but, rather, focuses on the origins and the intensity of one's emotional-existential commitments',[13] and later Golomb suggests that Kierkegaard adds another meaning to authenticity, 'namely, the return to the genuine origins of ourselves, our feelings and our beliefs'.[14] That authenticity expresses a return seems to imply a reversal of thought or commitment along some established lines to an initial point. Yet elsewhere Golomb points out that Kierkegaard argues that the 'self is something that should be created and formed, not something possessing an intrinsic essence to be further developed'.[15] Like nationalism, it is the 'genuineness' of 'genuine origins' that authenticity highlights rather than the materiality of origins; and 'genuineness', in a perfectly circular resistance to theory, is known by its authenticity. As with the nation in Benedict Anderson's famous formulation, authenticity wishes to be conceived of as 'moving steadily up (or down) history',[16] and as with the nation, authenticity 'proves' itself through its simultaneous and contradictory textual existence and refusal to be defined. In its own best scenario authenticity is thus what Golomb calls 'a state of integrity between the innermost self and its external manifestations, whatever their form and content';[17] an integrity (or 'loyalty') which

demands an unquestioning belief in a wholeness involving the individual and his/her social context.

If authenticity tends to a monologic unquestioning discourse
concurrent with that of the 'nation', it arises also out of contexts in
which the nation becomes an active arbiter between the past and a
'people'. Like the anti-colonial formation of nation, the 'quest for
authenticity becomes especially pronounced in extreme situations',
its 'birth' being 'rooted in revolution'.[18] Authenticity combines the
prioritisation of 'origins' with the 'pathos of incessant change' – again
moving steadily through history. Its definition is a set of contradictions,
static but changing, conservative but adaptable, originary but modern.

Golomb's book ends with a plea for the saving of a disintegrating
sense of authenticity, one of the rare moments when authenticity
allows its ideological susceptibilities to open out – Golomb's authenticity at this point reaches the limits of its ability to change, at the
point at which the humanism, the nationalism, the play of rationality
and love of the irrational it embodies, are consciously challenged.
The pathos of its plea, so obvious when placed in the context of
postmodernity, is made the centre of (Golomb's version of) authenticity's call for resurrection.

ADORNO AND BAUDRILLARD: SYSTEM TO SIMULATION

Although Golomb finishes with authenticity set against a vague
postmodernism, he is most vitriolic in his conclusions at the expense
of 'the ratiocinations of Adorno and his followers'.[19] Adorno's *The
Jargon of Authenticity* examines the points at which the authentic is
socialised and popularised; in Adorno the authenticities later traced
by Golomb become materiality, culture and policy. Adorno's attempt
to prick the bubble of authenticity is perhaps most effective in its
analysis of authenticity *in and as a language and as an ideology*.
Adorno sees 'authenticity' as a jargonised system, falsely constructing
itself as essence and origin: '[the language of authenticity] is a
trademark of societalized chosenness, noble and homely at once –
sub-language as superior language'[20] – coming from 'below' against
the once-dominant. Adorno's irritation with the jargon is furthered
by its exclusionism, identifying what is outside it:

'inauthentic', where something broken is implied, an expression which is
not immediately appropriate to what is expressed ... 'Inauthentic' ...
becomes a 'critical' term, in definite negation of something merely phenomenal.[21]

Authenticity is thus the inherent factor in the creation of an organicism which is ideologically charged, exclusivist, evaluative and almost a definition of the heroic ('noble and homely'). Adorno thus sees the authentic as not only a cultural ideology but as a way of thinking and being:

Whoever is versed in the jargon does not have to say what he thinks, does not even have to think it properly. The jargon takes over this task and devalues thought. That the whole man should speak is authentic, comes from the core . . . Communication clicks and puts forth as truth what should instead be suspect by virtue of the prompt collective agreement.[22]

Adorno's critique of authenticity hinges on disrupting the edges of its claims to wholeness and organicism, and its ability to become a self-sufficient ideology and way of speaking. Golomb's proposed search for authenticity, on the other hand, begins and ends with the self at the centre of authenticity, the site of definition and justification in which there is the continuously twisting paradox which suggests that authenticity and selfhood are both undefined until both can be defined by each other.

Before moving on to see how authenticity figures in Irish culture, it is useful to introduce Baudrillard's perspective on authenticity's role in simulation. While Adorno and Golomb can be placed in some sort of mutual dialogue which relies on agreement that authenticity is a dispute over possible truths, Baudrillard sees authenticity adopting a role in the fantasy of representation:

When the real is no longer what it used to be, nostalgia assumes its full meaning. There is a proliferation of myths of origin and signs of reality; of second-hand truth, objectivity and authenticity . . . there is a panic-stricken production of the real and the referential, above and parallel to the panic of material production.[23]

Authenticity here has ceased being a measurement of value (or even a proof of 'true' existence) and become a sign of the need for such values. In the midst of apparent disintegration, authenticity reverts to the (re)production of origins and of itself. Golomb's ending is perhaps a philosophical expression of what Baudrillard identifies: holding on nostalgically to a selfhood which justifies and is 'created' by being authentic. Golomb's strategy for the self in postmodernism thus overlaps with Baudrillard's identification of the processes of nostalgia and authenticity in postmodernism. To this extent we have reached a point where the authentic can be seen as a site of contestation across Golomb/Adorno, with Adorno identifying the authentic as a jargonised ideology travestying what it represents – and with Baudrillard seeing the authentic as evidence of a loss, or change in, the 'real', which in turn moves us, nostalgically, back through history.

POSTCOLONIALISM, IRELAND AND AUTHENTICITY

There are real dangers in recent representations of indigenous peoples in popular discourse, especially in the media, which stress claims to an 'authentic' voice. For these claims may be a form of overwriting the complex actuality of difference equal but opposite to the more overt writing out of that voice in earlier oppressive discourses of reportage.[24]

In his essay 'The Myth of Authenticity: Representation, Discourse and Social Practice', Gareth Griffiths suggests that the 'inauthenticity' once used to label the colonised, and which should have been subsequently 'reversed' by anti-colonialism, has transformed into an authenticity which is under the control of the 'West'. In other words, having rejected the 'inauthenticity' applied under colonialism, the once colonised now suffer their authenticity to be prescribed and hierarchised by the coloniser and by the malign after-effects of colonialism:

Whilst it is true that the various Australian Aboriginal peoples may increasingly wish to assert their sense of the local and the specific as a recuperative strategy in the face of the erasure of difference characteristic of colonialist representation, such representations, subsumed by the white media *under a mythologized and fetishized sign of the 'authentic'*, can also be used to create a privileged hierarchy of Australian Aboriginal voice.[25]

Given that we have seen David Lloyd apply the same prognosis to Irish culture under colonial rule, it must be seriously considered whether any certainties in expressions of authenticity in post-Independence Irish culture are prescribed or 'allowed' by the coloniser. Applied to the Irish situation, Griffiths' analysis of post-colonial power structures seems a little simplistic – the cultural interchanges between Britain/England and Ireland both during and after colonisation were never as settled or monolithic as Griffiths suggests they were and are in Aboriginal experience. Because of proximity, geography, race and religion the position of the Irish in colonial discourse was and is, as suggested in Chapter 4, 'liminal'.

Irish culture, at once western and colonised, white and racially other, imperial and subjugated, became marginal in the sense of existing at the edge of but within two experiences, with a culture that epitomises the hybridity, imitation and irony latent in colonial interchanges. 'Authenticity' may play a key role in Irish culture, but the function of authenticity in colonial and postcolonial terms in an Irish context will not, because of its liminality, follow the coloniser's trajectory in the way that Griffiths outlines. Colonialism's initial denial of 'authenticity' is at the root of the persistence of authenticity in Irish culture, but Ireland's colonially marginal, hybrid status allows authenticity a less stable role subsequently – thus authenticity becomes embedded as a feature of discourses of Irish culture, but its provenance ultimately resists limitation, making 'Ireland' spatially and temporally 'liminal' to its referent.

AN OLD AUTHENTICITY

The teleology of colonialism suggests that authenticity will be reclaimed as part of the '[bringing] into existence [of the] history of the nation' which Fanon sees as crucial in the process of decolonisation.[26] If authenticity is a tool for the justification of colonialism then, like (and as part of) the nation, it must be turned to face the coloniser. The history of nineteenth-century Irish cultural nationalism can be seen as such a process of reclamation, restaking the grounds for Irishness, 'proving' Irish authenticities.

Immediately we try to divide the tropes of Irish authenticities we are faced with contradiction and multiplicity. Is the predominant anti-colonial Irish authenticity of the de Valerean or Yeatsian version, for example? Folkish or rural? Irish Irish, Anglo-Irish or global Irish? These strains, along with many others overlapping and contesting, could be identified in a longer study. For the moment I wish to focus on claims to authenticity in a text which allows for some distinction in authenticities directed against the colonial claims to 'inauthentic-ity' Lloyd mentions – W. B. Yeats's *Fairy and Folk Tales of the Irish Peasantry* (1888). Yeats's collection of Irish 'peasant' tales is in one sense part of a continued popularisation of the antiquarianism which had begun in Ireland earlier in the century; Yeats's folk and fairy tales are not remarkable but typical in the way that they attempt to construct an Irishness which is from outside the social and sectarian remit of the collector, who through the act of collection, cataloguing, publishing and the accumulation of knowledge sees a potential for becoming 'of' what is collated. The Irishness of Yeats's collection is constructed as both other and part of him, and is thus doubly authenticated; discursively he attempts to act as intermediary between an Irishness which is 'authentic' and a receiver of claims to authenticity whose identity will never be fully articulated (Britain or Anglo-Ireland, Europe or a universal sense of nationhood?). As medium for the authentic, his knowledge of authenticity and his ability to recognise it 'infect' him with authenticity too.

Yeats's 'Introduction' to *Fairy and Folk Tales of Ireland* expresses as much concern with the authenticity attached to the gathering of material as it does to the material itself:

In the *Parochial Survey of Ireland* it is recorded how the story-tellers used to gather together of an evening, and if any had a different version from the others, they would all recite theirs and vote, and the man who had varied would have to abide by their verdict. In this way stories have been handed down with such accuracy, that the long tale of Dierdre was, in the earlier decades of this century, told almost word for word, as in the very ancient MSS. in the Royal Dublin Society. In one case only it varied, and then the MS. was obviously wrong – a passage had been forgotten by the copyist.[27]

The material of authenticity is here 'handed down' unchanged through history. This Irishness is certainly projected 'with anticipatory resoluteness towards one's future';[28] its trajectory begins in antiquity and survives history because it is a futurology. While Yeats is primarily seeming to stress the objectivity (even democracy) of the authentication of the Irishness of 'the people', this first-level authenticity is encapsulated by two processes for authentication – both the storytellers and at a different level the collector re-authenticate the tales; in the terms we uncovered in reading Golomb, by becoming 'genuine' the tales become authentic. And for Yeats the genuine 'proves' his loyalty[29] – the editorial ownership of authenticity may connect Yeats to his material but it also arguably anticipates the hierarchising of subaltern authenticities which Griffiths describes. From this point Yeats can retrace with yet greater assurance the nature and production of Irish authenticity:

[In Lady Wilde's *Ancient Legends* the] humour has all given way to pathos and tenderness. We have here the innermost heart of the Celt in the moments he has grown to love through years of persecution, when cushioning himself about with dreams, and hearing fairy-songs in the twilight, he ponders on the soul and on the dead. Here is the Celt. Only it is the Celt dreaming.[30]

As noted earlier, authenticity combines the prioritisation of origins with what Golomb calls the 'pathos of incessant change' – for Yeats, going more closely to the origins of the 'Celt' ('humour has given way') leads to the ultimate, unquestionable authenticity of 'pathos and tenderness', which has been, as Golomb says, 'especially pronounced in extreme situations'.[31] The ultimate collector of authenticated Irishness, in Yeats's 'Introduction', is Douglas Hyde:

He knows the people thoroughly. Others see a phase of Irish life; he understands all its elements. His work is neither humorous nor mournful; it is simply life.[32]

As Adorno suggested, against the 'inauthentic' as broken is the authentic as 'whole' – Yeats's Irish authenticity, by being 'simply life', trails off as authenticity must into a refusal to be defined[33] and 'in definite negation of something merely phenomenal'.[34]

This Irish authenticity is thus complicated and usefully foreshadows the warnings given by Griffiths that authenticity may be continually authorised by the 'coloniser'. It cannot be simply assumed that Yeats is entirely fulfilling the role of coloniser – in fact the authenticity of the text only makes sense if Yeats's position is not taken as colonial but as liminal and constituted by a rhetoric of showing, claiming and confirming, which both vindicates the colonised while implicating and elevating the collector of this authenticity in the vindication.

A New Authenticity

Griffiths' notion that postcolonial authenticity still lies in the hands of the coloniser accords with Yeats's version of the authentic, since Yeats can be understood as coloniser controlling the voice of the colonised. Griffiths places his argument over authenticity in a familiar sphere in postcolonial studies, questioning how and if the 'subaltern speaks'. To believe in an ability to utter authentically may be to fail to see the continuation of power structures existing as after-effects of colonialism.

In the Irish case we need to be aware both of the particular circumstances of colonialism in Ireland (in shorthand, its liminality) and more generally that Griffiths' one-way process of cultural control may be naive or at least lacking when applied to the Irish case. Authenticity, after all, appears to reverse itself during the anti-colonial process, and in the complicated and unstable cultural circumstances of Ireland this is unlikely to be simply an 'appearance'. Given Independence, how will authenticity, which is 'rooted in revolution',[35] move away from its origins?

Yeats's ambiguous control over the authenticity of his material reveals in its triple-level of authentication (tales, storytellers, folktale-collectors) that authenticity thrives on the textuality and substance of its medium – as suggested above it is the 'mass', not the media, which authenticity finds difficult. Textuality seems to provide the material existence which authenticity needs in tandem with its resistance to definition – its mystique is maintained and *evidenced*, while what is actually 'authentic' is filtered through further authenticating processes (folk tales are themselves authenticated democratically by their tellers, then approved and re-authorised by their collectors/editors).

How nineteenth- and early twentieth-century Irish modes of authenticity (of which there are many more than the example from Yeats suggests – Corkery might be a useful contrast) are played out in contemporary circumstances would be an obvious area of research in further examining authenticity in Irish culture. Anecdotally, one might suggest that 'authenticity' has increased in its value as a marker of what is Irish as Ireland has (partially) moved out of its anti-colonial mode. Authenticity's ability to coexist with the market has not only enabled it to survive after decolonisation but has allowed it to become, in some circumstances, as Griffiths says, a 'mythologised and fetished sign'.[36] What Griffiths calls 'an overdetermined narra-tive of authenticity and indigeneity'[37] characterises rebirths of the old authenticities, whether these are used to sell or purchase the 'authentic' once-colonised.

In the Irish context the tourist industry is an obvious site for the peddling of the authentic in an explicit and populist way. Luke Gibbons quotes Robert Ballagh on Bord Fáilte: 'you have Bord Fáilte eulogizing roads where you won't see a car from one day to the other: it's almost as if they're advertising a country nobody lives in'.[38] As Gibbons points out, the Bord Fáilte advertising which he discusses seems initially at odds with the Industrial Development Authority's (IDA) selling of Ireland economically as a marketplace and site for expansion; yet almost immediately the imagery and language of tourism becomes part of the IDA's marketing strategy: 'The factories and the bustling towns and cities exist in harmony with the Ireland the tourists flock to see, a land of unsurpassed natural beauty'.[39] Gibbons call this phenomenon the 'appeal of remote antiquity to today's filofax generation',[40] and it is an important feature of the ways in which older Irish authenticities have been retained in Irish contemporaneity. However, given that modernisation constitutes a necessary synchronicity in the path of 'Ireland' as it waits for its future self, the phenomenon of consumers now wanting Ireland then is less than peculiar. Brian P. Kennedy, discussing early visual images of the Irish Free State, strikes a note similar to Gibbons' when he writes about a tourist poster which promises, as Kennedy says, 'the clean, untramelled, quaint image of a country untouched by urban difficulties'.[41] The first line of the poster reads:

The ancient values still remain unchanged in Ireland: yet Catering and Transport, judged by modern standards, maintain a high level of comfort and efficiency.[42]

The poster's use of the word 'yet' looks initially like an admission of contradiction – but it might as easily demonstrate that what the poster calls 'paradise' (that is, 'Ireland') and the 'ancient values' which justify it are comfortably untouched and 'unchanged' by the modern.

Heritage Island[43] sell Ireland on the currency of its authenticity, marketing an organic vision of an Ireland layered with visible, visitable history. What follows comes under the heading of 'Irish Heritage Retold' in their marketing brochure:

The story of Ireland's heritage is a new reason for visiting Ireland. It is told in a modern but authentic style and mirrors European culture preserved in an island which makes it possible to visit centres from neolithic to 19th Century, even on a short visit.

Heritage Island properties can be found throughout Ireland and range from restored castles and historic houses to state-of-the-art story telling of the legends and history of Ireland.

All interpretation has been professionally researched and where there has been reproduction the style is authentic.[44]

Authenticity here relies on preservation; what is to be visited is not modern, new Ireland but authentic Ireland made modern and new. Thus Ireland is now 'modern *but* authentic' in *style*; *storytelling* is state-of-the-art, but uses legends and history. It is the media (style and story) which are able to embody this apparent dichotomy of old and new and in the process preserve the authentic.

Golomb, as we have already seen, pits authenticity against 'mass media', and I have been stressing that the simple fact of changing media is not necessarily a threat to the authentic. Here the attempt to cope with the changed social/political context for Irish authenticity is embodied in the notion that 'modern but authentic' Ireland's style

'mirrors European culture preserved in an island'. There is a nod here
to Irish post-nationalism and a valorising of the European context,
and yet 'mirrors' retains a distance from the possible inauthenticities
of what is outside Ireland undermining the indigenous authenticity
of the 'national culture' (with which authenticity so closely equates
itself). The word 'preserved' is crucial, implying not only that authentic Irishness is newly (and economically) available in Ireland, but
that this haven of authenticity includes (but is not swamped by) an
almost lost authentic European antiquity. Authenticity's claims may
always tend to such extravagance.

Heritage Island is a reworking of the Yeatsian authenticities of *Folk
and Fairy Tales of the Irish Peasantry*, showing how authenticities
are self-preserving through their willingness to reproduce themselves
in new media and new discourses. The structures of authentication
here are also those expressed by Yeats. Just as Yeats sees authenticity
at a base level in the Irishness of tales themselves, at another level in
the standardisation by tellers and at a final level by their collectors/
editors, so Heritage Island reassures its customers of Irish heritage's
authenticity through the same three levels. Ireland's history/legends
are the authentic material, but their (re)telling is further proof of
their authenticity since they are told in 'modern but authentic style'
('state-of-the-art'). And as a final affirmation that no inauthenticity
has corrupted the 'stuff' of the authentic, the authoritative validator
steps in, filling Yeats's role as collector/editor: 'All interpretation has
been professionally researched'.

There is certainly a tendency here to 'an overdetermined narrative
of authenticity and indigeneity';[45] Irish authenticity, in Yeats and
Heritage Island, displays the same characteristics of definition –
Heritage Island is arguably more aware of itself as a rewriting rather
than a creation, but both have a sense of the origins stretching back
into faded time. Just as Golomb sees authenticity as at its best a
'search', and Adorno condemns authenticity as a 'jargon', we can
now begin to see that Irish authenticity, through its very structures,
is a series of claims to authenticity which persist both despite changing cultural circumstances and media and in full knowledge of what
those circumstances and media are.

AN IRONIC AUTHENTICITY

If authenticity in Irish culture followed only the trajectory mapped
out above then its ability to order Irish cultural experience would be

almost unchallengeable. From the examples I have used it might be possible to see not only the authenticity of the folkish, rural and historical/legendary as nearly monolithically dominant, but to note that its repeated forms of self-sustenance and validation give it a layered authenticity which reinforces its desire for dominance. Is it then possible for this standardised authenticity to be challenged? And if it is challenged, how far is the notion of authenticity itself (as well as what is considered authentic) undermined?

Golomb's crusading restatement of the necessity for a search for authenticity is, as has already been noted, set against the postmodern, mass media and the 'attempt to dissolve the subjective pathos of authenticity'.[46] The rigour of Golomb's attack on these aspects of the postmodern may signal the way into reading against authenticity, or at least without the tyranny of authenticity as a central defining feature of cultural integrity. In the Irish case this would mean looking to new forms of culture as a means to disrupting the influence of old authenticities and their new forms – as Heritage Island shows, an apparently postmodern form (advertising tourism) does not guarantee such disruption.

To move towards a possible alternative formation of the authentic in Irish culture I want to discuss a television advertisement for Smithwick's beer, appropriately entitled 'Ireland' by its makers.[47] 'Ireland' takes as its theme the authenticity of advertising, the authenticity of Ireland and the authenticity of advertising Irish beer. The 20-second advertisement ironically constructs and deconstructs the Irish authenticity examined so far, and can be read as a possible attempt to posit a revised, ironic authenticity as a replacement.

Because of its overt iconophilia, 'Ireland' works by deploying the 'crise pléthorique' discussed in Chapter 1; it is almost stereotypically a postmodern montage, and in this bears a resemblance to Seán Hillen's work. 'Ireland' begins with the words 'GET' and then 'INTO' in white on red, with a Northern American voice-over saying: 'Get into . . . Ireland'. The complete screen then splits into a screen divided horizontally and vertically to make four squares, each of which has changing images and film clips throughout. The first four identifiable images are (clockwise from top left): a moving aerial shot of a rural landscape; a stained glass pattern with a shamrock; a Celtic cross (towards which the camera zooms); and a neon sign for 'Home Cookin''.

Here already we can begin to establish the patterning of authenticity in 'Ireland'. The four-part structure is undoubtedly a jokey reflection of the four provinces of Ireland – or the four green fields, given the top left shot. Rurality and standard cultural imagery (shamrock, Celtic cross) allow the viewer to 'get into Ireland' in an unchallenging, familiar way. The product here is on the verge of being made authentic because of its Irishness. And yet the bottom left of the four hints at what is to come. Neon and 'Home Cookin'' suggest an alternative cultural background to an authentic Irishness. This is quickly reinforced by the next series of images (again top left clockwise): Ronald and Nancy Reagan drinking Smithwick's on a trip to Ireland (they actually drank Guinness – the Smithwick's is self-consciously, badly airbrushed in), three pints of Smithwick's, a fiddler (a shot which fades into another of an Irish dancer) and Smithwick's advertising on a neon sign in Belfast. The neon and the lost 'g' in cooking ironise 'home', which has become Americanised (signified also by Reagan).

The globalisation and Americanisation of the authenticity of Irishness is overemphasised in the next series: a boot kicking a ball; 'I ⚽ [football, i.e. love] N.Y.': John F. Kennedy (who can be heard to say the word 'haemorrhage' – a reference to Irish emigration to the United States); the Statue of Liberty overwritten by the word 'Donnelly' (it would be too much to hope that Ignatius Donnelly was in mind here). Having made this point about Irishness in a global context, both as an exporter of Irishness to the States and as a culture existing in a global market, 'Ireland' reverts to an older Irishness in order to carry out another deconstruction. So a mountain/shepherd/sheep, waves, a dancer and a woman carrying pints of beer become a map of Ireland with 293,140 unemployed (with paper money slipping off the map), a picture of a banana with the word REPUBLIC underneath, a diver, and a condom advertisement. Here old Irish authenticities are truly challenged – a (post)modern and postcolonial, urban Ireland presents new realities of unemployment, sexual liberality and criticism of established state nationalism.

The advertisement, to which I have not done full justice here, ends with its lower two squares seeming to take on the possibility of reconciliation between north and south; a white dove flies across a plaque with a red hand (Ulster) and over a ceramic tile with a harp engraved on it (signifying Ireland in more nationalistic sense, as well as Guinness, Smithwick's corporate owners). If this appears to replace an old authenticity with a new liberal politics, such a notion is undercut by a simultaneous but opposite movement in the top two squares. While the peace and reconciliation theme is played out from right to left in the lower squares, the top squares have, on the left, a shot of graffiti ('Who stole my bike?') and on the right an image of a whitewashed (and rural) housefront across which (left to right) rides an old man in a long coat on a bicycle. The humour here is at the expense of the older political discourse of national politics (and the problem of Northern Ireland), raising again the prospect of an alternative focus, established through ironic versions of the past.

'Ireland' suggests that the older authenticities are simultaneously contradicted and yet established by Ireland's cultural representation in a context wider than the Irish. The United States is viewed both as a consumer and producer of Irishness, and its effects on the mainte-nance of Irishness are charted through the tongue-in-cheekness of the double representation of the American Presidential desire to affix an Irishness to the Presidency. Almost all the commentary to the adver-tisement is spoken in snippets of North American voices: 'It's great to be back here in mythical, mystical Ireland'; 'the most wonderful place in the world; home'. And yet 'home' has already been shown to be Americanised in the sign 'Home Cookin''; so 'Ireland' sees Ireland's attempts at established authenticated culture as pitifully denying the cultural matrix which preserves old Irish authenticities.

Does 'Ireland' then represent a form of culture which is anti-authen-tic, or is it more interested in the establishment of an alternative authenticity? Certainly the movement from the old rural authenticity of the shepherd, or the pub scene with the woman carrying pints of beer, to, respectively, the map with unemployment figures and a con-dom advertisement would suggest that 'Ireland' is altering the rural, folkish, tourist authenticities in favour of urban, socialised, radicalised versions of Ireland (which are nevertheless still reliant on the notion that they are more authentic than previous versions of Ireland). This challenging of old authenticities and their newer resurrections (in tourism, in exile stereotypes of Irishness) is noteworthy in itself. But 'Ireland' does not rest there; its irony is finally turned on itself. The only (Northern) Irish voice used in the commentary says: 'Are ye going for a pint?' A totally unrevealing comment? A stereotype? As another (North American) voice says: 'You just can't handle the truth' – in this Ireland the truth is impossible to pin down; competing claims to authenticity (which are allowed to compete in 'Ireland') have rendered their truths and their authentic origins obscure and unstable. 'Ireland' ends with the wonderfully ironic and destabilis-ing comment (again in North American voice): '. . . maybe that's just Blarney'. Finally the whole process of authentication, claims to authenticity and the pathos of those claims is questioned and maybe dismissed in a double-edged use of a stereotype ('Blarney') culled from the excesses of populist versions of restored Irish authenticity. 'Ireland' almost undoes its own undoing of the authentic through a near sliding back into 'the jargon of authenticity', and yet in doing so it both reveals the power and dissects the pathos of established Irish authenticity.

According to Baudrillard, '[when] the real is no longer what is used to be . . . [there] is a proliferation of myths of origin and signs of reality; of second-hand truth, objectivity and authenticity'.[48] 'Ireland', in its joyous uncovering of myths of origins *as myths*, and signs of reality *as signs*, is able to question the objectivity and authenticity of old and renewed claims in Irish culture – its processes uncover both the mechanics of authenticity and the cultural desire for authenticity. 'Ireland' toys with an alternative authenticity, but finally cannot rest on anything but its ironic 'maybe that's just Blarney'.

The persistence of authenticity in Irish culture is best seen, then, as a series of claims, a desire for validation. There can be no doubt that this persistence arises from the cultural crises of colonialism and its de-authenticating of the colonised. Against this Irish authenticities can be read as movements against colonialism, (re-)establishing authenticity. And yet this anti-colonial authenticity is not purely formed; the Yeats example used above suggests that any Irish authenticity will be complex, layered and affected by the liminal space of colonialism in Ireland, never securely other than the colonised itself. While such old authenticities can be re-established after colonialism, the paradox of their reconstitution as authentic is central to the fate of the notion of authenticity in Irish culture. 'Ireland' may tend towards an authenticity which is urban and contemporary but its initial destabilisation of an old authenticity means that it cannot trust claims to the authentic again. And still 'Ireland' is not an entire rejection of authenticity but an ironic acknowledgement of its persistence in Irish culture.

Reading Irish culture in terms of authenticity can allow cultural criticism to trace changes and consistencies in cultural production and reception arising out of the power structures of colonialism. Authenticity as a focus potentially shifts Irish cultural criticism away from the often reified pre-existing terms of debates in literary studies, and allows cultural theory to enter Irish cultural criticism in a way which can, when necessary, deny the sacred status of established politicised readings of Irish culture, which can question the production processes of material culture in relation to history, and which can send us back through history via the ironies of origin and originality.

Notes

1. David Lloyd, *Anomalous States: Irish Writing and the Post-Colonial Moment* (Dublin: Lilliput, 1993), p. 112.
2. Heritage Island marketing brochure, c. 1994.
3. 'The shawl makes a comeback', *The Irish Times*, 27 December 1999, p. 2.
4. 'The shawl makes a comeback', p. 2.
5. 'The shawl makes a comeback', p. 2.
6. Jacob Golomb, *In Search of Authenticity* (London: Routledge, 1995), p. 12.
7. Theodor Adorno, *The Jargon of Authenticity* (London: Routledge, 1986 [1964]).
8. Golomb, *In Search of Authenticity*, p. 7.
9. Golomb, *In Search of Authenticity*, p. 205.
10. Golomb, *In Search of Authenticity*, p. 205.
11. Golomb, *In Search of Authenticity*, p. 117.
12. Benedict Anderson, *Imagined Communities: Reflections on the Origin and Spread of Nationalism*, revised edition (London: Verso, 1991), p. 25.
13. Golomb, *In Search of Authenticity*, p. 9.
14. Golomb, *In Search of Authenticity*, p. 39.
15. Golomb, *In Search of Authenticity*, p. 54.
16. Anderson, *Imagined Communities*, p. 26.
17. Golomb, *In Search of Authenticity*, p. 79.
18. Golomb, *In Search of Authenticity*, pp. 3 and 12.
19. Golomb, *In Search of Authenticity*, p. 204.
20. Adorno, *The Jargon of Authenticity*, p. 5.
21. Adorno, *The Jargon of Authenticity*, pp. 7–8.
22. Adorno, *The Jargon of Authenticity*, p. 9.
23. Jean Baudrillard, *Simulations*, trans. Paul Foss, Paul Patton and Philip Beitchman (New York: Semiotext(e), 1983), pp. 12–13.
24. Gareth Griffiths, 'The Myth of Authenticity: Representation, Discourse and Practice', in Chris Tiffin and Alan Lawson (eds), *De-scribing Empire: Post-Colonialism and Textuality* (London: Routledge, 1994), p. 70.
25. Gareth Griffiths, 'The Myth of Authenticity', p. 71.
26. Frantz Fanon, *The Wretched of the Earth* (Harmondsworth: Penguin, 1990 [1961]), p. 40.
27. W. B. Yeats, *Fairy and Folk Tales of the Irish Peasantry* in *Fairy and Folk Tales of Ireland* (London: Picador, 1973), p. 4.
28. Golomb, *In Search of Authenticity*, p. 117.
29. Golomb, *In Search of Authenticity*, p. 117.
30. Yeats, *Fairy and Folk Tales of the Irish Peasantry*, p. 7.
31. Golomb, *In Search of Authenticity*, p. 3.
32. Yeats, *Fairy and Folk Tales of the Irish Peasantry*, p. 7.
33. Golomb, *In Search of Authenticity*, p. 7.
34. Adorno, *The Jargon of Authenticity*, p. 8.
35. Golomb, *In Search of Authenticity*, p. 12.
36. Griffiths, 'The Myth of Authenticity', p. 71.
37. Griffiths, 'The Myth of Authenticity', p. 84.
38. Luke Gibbons, 'Coming Out of Hibernation?: The Myth of Modernity in Irish Culture', in Richard Kearney (ed.), *Across the Fontiers: Ireland in the 1990s* (Dublin: Wolfhound, 1988), p. 210.

39. Quoted in Gibbons, 'Coming Out of Hibernation?', p. 211.
40. Gibbons, 'Coming Out of Hibernation?', p. 213.
41. Brian P. Kennedy, 'The Irish Free State 1922–49: A Visual Perspective', in Raymond Gillespie and Brian P. Kennedy (eds), *Ireland: Art into History* (Dublin: Town House, 1994), p. 140.
42. Poster reproduced in Kennedy, 'The Irish Free State 1922–49', p. 139.
43. Heritage Island, established in 1992, is a private company offering tourist marketing services 'to a select number of the best Heritage Centres in [Ireland]': Cartan Finegan, 'Marketing Ireland's Heritage to the International Market', paper given at Tourism Development Conference, Killarney, 1996. I am grateful to Cartan Finegan, Managing Director of Heritage Island, for supplying me with a copy of this paper.
44. Heritage Island marketing brochure, c. 1994.
45. Griffiths, 'The Myth of Authenticity', p. 84.
46. Golomb, *In Search of Authenticity*, p. 204.
47. 'Ireland' was made and broadcast in 1994 and shown on network television and in cinemas on both sides of the border. My thanks to McConnell's Advertising Services Limited and Guinness Ireland for supplying me with material relating to Smithwick's advertising.
48. Baudrillard, *Simulations*, p. 12.

Punch Drunk: Irish Ephemera

Beginning his essay 'Race Against Time: Racial Discourse and Irish History', Luke Gibbons draws attention to a children's game 'circulated in the "Big Houses" of the Irish Ascendancy'.[1] This purported by its title to give the 'British Empire at a Glance', and as Gibbons notes, it understood the empire in terms of 'white' or 'native' populations. Gibbons points to the fact that:

When it came to Ireland, the wheel ground to a halt for here was one colony whose subject population was both 'native' and 'white' at the same time. This was one corner of the Empire, apparently, that could not be taken in at a glance.[2]

Against this seemingly paradigmatically colonial instance of the representation of Ireland in British, metropolitan terms, I want to set another children's game, this one to be found in the Museum of Childhood, Bethnal Green, London. At Bethnal Green there is a jigsaw puzzle, called 'Europe Delineated', which was first manufactured around 1830; it has a map of Europe at its centre with vignettes of European countries around the outside. Each country is represented through some form of indigenous transport and/or work, and is explained by an accompanying text. For Ireland there is a horse and cart with the following text (Figure 4):

Ireland is a small island about one third the size of Great Britain. The peasantry are very poor and live in small cabins or huts along with their pigs or whatever animals they keep. We cannot therefore wonder at the homeliness of the conveyance here represented.[3]

Set against each other, these two items of what can only imprecisely be called popular culture make a glaringly obvious (and potentially

IRELAND

ned to Europe, and that the names of all the countries they repres

s those *Ireland is an Island about one third the size of Great*   *The Wel*
the most *Britain. The peasantry are very poor, and live in small*   *tains, t*
well as *cabins or huts along with their pigs or whatever animals*   *and ar*
for this *they keep; we cannot therefore wonder at the homeliness*   *ral pa*
of the conveyance here represented.

FIGURE 4 Detail from 'Europe Delineated', child's jigsaw puzzle, *c.* 1830, Museum of Childhood, Bethnal Green. © The Board of Trustees of The Victoria and Albert Museum.

revisionist) point – that Ireland can be understood as European as well as colonial. That, however, would be a slightly false opposition; one that overestimates the catch-all validation of being European, underplays the hierarchies within the European itself, and forgets the extent to which 'Europe' is made by its absent Others.[4] More usefully, these two texts reveal that there coexist conflicting possibilities in the representation of Ireland in popular culture during the period of British rule in Ireland (and after). The coexistence of these texts seems to suggest that, in one sense, Ireland *can* be 'taken in at a glance' – in 'Europe Delineated' Ireland *is* glanced at; it is understood, catalogued and shuffled off into the structures of what Edward Said calls the 'family of ideas',[5] offering itself as a homology of adult knowledge which is to be created during childhood play: 'Toys here reveal the list of all the things the adult does not find unusual'.[6] To read these children's games as texts which are partially contradictory is not to diminish their ideological significance, nor is it to suggest that their establishment of patterns of cultural knowledge are annulled through their comparison – rather it is to stress alongside this potential existence as cultural evidence their fleeting nature, their status as ephemera, their representational instabilities. They are, quite literally, both ideological and playful. This chapter suggests that it is the generic *and* cultural status of popular texts which gives them a potential as a resource in cultural history and in cultural theory, and, most crucially, in the ability of Irish cultural criticism to trace possible 'Irelands' which are normally outside its view.

The standard work on the representation of Ireland and Irishness in what is recognisably popular culture is L. P. Curtis's *Apes and Angels*,[7] while the most significant expression of dissent from Curtis, in as much as it does dissent, is Roy Foster's essay 'Paddy and Mr Punch'.[8] Curtis's work has become influential largely because it offers a material cultural history as 'evidence' to a cultural critique which is dependent on a neat and precise argument for Irishness as an 'other' to Englishness;[9] as a result, Curtis's implicit and methodological insistence on *Punch* as the primary site in which popular culture in Britain constructed its 'Other' Ireland has gained a hegemonic status which would be extraordinary in any other area of academic research.[10] When Foster challenges Curtis the position of *Punch* as paradigmatic looking-glass for Victorian visualisations of Ireland is reaffirmed. Foster's reply to Curtis relies on arguments about the veracity and accuracy of stereotypes (as if a stereotype was neutralised by being 'true'). This method disables Foster's ability to discuss the politics of representation in any theoretical way, while his attention to genre goes only so far as to imply that stereotypes are typical of *Punch* and that Ireland was not therefore singled out for special treatment. Beyond that, Foster argues for a recognition of the variety in *Punch*'s representation of the Irish; this is useful and necessary, but it maintains the monopoly of *Punch* as the source (and type of source) to be used in examining British attitudes to Ireland. And of course this in itself negates any notion that popular cultural forms may be different from high cultural forms, or from 'official' political discourse, so that the 'popular' is a mode which is readily interpretable by History. For these reasons I would argue that we need to begin to look again at popular culture as a source for the representation of Ireland in and beyond the colonial metropolis, and that, in tandem with this material methodological change, there is a need for a theoretical shift away from the binaries of the 'Other' which this material base has supported, towards categories which attempt to give due credence to the ephemeral as cultural form.

Placing 'popular' cultural texts in the theoretical framework of postcolonial criticism is a largely untested discursive intersection.[11] Hybridity as a conceptual framework for understanding colonial and postcolonial culture has the advantage of acknowledging culture, when caught between centripetally organised ideological entities, as an often unstable state of affairs in which categories are maintained as ghosts of their original presences. Homi Bhabha usefully argues that colonial domination is reliant on a denial of 'its dislocatory presence in order to preserve the authority of its identity'.[12] Bhabha's initial illustration in his essay is a translated Bible, an 'authoritative' cultural text propelled into the domain of the 'low' and colonised, and this can enable the levering of a potential space in which the cultural and colonial statuses which seek to construct the text allow cross-hatched reading trajectories. The 'fall' from high to 'low' may be as much a process or series of stages as it is a choice between two levels – and determining the relation of this process to the dynamics of colonial interaction thus becomes more fluid and potentially indefinite. Following Bhabha, it can certainly be argued that the 'colonial' text's pressure to 'authorise' itself, to deny its own dislocation, is eased when that text is placed within what is already a discourse of authority (and in this sense Bhabha sees this struggle to deny dislocation as the weakness and force of colonial texts). Put simply for the case of Irish culture, it may be that it is now only partially possibly to read hybridity in Joyce or Yeats since the discourses in which these texts exist (that of Joyce scholarship, for example, or of Irish literature) are already established within what Bhabha calls 'teleological narratives of historical and political evolutionism'[13] (for example, the history of literature, or modernism, or indeed cultural or literary nationalism).[14]

To see textuality at play in marginality in the Irish case we might be able to turn to the sorts of texts which are discussed below, texts which are themselves marginal, and whose cultural status is indeterminate. The remainder of this chapter attempts to follow through some of the potentialities and difficulties of reading these marginalised, 'producerly' texts,[15] characterised by popular production, vulnerability, self-exposure and by having 'meanings [which] exceed [their] own power to discipline them'.[16] Brian Maidment's discussion of prints in the Victorian period makes these textual/theoretical possibilities more concrete. Maidment suggests that the 'unselfconscious and unambitious' nature of such texts allows them to contain a 'spontaneous response to an ephemeral social event or commercial opportunity',[17] an observation which importantly highlights the awkward negotiation involved in reading such texts in which the differentials of the ideologically reflective work against a generic and structural (lack of) depth, both of which in turn can only have a degree of dependence on audience ('commercial opportunity').

With these contingencies in mind, I will initially be moving backwards chronologically in reading these texts – the reasons for doing so should become clearer as the chapter progresses. However, it is worth stating at this point that I want to use these examples to look at the possibilities of complicating the understanding of the representation of Ireland in British popular culture which is currently available in Irish studies. This backwards look also allows me to end before *Punch* begins in an attempt to dislodge the dominance of the magazine from the status Curtis and others have given it. After this the chapter moves to a discussion on that most ephemeral of all cultural forms, kitsch.

The embodiment of Fiske's 'producerly' notion of 'popular' textuality, and its possibilities in an Irish context, are at their most 'indisciplined' in a 'text' which was a 'gift' series of collectors' items given away with Kensitas cigarettes (presumably some time in the 1920s or 1930s[18]). The item is a small silk banner and comes from a series called 'Flags of the Empire' (which also included flags from both white and non-white parts of the Empire). It has the 'new' Irish tricolour, below which are the words 'British Empire' and then 'Irish Free State'; and in the smallest of print above the flag 'Kensitas Cigarettes'. Before beginning to struggle with what might be said about this item, it needs to be placed in its widest possible context. The other similar types of collector's items and series issued with tobacco products at this time were often, as far as it is possible, ideologically innocuous, or at least less obviously political (from wildlife and flora to footballers and cricketers). This is not to downplay the cultural significance of collecting images of footballers; rather it should emphasise the 'ordinariness' of this type of cultural text, while comprehending the 'shapes', 'purposes' and 'meanings'[19] which this ordinariness draws into the 'passionate game' of collecting.[20]

The Kensitas flag embodies one delicious irony, of course: the coexistence of the word 'Free' with the word 'Empire'. Its ordinariness sits blandly beside its politicality as if both speak with equal weight. As a text it is placed at that anomalous, paradoxical, pre-Constitutional period of Irish history. Certainly that paradox is made less evenly balanced by the fact that the typeface of 'BRITISH EMPIRE' is larger than that of 'IRISH FREE STATE'; however, the contradiction and ultimately the bizarre hybrid nature of this text is clinched by the flag itself – an expression of independence and nationality which is,

through the (proposed) act of collecting the entire set of 'Flags of
the Empire', dragged unhappily and illogically into the awkward
constitution of the empire. Faced with the 'Plates of the *Encyclopedia*',
Roland Barthes notes appositely that we are lured into its structuring
of knowledge in the following way: 'the fracture of the world is
impossible; a glance suffices . . . for the world to be eternally complete',
and thus the act of collecting resolves the political contradiction by
prioritising the completeness of the collection over the individuality
of the object.[21] What we are left with in reading the Kensitas flag is
an ideological connotation that is in the process of erasure; inherent
in the compulsiveness of the collector is a blindness to the political
reality which the collected item loudly proclaims. The world in the
text (here in its individual and serial form) in this case stands at
the edge of being an 'act' (collecting for its own sake) rather than a
signification (Ireland in the Empire) – such balances of genre, audience,
consumption and ideology are crucial to readings of these texts
since the insistences they bring introduce a different theoretical and
contextual domain to that used to read standard Irish 'cultural' texts.

It would be a false methodological and theoretical construction to
use the backwards historical movement in this chapter as an attempt
at a history of images of Ireland in British popular culture. The cumu-
lative argument here is in fact tangential to and partly in conflict
with the notion of a cultural history in the way that Curtis and Foster
allow it. While the Kensitas flag shows an incongruity embodied in
one text to the extent that we are left resisting the text's tendency to
closure if not contradiction, my next examples can be used to open a
similar textual space in a different genre and context. These are two
late Victorian song sheets, both concerning Charles Stewart Parnell
and both produced at around the same time (after Parnell was cited
as co-respondent in O'Shea's divorce case in 1890, an event which
they both refer to). The songs and the texts they form (including the
covers) were part of a long series produced by Francis, Day & Hunter
(again it is important to stress that the rest of the series is by no
means solely about Ireland, nor even solely about politics). The first
song, 'Now What will Become of Poor Old Ireland? or, Charlie Parlie'
is a satire on Parnell, attacking him for his adultery (the cover depicts
Parnell infamously escaping from O'Shea down a fire-escape – Figure
5), for his law-breaking and (almost) accusing him of money laun-
dering and neglecting his mother. The song itself, playing on Parnell's
difficulty, contains the marvellously devastating lines:

> Won't the lawyers giggle and grin when they take up his pelf;
> He wants Home Rule for Ireland, but he can't Home Rule himself.

FIGURE 5 Cover of 'Now What Will Become of Poor Old Ireland?', by
Charles Bignell (London: Francis, Day & Hunter, n.d.).

There are no surprises here – this is satire of the *Punch*-type, with an
added sense of ribaldry and sexual innuendo, reflections, no doubt,

of its music hall context. But the second song (Figure 6), 'O'Shea's My Sweetheart I'm Her Beau', contains an entirely different version of Parnell in which he is a romantic hero and a tragic lover, exemplified in the lines:

> Perhaps we'll marry, never to part,
> Little Kitty O'Shea's
> The girl that broke my heart

These are uttered entirely without irony, without satire and with immense affection. How then can these conflicting views of Parnell be held simultaneously in one cultural form, at one brief historical moment, produced by one music publisher? One obvious way to understand this would be to revert to the trope of what is here quite literally stage-Irishness; the sentimentality attached to Parnell could be envisaged as the light side of the Othering of Ireland, part of the marrying of the exotic and threatening which characterises Orientalist discourses. If this is so, then the switch from one side to another, from exotic to dark, is shockingly immediate and above all arbitrary. This arbitrariness can only disturb to some extent the apparently definitive nature of the binaries of the Other and this may tell us something significant about popular culture – that in a very particular way it is fickle, its representational categories having peculiarly porous, reversible, even shifting boundaries. This is certainly convincing, but there is another factor here. The audience that listens to these songs is of course largely working-class, Victorian and English – but a significant part of that audience could, under certain circumstances, be of Irish origin. How far this affects this cultural text is impossible to tell quantitatively without extensive research on the ethnic make up of Victorian music hall audiences.[22] But an important point is nevertheless enforceable – these cultural texts are moving in ways we are only partially able to grasp (being both methodological and conceptually 'new'), and the glimpses that we see of their resonances implies that they exist in an order of discourse which at the very least cross-cuts that which we usually assume for 'Ireland' as it is figured in 'British' culture (additionally questioning Irish criticism's understanding of how 'British' culture is made).

To reach concrete conclusions on this topic would in a sense be self-defeating since the 'field' of study outlined here is essentially unpredictable and unmapped. It seems appropriate then to conclude this backward progression with an image which is typically astonishing,

in a genre about which too little is known and the 'meanings' of
which could be endlessly contended.

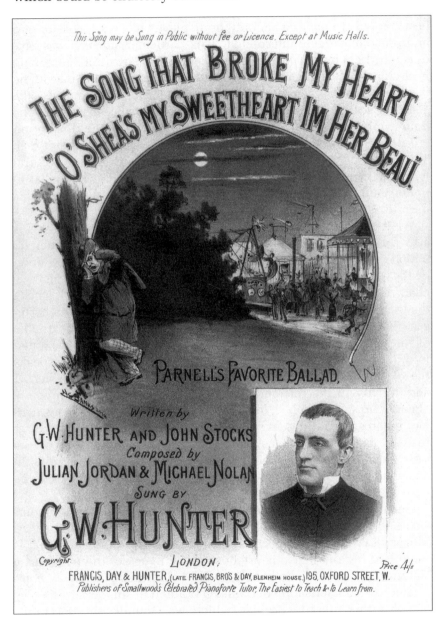

FIGURE 6   Cover of 'The Song That Broke My Heart: "O'Shea's My
Sweetheart I'm Her Beau"', by G. W. Hunter and John Stocks, music by
Julian Jordan and Michael Nolan (London: Francis, Day & Hunter, n.d.).

This final nineteenth-century item is principally a satiric version of the almanac, a cultural form which gained in popularity over the early nineteenth century (Figure 7). It is likely that this would have been passed around as a handbill or displayed in a workplace or pub and thus collectively interpreted. This particular almanac was produced in 1838 by J. L. Marks – at its centre is a harlequin figure, who is obviously Irish, given the text above him[23] and his potato head; he is surrounded by gestures towards typical features of the almanac – the changing seasons, meteorological 'information', predictive powers. The figures circulating the zodiacal dial at the bottom of the illustration are also typical of the form (and are excellent examples of their type). To this extent this almanac contains standard elements of a cultural form we know too little about, yet as I argue below it is crucial to understand that this text actually constitutes an attack on the almanac form itself.

What is of further interest, of course, is the extent to which this is also a representation of Irishness, and additionally, the extent to which this Irishness is of its time or is anticipated or insisted upon by the genre. From our knowledge of later *Punch* images we can trace characteristics of Irishness which became (or already were) 'stock': the Irish bull, for example, contained in the text at the top which suggests beginning at the 59th edition of the almanac to save the trouble of the printer; the meteorological symbolism, which is transmuted into the 'blowing hot & cold' of the pipe smoke and which bespeaks the supposed intemperance of the Irish (this is of course transferred additionally in the references to alcohol[24]). In parallel to this, the almanac form arguably allows for both Catholicism (perceived as tending to superstition) and 'stupidity' to be woven into this text, so that while these work as essential structural principles of the satirised almanac (the religious ordering of the year and the belief in almanacs as predictive) they are also able to function as tropes of the Irish stereotype alluded to.

One element which is central to the illustration and to any understanding of it is the central harlequin figure with the potato head (A. Murphy). From the perspective of representations of Ireland what is important here is that this establishes the image of the potato as a signifier of 'Ireland' both before the Famine and before *Punch*'s infamous characterisation of Daniel O'Connell in similar terms.[25] The fact that this precedes *Punch* (which was founded in 1841) puts the structures of knowledge we have on this area of visual/popular culture further into question. This image represents some sort of ideological battle in which Irishness is implicated but is not necessarily

FIGURE 7 'The Modern Phenomenon of a Murphy, or the Gullcatcher of 1838' (Long Lane, Smithfield, London: J. L. Marks, n.d.).

central. The 'Gullcatcher' (Murphy) is predominantly 'catching' those who 'live by' the almanac. The anti-rationalism of almanac forms of knowledge is then arguably further 'discredited' by the conjunction of Irishness (stupidity, drunkenness, superstition) and the form. Yet interestingly this is a debate the satire of which tends to suggest an uncertainty about the dominance of the almanac itself. It is surely a useful and potentially extraordinary spectacle to see Irishness involved in this way in a cultural friction in which a 'low' cultural form may be undermined and mimicked from 'above', and which leaves the status of that 'low' form unresolved. 'Ireland' signifies tangentially here, entangled in an ideological, class war over the dominance of rationality and the degradation of popular superstition in Britain.

Finally we might speculate on the detail of this almanac, always being thrown by its inability or unwillingness to prioritise and order what it contains. How, for example, are we to understand the figures on the right-hand side labelled 'Northern-lights'? The temptation is here surely to look at the geography of the landscape in the print, the exclusionism of the text ('we Green-landers are too Far North'), the play on the North itself, the border of ice between the 'Green-landers' and the other figures, and to see pre-echoes of Partition (thus separating off Protestantism from the 'Catholicism' of the main section of the illustration?). And yet could we ever substantiate such a reading?

The problem here is not simply retrospective projection of our own ideological obsessions. We are faced with this image as an 'object' in the sense in which Barthes understands the term, something which is 'at once a perfection and an absence of origin'.[26] In many ways this is the case for all of the images discussed above. These texts are on the verge of a new archaeology of knowledge about which we know little. As Foucault suggests under different circumstances, we are left with the 'never completed, never wholly achieved uncovering of the archive [which] forms the general horizon to which the description of discursive formation . . . belongs';[27] this is an archive which can only complicate and expand our notions of the meeting of cultural monoliths in Irish colonised history. How these popular cultural representations coincide with or have any knowledge of other forms of political and cultural discourse remains equally unknown. Summarising the conditions for the reception and the reading of prints, Brian Maidment says:

In seeking to represent the immediate, the topical, and the ephemeral within their own cultures, these images instead describe for us the complex and not entirely conscious exchange of cultural values which is characteristic of discourse. Such discourses are dependent on representational codes which we can never decipher with absolute confidence.[28]

We are still, arguably, a long way from understanding the 'representational codes', patterns and structures of ideology expressed about Ireland in texts such as these – and as a result the predominantly high literary version of 'theory' we use in the Irish context is still skewed by readings of Ireland as a *literary* analogue to the Empire elsewhere, just as the version of 'culture' we assume for Britain and Ireland across cultural history is hierarchised and static. Reading these texts suggests that the negotiation between particularity and typicality, discourse and genre, text and ideology needs to be carried over into a critique of 'Ireland' as generically and marginally unsettled, both in its cultural status and in *all* its cultural textuality.

'THE FIRST UNIVERSAL CULTURE': IRISH KITSCH[29]

BROADBENT: But he spoke – he behaved just like an Irishman.
DOYLE: Like an Irishman!! Man alive, dont you know that all this top-o-the-morning and broth-of-a-boy and more-power-to-your-elbow business is got up in England to fool you, like the Albert Hall concerts of Irish music?[30]

Larry Doyle's warning to Tom Broadbent about the fakery of circulating versions of Irishness plays on anatomies of Irish authenticity (discussed in the previous chapter), on the gap between 'Ireland' and its receivers, and on the formation of 'Ireland' by Britain. In allowing Broadbent to be duped by Tim Haffigan, a Glasgow-born non-Irishman who has never been in Ireland, Shaw politicises the idea of 'Ireland' as floating signifier, not just as it is made by Britain in an Orientalist form of Othered self-fashioning, but as having already been built into that capacity for 'sly civility' which Bhabha describes as inherent in the split at the enuniciative moment of the sign[31] – Tim Haffigan's appropriated performance of servile Irishness earns him half a bottle of whisky from Broadbent, while Broadbent is a willing participant in a formula in which Ireland becomes 'Ireland'. Derrida describes the structure, perhaps the inevitability, of this process:

Every sign, linguistic or non-linguistic, spoken or written (in the current sense of this opposition), in a small or large unit, can be *cited*, put between quotation marks; in so doing it can break with every given context, engendering an infinity of new contexts in a manner which is absolutely illimitable.[32]

Succinctly put here by Derrida, this is the premise at the basis of much that this book has been arguing: that the possibility of being *cited* is used by an entity which moves from being Ireland to being 'Ireland'

and which in doing so avoids becoming fixed and 'sited'. To attribute the cause of this propensity to citation to the unfinished struggle for unity, or the unhealed scar of Partition, or the utopianism of the idea of the nation, is to forget the innate capacity of signs to leave their pristine state of signification and to be produced, re-produced, 'put in quotation marks' and then mark-eted. For all his whimsy, Tom Broadbent is capable of both attempting to replace the sign of Ireland into a knowledge system (as when he consults his Murray travel book on druidic stones) and then, when the sign escapes his ratio-nalisation, giving in to the marketable value of the sign in 'quotation marks' – his, and the play's last words, are 'Come along and help me choose a site for the hotel'.[33]

As indicated by Broadbent, the place of tourism in this process of 'citation' is crucial, in that tourism gives a schematic form to the disassociation, the break from context, so that the sign 'Ireland' is given its weight in an utterance outside its own provenance. This leads to a paradoxically continuous series of moments of uncovering, in which the tourist 'finds' the sign and gives it meaning. The fol-lowing example is from *Time Off In Ireland*, a book published by the (British) newspaper *The Observer* in 1966:

Ireland is being discovered by the British. Of course they have always known the thing was there and for most of our history have resented the fact. But now it is being seen, not through the dark glasses of politics and of fear and contempt, but through spectacles that are almost rose-coloured.[34]

In theoretical terms this fate of the sign is easily described: the erasure of history which is not an erasure reveals the fantasy of discovery. The word 'our' here also has strange effect, 'the British' being addressed by an Irish metonymic voice and told about their own changing habits. If this verges on a Shavian moment of didacticism, its intention is more Haffigan than Broadbent – the point is to issue a convoluted invitation to the British traveller to enjoy the 'innocent and delicious' 'illusion' that in Ireland can be found 'the sort of living that might have existed 60 years ago'.[35] Fintan O'Toole suggests that tourism

has completed and commodified the process that Romanticism and Celticism started in the last century. It has made the exotic and archaic aspects of Irish culture not merely acceptable to but desirable for the centre.[36]

Following this line, then, the contemporary marketing of 'Ireland' becomes part of a wider system of globalisation in which cultural signifiers circulate at the behest and under the aegis of powerful national/corporate formations, replicating the earlier colonial heritage which the sign 'Ireland' sought to outwit, and forcing 'Ireland' to go on deferring itself again. But does this explain and account for the outer edges of Derrida's perception that the sign-in-marks has a capacity for 'an infinity of new contexts in a manner which is absolutely illimitable'? Can 'Ireland' be seen or given meaning outside the ideological trammelling of neo-imperialist tourism? How could 'Ireland' be 'illimitable'? The introductory chapter of this book attempts some answers to these questions; the discussion which began this chapter moved towards the suggestion that marginal cultural forms of 'Ireland' find their often uncatalogued place both easily within and challengingly beyond the epistemologies which proclaim a certain ability to describe and define Ireland. If tourism circulates 'Ireland' within itself, then the marginalia of cultural form which offers itself as the place for this transgressive show of conformity and the illimitable is kitsch, 'which proliferates everywhere, with a decided preference for holiday and tourist shops'[37] – Irish kitsch arguably plays Tim Haffigan's role, peddling 'Ireland', making the gestures of authentic connection, but finally annulling the connectivity promised by authenticity and replacing them with a mixture of commercial transaction and cultural aporia.

Irish kitsch is many possible things and objects: model country cottages which burn tiny blocks of peat to recreate the smell of 'real' Ireland; John Hinde postcards; Connemara marble ashtrays; a leprechaun in a tin; a fridge magnet picture of Belfast City Hall; a door mat on which are the words 'Céad Míle Fáilte' and which plays 'Danny Boy' when stepped on. Kitsch may be, as Baudrillard suggests, a 'cliché' and a 'cultural category', but it is also characterised by its 'plethora' and 'overabundance'.[38] In its excessive replication of the absolutely normative kitsch becomes 'absolutely illimitable', and in this, its 'glanced at' quality, it tantalises with the possibility of an 'Ireland' which is either entirely replete or entirely emptied of meaning.

In *Kitsch and Art* Tomas Kulka writes *against* kitsch and offers three tentative, defining characteristics:

1. Kitsch depicts objects and themes that are highly charged with stock emotions.
2. The objects or themes depicted by kitsch are instantly and effortlessly identifiable.
3. Kitsch does not substantially enrich our associations relating to the depicted objects or themes.[39]

Kulka's recalcitrant aesthetic response is useful in that it clarifies what kitsch is defined against. Kulka is aware of the blurred bound-aries of genre and style which he solidifies, of the possibility of cultural relativism as a mode of objection to his characteristics, and the charges that could be made about his universalising aesthetic. Nevertheless, Kulka sticks by these three defining features, and in doing so keeps kitsch alive and well again. Because in one crucial way kitsch could not survive without being oppositional and in 'bad taste'. The act of buying and owning kitsch is set against the standards of 'good taste', sometimes as an 'unthinking' alternative, sometimes as an ironic critique, but, whichever, kitsch needs oppositionality to be itself – its relationship to not-kitsch is thus necessarily one of potential hostility. In this lies its capacity for subversion and/or submission; kitsch is and must be akin to that which it isn't, and its hostile proximity is then its dangerousness and its future.

As Kulka points out to his continual irritation, kitsch deploys the culturally 'stock', or clichéd, and so its definition against what is in 'good' taste always moves towards the disabling of artistic and seman-tic content, since kitsch can contain the same sign as not-kitsch and yet empty it of significance. Hence Kulka must always indecisively match 'object and theme' and move between the two, searching for the space which kitsch has not already infected.

In the Irish context, kitsch has been most recently and provoca-tively theorised by David Lloyd in his essay 'The Recovery of Kitsch'; here Lloyd gives kitsch an active role in the articulation of subalter-nity's oppositionality and so emphasises *one* possible mode of kitsch's dual cultural status. For Lloyd kitsch must be 'recovered' because

what passes for kitsch in the light of aesthetic judgment [can be] recovered as the emblem of cultures that have been cast from futurity by the state, as commodities are thrown out of circulation, only to discover in their wasted particulars the elements of another living.[40]

Lloyd's subaltern, as discussed in Chapter 5, has a dependency on *recovery* by the academic voice, and yet can have its own agency in tandem with (rather than despite) that form of secondary articulation. For Lloyd the oppositional status of kitsch is always going to be cemented by the subaltern model in which the distinction between dominant ideology and subaltern is impermeable, fixed and binate. For this reason Lloyd's notion of what kitsch is ultimately and curiously relies in its proper form on an intentionality which is the evidence of subaltern agency. As a result Lloyd must reintroduce into the

anti-aesthetic of kitsch a distinction which is close to and uses the
forms of aesthetic judgement which kitsch rejects. Lloyd, in other
words, outlines two types of kitsch: one which sees itself as so transparently obvious that it needs all its connotations to be described
by the critical voice (this kitsch does have a shadowed sense of
intention behind it); and a preferred version of kitsch in which the
subaltern agent as kitsch *artist* recovers the 'wasted' 'emblems of
cultures' – this process is then described with relative transparency
by the interested radicalism of the subaltern critic.

So Lloyd's first example of Irish kitsch is the 'image above the bar
of the Irish Cultural Center in San Francisco', which in its depiction
of emigration both preserves and suppresses the trauma of mass
population movement and the Great Hunger. The psychosis of duality in this image (able to be both . . . and) reveals, Lloyd usefully
points out, 'the secret of the sudden mobility to which the icon can
attain in spite of its debasement and devaluation as mere kitsch'.[41]
Yet this 'sudden mobility' is the prelude to a reattachment of the
icons of kitsch to full meaning in the subaltern use of kitsch which
Lloyd describes in John Kindness's art and Gerry Kelly's wall murals.
While the status of kitsch in Kindness's work might be questioned
(hasn't Kindness recovered kitsch *for* art?), it is in analysing Kelly's
murals that Lloyd both raises the potential of kitsch and then disables
it *for* subalternity.

Lloyd describes and makes significant Kelly's mural of eight IRA
members killed at Loughgall in this way:

When Gerry Kelly juxtaposes the images of IRA volunteers ambushed at
Lough Gall with a stylized Irish landscape retrieved from Jim Fitzpatrick, the
appeal is not to nostalgia for an unbroken spirit of Irish identity but to
the fragmentary tableau that constitutes the memory of constant efforts to
realize other ways of living in the face of unrelenting domination.[42]

Lloyd's subalternity homogenises the subaltern and blinds itself to
hierarchisation and power within subalternity itself (here the effect
on the community of this 'site', and the fact that it proclaims a collective ideology of the subaltern which may not be shared entirely by
that community, but is assumed to do so). There is also a fine line to
be drawn between the 'unbroken' (which, Lloyd says, this mural is
not) and the 'constant' (which it is). It is only by attaching the identitarian 'spirit' to 'unbroken' that Lloyd can reject nostalgia, while
the sign of agency, 'efforts', is allowed the solidity and history of
constancy. Lloyd's analysis of this 'kitsch' is more about the war over

the fate of republicanism in Ireland than it is about the political potentiality of kitsch itself, and thus Lloyd's idea of kitsch as an 'emblem of cultures that have been cast from futurity by the state' becomes suspect in its ability to define kitsch as anything other than that which is evidence of (a particular type of) subaltern agency. A kitsch that must 'retrieve' Jim Fitzpatrick's already kitsch landscapes, suggests a kitsch which has its boundaries firmly set, and those are partly, it becomes clear, drawn in the unlikely place of commodification. Gerry Kelly's mural cannot, very obviously, be bought or sold as an item itself. What would be more properly kitsch would be its existence on a postcard, or as a site on a guided tour around West Belfast – but here agency would be lost and critique would have to return, losing its transparency and being propelled towards that Micheletean dilemma of fracture discussed in Chapter 3.

That kitsch might signify 'elements of another living' is then to place within kitsch the expectation of a germination of political meaning which kitsch cannot sustain, since it is reliant on production, overproduction and a plethora of meanings which verge on overwhelming the capacity to mean. Where John Kindness ironically uses kitsch in the context of artistic production, Gerry Kelly deploys kitsch in the name of ideology, and both can only partially account for the meaninglessness which kitsch seems to exclaim. Indeed Kelly and Kindness both arguably *critique* kitsch rather than make it – the very fact that their names, their '*creator's mark*',[43] can be applied to what they do suggests that in discussing kitsch Lloyd seeks to return authenticity to the cultural form which most clearly challenges authenticity's hold on cultural identity.

So what of these other items of Irish kitsch, those found at tourist shops and in airports? A typical enough example is the leprechaun in a snow storm. About two inches high, a green base ('Lucky Irish Leprechaun' in gold letters), a clear plastic dome on top of which is a green plastic top hat. Inside a leprechaun, sitting on 'grass', white-beard, no moustache, relatively gleeful expression, arms out wide. Beside him a pot of gold, behind him a wooden sign with green lettering: 'I ♥ the IRISH!'; on top of the sign a snail. Give it a shake and the 'snowstorm' is of gold coins. It is difficult to transfer any of Lloyd's readings onto this piece of kitsch: it happily bypasses trauma and shows little or no signs of 'another living'. This could simply be a case for the *Punch*-like stereotype at its most successful, persuading those stereotyped of the 'truth' of the image, though as Bhabha points out even the generation of the colonial 'coercive image' tends to the uncanny, and to point to a 'loss or lack of truth' at the very moment

at which it is figured.[44] Arguably this kitsch calls to account that lack
of truth, its moment of agency evident in the way in which it imitates
its own colonially coercive image for commercial ends. In this reading
the act of buying and possessing the artefact becomes meaningful
while the thing itself is semiotically empty; in Kulka's words everything it signifies is 'instantly and effortlessly identifiable', and as an
object it accepts this fate, playing on its own emptiness as all it has
left, and equally accepting its degradation as non-'enriching'.

Finding meaning in kitsch is troublingly paradoxical. The leprechaun in a snowstorm is replete with the signs of 'Ireland', from
happiness to sloth, from nature to supernatural lucre, and yet to give
any of these a meaning beyond their own proclamation of exported
Irishness is to meet the recalcitrance of kitsch itself. Or, put another
way, to be serious about kitsch is to sound ridiculous. If we search
for the truly unutterable, subaltern status in Irish culture, it may
be that we meet it most clearly not in a 'hidden' Ireland, but in the
obvious, crude, brash, blatant and garish 'Ireland' all around us.
Easily dismissed by analysis, it has the ability to undermine the very
nature of critique itself and to throw the critical voice back at itself
in a form of self-parody. Baudrillard, discussing kitsch, finds himself
faced with exactly same dilemma. Kitsch, for Baudrillard, is caught
somewhere between the authenticity sought for by the fetish for
'bygone objects' and the functionality of the modern gadget. Our
kitsch item, this leprechaun in a snowstorm, is neither functional nor
bygone (though it may *signify* something perhaps bygone) and is
what Baudrillard identifies as 'anachronic', out of the synchronous
and diachronous systems: '[testifying] to the relative failure of the
system, this regressive dimension nonetheless takes refuge in the
system, by which it paradoxically permits it to function'.[45] But for
Baudrillard kitsch is ultimately about the reintroduction of (class)
distinction into the world, where the kitsch object in its infinite
reproducibility is contrasted to the exclusive collectability of the
antique. As Baudrillard says, '[kitsch] and the authentic object con-
spire to organise the world of consumption',[46] and this curiously
resolves that initial anachronism.

Perhaps the possibilities of kitsch, and the popular more generally,
are held in these circulations around its strangeness and its reluctance to be explained. Signifying 'Ireland' painlessly, kitsch is the
exportation and ownership of 'Ireland'; in its reproducibility it may be
a sign of the commercialisation of 'Ireland' and an ironisation of that
commercialisation at the same time. But the key is in the ownership
of the sign of 'Ireland' which it in turn signifies. Kitsch scatters the

remnants of Irish authenticity around the globe, allowing forms of ownership to visitor, emigrant and citizen alike. By celebrating the second-hand, irretrievable nature of the authentic, kitsch is closer to 'Ireland' than it might seem – because kitsch is the knowledge, the panic and the relief that the future 'Ireland' is never going to remove its marks of citation. By accepting that 'nostalgia, the phantasmal parodic rehabilitation of all lost referentials',[47] *is* phantasmal, kitsch is one version of 'Ireland' which knows the eternally delayed utopian nature of its master-discourse. Selling itself and 'Ireland', kitsch recognises the brand name as the sign of a never-to-be-realised and thus never-to-be-broken promise. And so our leprechaun can continue eternally in his plastic bubble, smiling forever, at snail's pace, while any stimulation allows his gold coins to float around him.

THE ATLANTIC FLYOVER

At the beginning of *Riverdance: The Homecoming*, the Irish emerge from the sea in a temptingly Atlantean way to populate the land. By the second half of the performance they have begun to emigrate to the United States, mix with Afro-American culture, and begin to return to Ireland. The message is similar to Ignatius Donnelly's – movement is the fate of the world, culture is an origin that moves too.

In 1991 the comic book *2000AD* ran a six-part 'Judge Dredd' story set in a future, post-apocalypse Ireland in which the entire island had been set aside as a holiday resort. Judge Dredd is sent to deal with the 'Sons of Erin', a terrorist group hiding in the Charles Haughey Memorial Village, who want to stage a 'spectacular' to kill off the tourist industry ('No more leprechaun suits . . . No more top o' the mornin' to ye . . . No more patronising our entire nation for the stereotyped garbage in a tourist brochure by some jerk who thinks this country's just one big joke'[48]). Having eliminated the Sons of Erin in his usual way Judge Dredd leaves 'Emerald Isle' by the Atlantic Flyover and through the Black Atlantic Tunnel. The Flyover has directions to Mega-City (America), Brit-Cit (Britain) and, of course, . . . to Atlantis.

Notes

1. Luke Gibbons, 'Race Against Time: Racial Discourse and Irish History', in *Transformations in Irish Culture* (Cork: Cork University Press/Field Day, 1996), p. 149.

2. Gibbons, 'Race Against Time: Racial Discourse and Irish History', p. 149.
3. 'Europe Delineated', produced by John Betts *c.* 1830. This is a 57-piece jig-saw cut from a hand-coloured steel engraving mounted on wood; when assembled it was used as a 'race' game. John A. Betts published various educational materials such as maps, globes and puzzles. After 1875, Betts' stock was sold by the importers A. N. Myers & Co. George Phillip & Son took over the puzzle publication, to be listed as Betts Dissected Puzzles. I am grateful to Susan Smith of the Bethnal Green Museum of Childhood for her generosity in supplying information on this item. 'Europe Delineated' is catalogued at Bethnal Green as MISC 6-1936.
4. The text for 'England' reads: 'Harvest Home This is a cheerful sight indeed! The last load is going home and the reapers are no doubt thinking of the hearty supper which the farmer gives them on this occasion. It is hoped that they will not abuse his kindness by taking more than will do them good'.
5. Edward W. Said, *Orientalism: Western Conceptions of the Orient* (London: Penguin, 1991 [1978]), p. 41. Said takes the phrase from Ian Hacking, *The Emergence of Probability* (Cambridge: Cambridge University Press, 1975), p. 17.
6. Roland Barthes, 'Toys' in *Mythologies* (London: Vintage, 1993), p. 53.
7. L. P. Curtis, *Apes and Angels: The Irishman in Victorian Caricature* (London and Washington: Smithsonian Institution Press, 1971). See also Curtis's *Anglo-Saxons and Celts* (Bridgeport, CT: Conference on British Studies, 1968).
8. R. F. Foster, 'Paddy and Mr Punch', in *Paddy and Mr Punch: Connections in Irish and English History* (Harmondsworth: Allen Lane, 1993), pp. 171–94.
9. The idea which underpins Declan Kiberd's *Inventing Ireland: The Literature of the Modern Nation* (London: Jonathan Cape, 1995), though of course Curtis is in no way the sole or even main source for this thesis in Kiberd.
10. Vincent J. Cheng's *Joyce, Race and Empire* (Cambridge: Cambridge University Press, 1995), for example, repeats many of Curtis's assertions with little fundamental questioning of the method or remit of Curtis's work.
11. Though see Kevin Barry, 'Critical Notes on Post-Colonial Aesthetics', *Irish Studies Review*, 14 (1996), 2–11 for largely incidental usages of 'popular' visual culture, and David Lloyd's discussion of ballads, especially in 'Adulteration and the Nation' in *Anomalous States: Irish Writing and the Post-Colonial Moment* (Dublin: Lilliput, 1993), pp. 88-124.
12. Homi K. Bhabha, *The Location of Culture* (London: Routledge, 1994), p. 111.
13. Bhabha, *The Location of Culture*, p. 111.
14. For more recent work on popular representations of Ireland see J. R. R. Adams, *The Printed Word and the Common Man: Popular Culture in Ulster, 1700–1900* (Belfast: Institute of Irish Studies, 1987); J. S. Donnelly and Kerby A. Miller (eds), *Irish Popular Culture, 1650–1850* (Dublin: Irish Academic Press, 1998); and Niall Ó Ciosáin, *Print and Popular Culture in Ireland, 1750–1850* (London: Macmillan, 1997).
15. John Fiske, *Understanding Popular Culture* (London: Routledge, 1989), pp. 103–4.
16. Fiske, *Understanding Popular Culture*, p. 104.
17. B. E. Maidment, *Reading Popular Prints, 1790–1870* (Manchester: Manchester University Press 1996), pp. 17, 18. I am grateful to Professor

Maidment for generously sharing his expertise on nineteenth-century popular cultural forms and especially his knowledge of the almanac form (discussed below).

18. I have been unable to find an exact date for this series.

19. Alluding to Raymond Williams, 'Culture is Ordinary', collected in *Studying Culture*, eds Ann Gray and Jim McGuigan (London: Edward Arnold, 1993).

20. Maurice Rheims's description of the 'taste for collecting' quoted in Jean Baudrillard, *Revenge of the Crystal: Selected Writings on the Modern Object and Its Destiny, 1968–1983*, eds and trans. Paul Foss and Julian Pefanis (London: Pluto, 1990), p. 44.

21. Roland Barthes, 'The Plates of the Encyclopedia', in *Selected Writings* (London: Fontana, 1982), p. 234.

22. The work of Professor David Mayer of Manchester University on early films in the United States is instructive here. Professor Mayer's archive material includes many films which depend on 'ethnic' jokes and the representation of ethnic types (including the Irish). Professor Mayer suggests that these jokes were often 'for' rather than aimed against the immigrant groups represented, who would often have *been* the audience.

23. This reads: 'In returning my grateful acknowledgment for the liberal patronage which an "**enlightened Public!**" has bestowed on my "**Weather Almanac**" and the **increasing demand** for it proves my **theory** is **sound**!! and that I'm quite a Pat!!! I beg to state that I am preparing another for the Year 1839 and intend to publish it on the **1st of April** next (all Fools day) with many improvements, and to save my Printer time and trouble I shall **commence** with the **59th Edition**.'

24. Father Mathew's abstinence movement was founded in 1838, the year of this almanac.

25. 'The Real Potato Blight', in *Punch*, 9 (July–December 1845), p. 255.

26. Roland Barthes, 'The New Citroën' in *Mythologies* (London: Vintage, 1993), p. 88.

27. Michel Foucault, *The Archaeology of Knowledge*, trans. A. M. Sheridan Smith (London: Tavistock, 1972), p. 131.

28. Maidment, *Reading Popular Prints*, p. 19.

29. Clement Greenberg's description of kitsch, cited in Wayne Hemingway, *20th Century Icons: Kitsch* (Bath: Absolute, 1999), p. 13.

30. From George Bernard Shaw's *John Bull's Other Island*, in Seamus Deane (ed.), *The Field Day Anthology of Irish Writing* (Derry: Field Day, 1991), II, p. 429.

31. See Bhabha, *The Location of Culture*, pp. 93–101.

32. Jacques Derrida, from 'Signature Event Context', quoted in Gregory L. Ulmer, 'The Object of Post-Criticism', in Hal Foster (ed.), *Postmodern Culture* (London: Pluto, 1985), p. 89.

33. Shaw, *John Bull's Other Island*, p. 472.

34. Patrick O'Donovan, 'Introduction', in *Time Off In Ireland* (London: Hodder & Stoughton, 1966), p. 11.

35. Patrick O'Donovan, 'Introduction', p. 11.

36. Fintan O'Toole, *The Ex-Isle of Erin: Images of a Global Ireland* (Dublin: New Island Books, 1996), p. 159.

37. Baudrillard, *Revenge of the Crystal*, p. 75.

38. Baudrillard, *Revenge of the Crystal*, p. 75.

39. Tomas Kulka, *Kitsch and Art* (University Park: Pennsylvania State University Press, 1996), pp. 37–8.

40. David Lloyd, *Ireland After History* (Cork: Cork University Press/Field Day, 1999), p. 100.
41. Lloyd, *Ireland After History*, p. 94.
42. Lloyd, *Ireland After History*, p. 98.
43. Baudrillard, *Revenge of the Crystal*, p. 37.
44. Bhabha, *The Location of Culture*, p. 135.
45. Baudrillard, *Revenge of the Crystal*, p. 41
46. Baudrillard, *Revenge of the Crystal*, p. 76.
47. Jean Baudrillard, *Simulations*, trans. Paul Foss, Paul Patton and Philip Beitchman (New York: Semiotext(e), 1983), p. 72.
48. 'Emerald Isle', Part 2, *2000AD*, 27 April 1991.

Bibliography

Adams, Gerry, *Falls Memories* (Dingle: Brandon, 1982)

Adams, Gerry, *The Street and Other Stories* (Dingle: Brandon, 1992)

Adams, J. R. R., *The Printed Word and the Common Man: Popular Culture in Ulster, 1700–1900* (Belfast: Institute of Irish Studies, 1987)

Adorno, Theodor, *The Jargon of Authenticity* (London: Routledge, 1986)

Ahmad, Aijaz, *In Theory: Classes, Nations, Literatures* (London: Verso, 1992)

Allingham, William, *William Allingham's Diary*, intro. Geoffrey Grigson (London: Centaur, 1967)

Anderson, Benedict, *Imagined Communities: Reflections of the Origin and Spread of Nationalism*, revised edition (London: Verso, 1991)

Ashcroft, Bill, Griffiths, Gareth and Tiffin, Helen, *The Empire Writes Back: Theory and Practice in Post-colonial Literatures* (London: Routledge, 1989)

Baldick, Chris, *Criticism and Literary Theory: 1890 to the Present* (London: Longman, 1996)

Barry, Kevin, 'Critical Notes on Post-Colonial Aesthetics', *Irish Studies Review*, 14 (1996), 2–11

Barthes, Roland, *Michelet*, trans. Richard Howard (Oxford: Basil Blackwell, 1987)

Barthes, Roland, *Selected Writings* (London: Fontana, 1982)

Barthes, Roland, *Mythologies* (London: Vintage, 1993)

Baudrillard, Jean, *Simulations*, trans. Paul Foss, Paul Patton and Philip Beitchman (New York: Semiotxt(e), 1983)

Baudrillard, Jean, *Revenge of the Crystal: Selected Writings on the Modern Object and its Destiny, 1968–1983*, eds and trans. Paul Foss and Julian Pefanis (London: Pluto, 1990)

Bell, Desmond, 'Ireland Without Frontiers? The Challenge of the Communications Revolution', in Richard Kearney (ed.), *Across the Frontiers: Ireland in the 1990s* (Dublin: Wolfhound, 1988), pp. 219–30

Bhabha, Homi K. (ed.), *Nation and Narration* (London: Routledge, 1990)

Bhabha, Homi K., *The Location of Culture* (London: Routledge, 1994)

Blackburne, E. Owens, *Illustrious Irishwomen* (London: Tinsley, 1877)

Blavatsky, H. P., *The Secret Doctrine: The Synthesis of Science, Religion, and Philosophy: Volume II – Anthropogenesis*, Third Point Loma Edition (Point Loma: Aryan Theosophical Society, 1925)

Bleiler, E. F., 'Ignatius Donnelly and Atlantis', in Ignatius Donnelly, *Atlantis: The Antediluvian World* (New York: Dover, 1976 [1882]), pp. v–xx

Boland, Rosita, 'Hillen's Hinde-sight', *Irish Times* (Weekend), 9 October 1999, 5

Boyd, Ernest, *Ireland's Literary Renaissance* (London: Grant Richards, 1923)

Brown, Terence, *Ireland: A Social and Cultural History, 1922–1985* (London: Fontana, 1985)

Brown, Terence, *Ireland's Literature: Selected Essays* (Mullingar: Lilliput, 1988)

Burgess, Anthony, *Here Comes Everybody* (London: Arena, 1982)

Butler, Christopher, *Interpretation, Deconstruction and Ideology* (Oxford: Clarendon, 1984)

Butler, Hubert, *In the Land of Nod* (Dublin: Lilliput, 1996)

Cairns, David and Richards, Shaun, *Writing Ireland: Colonialism, Nationalism and Culture* (Manchester: Manchester University Press, 1988)

Cheng, Vincent J., *Joyce, Race and Empire* (Cambridge: Cambridge University Press, 1995)

Clancy, Tom, *Patriot Games* (London: Collins, 1987)

Cleary, Joe, '"Fork-Tongued on the Border Bit": Partition and the Politics of Form in Contemporary Narratives of the Northern Irish Conflict', *South Atlantic Quarterly*, 95:1 (1996), 227–76

Collins, Jim, *Uncommon Cultures: Popular Culture and Post-Modernism* (London: Routledge, 1989)

Comerford, R. V., 'Political Myths in Ireland', in The Princess Grace Irish Library (ed.), *Irishness in a Changing Society* (Gerrards Cross: Colin Smythe, 1988), pp. 1–17

Connolly, Claire, 'Reflections on the Act of Union', in John Whale (ed.), *Edmund Burke's 'Reflections on the Revolution in France': New Interdisciplinary Essays* (Manchester: Manchester University Press, 2000), pp. 168–92

Connolly, Claire, 'Introduction: Ireland in Theory', in *Theorising Ireland* (London: Macmillan, forthcoming)

Connolly, James, *Labour in Irish History* (Dublin: New Books, 1983 [1910])

Connolly, S. J. (ed.), *The Oxford Companion to Irish History* (Oxford: Oxford University Press, 1999)

Corcoran, Neil, *After Yeats and Joyce: Reading Modern Irish Literature* (Oxford: Oxford University Press, 1997)

Corkery, Daniel, *The Hidden Ireland: A Study of Gaelic Munster in the Eighteenth Century* (Dublin: Gill & Macmillan, 1989 [1924])

Coulter, Carol, *The Hidden Tradition: Feminism, Women and Nationalism in Ireland* (Cork: Cork University Press, 1993)

Craig, Edward Thomas, *An Irish Commune* (Dublin: Irish Academic Press, 1983 [c. 1920])

Cullen, Louis M., *The Hidden Ireland: Reassessment of a Concept* (Mullingar: Lilliput, 1988)

Culler, Jonathan, *On Deconstruction: Theory and Criticism After Structuralism* (London: Routledge & Kegan Paul, 1983)

Cullingford, Elizabeth Butler, *Gender and History in Yeats's Love Poetry* (Cambridge: Cambridge University Press, 1993)

Curtis, L. P., Jr, *Anglo-Saxons and Celts: A Study of Anti-Irish Prejudice in Victorian England* (Bridgeport, CT: Conference on British Studies, 1968)

Curtis, L. P., Jr, *Apes and Angels: The Irishman in Victorian Caricature* (London and Washington, DC: Smithsonian Institution Press, 1971)

Davidson, Basil, *The Black Man's Burden: Africa and the Curse of the Nation State* (London: James Curry, 1993)

Davie, Donald, 'Reflections of an English Writer in Ireland', *Studies*, 44 (1955), 439–45

Deane, Seamus, *Heroic Styles: The Tradition of an Idea* (Derry: Field Day, 1986)

Deane, Seamus, *Celtic Revivals: Essays in Modern Irish Literature* (Winston-Salem, NC: Wake Forest University Press, 1987)

Deane, Seamus, 'Joyce the Irishman', in Derek Attridge (ed.), *The Cambridge Companion to James Joyce* (Cambridge: Cambridge University Press, 1990), pp. 31–53

Deane, Seamus (ed.), *Nationalism, Colonialism and Literature* (Minneapolis, MN: Minneapolis University Press, 1990)

Deane, Seamus, 'Wherever Green is Read', in Máirín ní Dhonnchadha and Theo Dorgan (eds), *Revising the Rising* (Derry: Field Day, 1991), pp. 91–105

Deane, Seamus, *Strange Country: Modernity and Nationhood in Irish Writing Since 1790* (Oxford: Clarendon, 1997)

Delaney, Frank, *Telling the Pictures* (London: HarperCollins, 1994)

Derrida, Jacques, *Of Grammatology*, trans. Gayatri Chakravorty Spivak (London: Johns Hopkins University Press, 1976)

Derrida, Jacques, *Writing and Difference*, trans. Alan Bass (London: Routledge & Kegan Paul, 1978)

Derrida, Jacques, *The Post Card: From Socrates to Freud and Beyond*, intro. and trans. Alan Bass (London: University of Chicago Press, 1987)

Derrida, Jacques, *Aporias*, trans. Thomas Dutoit (Stanford, CA: Stanford University Press, 1993)

Derrida, Jacques, *Spectres of Marx: The State of Debt, the Work of Mourning and the New International*, trans. Peggy Kamuf, intro. Bernd Magnus and Stephen Cullenberg (London: Routledge, 1994)

Derrida, Jacques, *Archive Fever: A Freudian Impression*, trans. Eric Prenowitz (Chicago: Chicago University Press, 1996)

Derrida, Jacques, *Monolingualism of the Other; or, the Prosthesis of Origin*, trans. Patrick Mensah (Stanford, CA: Stanford University Press, 1998)

Dobbins, Gregory, '"Scenes of Tawdry Tribute": Modernism, Tradition and Connolly', in P. J. Mathews (ed.), *New Voices in Irish Criticism* (Dublin: Four Courts, 2000), pp. 3–12

Donaldson, Laura E., *Decolonizing Feminisms: Race, Gender and Empire-Building* (London: Routledge, 1992)

Donnelly, J. S. and Miller, Kerby A. (eds), *Irish Popular Culture, 1650–1850* (Dublin: Irish Academic Press, 1998)

Donoghue, Denis, 'Notes Towards a Critical Method: Language as Order', *Studies*, 42 (1955), 181–92

Donoghue, Denis, *Yeats* (London: Fontana, 1971)

Donoghue, Denis, 'Afterword', in The Field Day Theatre Company (ed.), *Ireland's Field Day* (London: Hutchinson, 1985), pp. 107–12

Donnelly, Ignatius, *Atlantis: The Antediluvian World* (New York: Dover, 1976 [1882])

Eagleton, Terry, *Crazy John and the Bishop and Other Essays on Irish Culture* (Cork: Cork University Press/Field Day, 1998)

'Emerald Isle', *2000AD*, 6 parts (beginning 20 April 1991): scripted by Garth Ennis, drawn by Steve Dillon and Wendy Simpson

Engels, Frederick, *Socialism: Utopian and Scientific*, trans. Edward Aveling (London: George Allen & Uwin, 1936)

Fanon, Frantz, *The Wretched of the Earth* (Harmondsworth: Penguin, 1990)

Finegan, Cartan, 'Marketing Ireland's Heritage to the International Market', paper given at Tourism Development Conference, Killarney, 1996

Fiske, John, *Understanding Popular Culture* (London: Routledge, 1994)

Foster, R. F., *Paddy and Mr Punch: Connections in Irish and English History* (Harmondsworth: Allen Lane, 1993)

Foucault, Michel, *The Archaeology of Knowledge*, trans. A. M. Sheridan Smith (London: Tavistock, 1972)

Gibbons, Luke, 'Coming Out of Hibernation? The Myth of Modernity in Irish Culture', in Richard Kearney (ed.), *Across the Fontiers: Ireland in the 1990s* (Dublin: Wolfhound, 1988), pp. 205–18

Gibbons, Luke, 'Constructing the Canon: Versions of National Identity', in Seamus Deane (ed.), *The Field Day Anthology of Irish Literature* (Derry: Field Day, 1991), II, pp. 950–1020

Gibbons, Luke, 'Challenging the Canon: Revisionism and Cultural Criticism', in Seamus Deane (ed.), *The Field Day Anthology of Irish Writing* (Derry: Field Day, 1991), III, pp. 561–680

Gibbons, Luke, *Transformations in Irish Culture* (Cork: Cork University Press/Field Day, 1996)

Gifford, Don, with Seidman, Robert J., *'Ulysses' Annotated: Notes for James Joyce's 'Ulysses'* (London: University of California Press, 1989)

Godzich, Wlad, 'Language, Images, and the Postmodern Predicament', in Hans Ulrich Gumbrecht and K. Ludwig Pfeiffer (ed.), *Materialities of Communication*, trans. William Whobrey (Stanford, CA: Stanford University Press, 1994), pp. 355–70

Golomb, Jacob, *In Search of Authenticity* (London: Routledge, 1995)

Gramsci, Antonio, *Selections from the Prison Notebooks*, eds and trans. Quintin Hoare and Geoffrey Nowell Smith (London: Lawrence & Wishart, 1971)

Gray, Ann and McGuigan, Jim (eds), *Studying Culture* (Edward Arnold, 1993)

Griffiths, Gareth, 'The Myth of Authenticity: Representation, Discourse and Practice', in Chris Tiffin and Alan Lawson (eds), *De-scribing Empire: Post-Colonialism and Textuality* (London: Routledge: 1994), pp. 70–85

Guha, Ranajit, 'On Some Aspects of the Historiography of Colonial India', in Ranajit Guha (ed.), *Subaltern Studies: Writings on South Asian History and Society*, vol. I (Delhi: Oxford University Press, 1982)

Gwynn, Stephen, *Today and Tomorrow in Ireland* (Dublin: Hodges Figgis, 1903)

Gwynn, Stephen, *Irish Literature and Drama in the English Language: A Short History* (London: Thomas Nelson, 1936),

Habermas, Jürgen, 'Modernity – An Incomplete Project' in Hal Foster (ed.), *Postmodern Culture* (London: Pluto, 1985), pp. 3–15

Harvey, David, *The Condition of Postmodernity: An Enquiry into the Origins of Cultural Change* (Oxford: Blackwell, 1989)

Hemingway, Wayne, *20th Century Icons: Kitsch* (Bath: Absolute, 1999)

Henke, Suzette A., *James Joyce and the Politics of Desire* (London: Routledge, 1990)

Hill, Constance, *Maria Edgeworth and Her Circle in the Days of Buonaparte and Bourbon* (London: John Lane, 1910)

Hill, Myrtle and Pollock, Vivien, *Image and Experience: Photographs of Irishwomen* (Belfast: Blackstaff, 1993)

Hillen, Seán, *Irelantis* (Dublin: Irelantis, 1999)

Hofheinz, Thomas, *Joyce and the Invention of Irish History: 'Finnegans Wake' in Context* (Cambridge: Cambridge University Press, 1995)

Holton, Robert J., *Globalization and the Nation-State* (London: Macmillan, 1998)

Howe, Stephen, *Ireland and Empire: Colonial Legacies in Irish History and Culture* (Oxford: Oxford University Press, 2000)

Howes, Marjorie, *Yeats's Nations: Gender, Class, and Irishness* (Cambridge: Cambridge University Press, 1996)

Hume, John, 'Europe of the Regions', in Richard Kearney (ed.), *Across the Frontiers: Ireland in the 1990s* (Dublin: Wolfhound, 1988), pp. 45–57

Hyde, Douglas, 'The Necessity for De-Anglicising Ireland', in Mark Storey (ed.), *Poetry and Ireland Since 1800: A Source Book* (London: Routledge, 1988), pp. 78–84

Jameson, Fredric, *The Political Unconscious: Narrative as Socially Symbolic Act* (Ithaca, NY: Cornell University Press, 1982)

Jameson, Fredric, *'Ulysses* in History', in W. J. McCormack and Alistair Stead (eds), *James Joyce and Modern Literature* (London: Routledge and Kegan Paul, 1982), pp. 126–41

Jameson, Fredric, *Postmodernism; or, the Cultural Logic of Late Captialism* (London: Verso, 1993)

Jones, Derek and Stoneman, Rod (eds), *Talking Liberties* (London: Channel Four/BSS, 1992)

Joyce, James, *Ulysses: The Corrected Text*, ed. Hans Walter Gabler (London: Bodley Head, 1989)

Joyce, James, *A Portrait of the Artist as a Young Man*, ed. Seamus Deane (Harmondsworth: Penguin, 1992)

Kandiyoti, Deniz, 'Identity and its Discontents: Women and the Nation', in Laura Chrisman and Patrick Williams (eds), *Colonial Discourse and Post-Colonial Theory: A Reader* (Hemel Hempstead: Harvester, 1994), pp. 376–91

Kateb, George, *Utopia and its Enemies* (New York: Schoken, 1972)

Kearney, Richard, 'Introduction: Thinking Otherwise', in Richard Kearney (ed.), *Across the Frontiers: Ireland in the 1990s* (Dublin: Wolfhound, 1988), pp. 7–28

Kearney, Richard, *Transitions: Narratives in Modern Irish Culture* (Manchester: Manchester University Press, 1988)

Kearney, Richard, *Postnationalist Ireland: Politics, Culture, Philosophy* (London: Routledge, 1997)

Kelly, Aaron, '"A Sense of Stasis, Fear and Hatred": The Politics of Form in Representations of Northern Ireland Produced by the "Troubles" Thriller', in P. J. Mathews (ed.), *New Voices in Irish Criticism* (Dublin: Four Courts, 2000), pp. 109–15

Kelly, John and Domville, Eric (eds), *The Collected Letters of W. B. Yeats: Volume I, 1865–1895* (Oxford: Oxford University Press, 1986)

Kelly, Margaret, 'Women in the North', in Thérèse Caherty, Andy Storey, Mary Gavin, Máire Molloy and Caitríona Ruane (eds), *Is Ireland a Third World Country?* (Belfast: Beyond the Pale, 1992), pp. 51–3

Kennedy, Brian P., 'The Irish Free State 1922–49: A Visual Perspective', in Raymond Gillespie and Brian P. Kennedy (eds), *Ireland: Art into History* (Dublin: Town House, 1994), pp. 132–52

Kennedy, Harlan, 'Shamrocks and Shillelaghs: Idyll and Ideology in Irish Cinema', in James MacKillop (ed.), *Contemporary Irish Cinema: From 'The Quiet Man' to 'Dancing at Lughnasa'* (Syracuse, NY: Syracuse University Press, 1999), pp. 1–10

Kennedy, Liam, 'Modern Ireland: Post-Colonial Society or Post-Colonial Pretensions?', *Irish Review*, 13 (1992/93), 107–21

Kiberd, Declan, 'Anglo-Irish Attitudes', in The Field Day Theatre Company (ed.), *Ireland's Field Day* (London: Hutchinson, 1985), pp. 83–105

Kiberd, Declan, *Inventing Ireland: The Literature of the Modern Nation* (London: Jonathan Cape, 1995)

Kirkland, Richard, *Literature and Culture in Northern Ireland Since 1965: Moments of Danger* (Harlow: Longman, 1996)

Kirkland, Richard, 'Questioning the Frame: Hybridity, Ireland and the Institution', in Colin Graham and Richard Kirkland (eds), *Ireland and Cultural Theory: The Mechanics of Authenticity* (London: Macmillan, 1999), pp. 210–28

Kulka, Tomas, *Kitsch and Art* (University Park: Pennsylvania State University Press, 1996)

Law, Hugh Alexander, *Anglo-Irish Literature* (Dublin: Talbot Press, 1926)

Lawless, Emily, *Maria Edgeworth* (London: Macmillan, 1904)

Ledbetter, Gordon T., *The Great Irish Tenor* (London: Duckworth, 1977)

Leerssen, Joep, *Mere Irish and Fíor Gael: Studies in the Idea of Nationality, its Development and Literary Expression Prior to the Nineteenth Century* (Cork: Cork University Press/Field Day, 1996)

Leerssen, Joep, *Remembrance and Imagination: Patterns in the Historical and Literary Representation of Ireland in the Nineteenth Century* (Cork: Cork University Press/Field Day, 1996)

Leslie, Peter, *The Extremists* (London: New English Library, 1970)

Levinas, Emmanuel, *The Levinas Reader*, ed. Seán Hand (Oxford: Blackwell, 1996)

Livesey, James and Murray, Stuart, 'Post-colonial Theory and Modern Irish Culture', *Irish Historical Studies*, 30:119 (1997), 452–61

Lloyd, David, *Anomalous States: Irish Writing and the Post-Colonial Moment* (Dublin: Lilliput, 1993)

Lloyd, David, 'Nationalisms Against the State: Towards a Critique of the Anti-Nationalist Prejudice', in T. P. Foley, Lionel Pilkington, Sean Ryder and Elizabeth Tilley (eds), *Gender and Colonialism* (Galway: Galway University Press, 1995), pp. 256–81

Lloyd, David, *Ireland After History* (Cork: Cork University Press/Field Day, 1999)

Longley, Edna, *Poetry in the Wars* (Newcastle upon Tyne: Bloodaxe, 1986)

Longley, Edna, *From Cathleen to Anorexia: The Breakdown of Irelands* (Dublin: Attic, 1990)

Longley, Edna, 'Writing, Revisionism and Grass Seed: Literary Mythologies in Ireland', in Jean Lundy and Aodán Mac Póilin (eds), *Styles of Belonging: The Cultural Identities of Ulster* (Belfast: Lagan Press, 1992), pp. 11–21

Longley, Edna, *The Living Stream: Literature and Revisionism in Ireland* (Newcastle upon Tyne: Bloodaxe, 1994)

Longley, Edna, '"A foreign oasis"? English Literature, Irish Studies and Queen's University Belfast', *Irish Review*, 17/18 (Winter 1995), 26–39

McAleavy, James, 'The Imagination of Contemporary Republicanism' (MA Dissertation, University of Dublin, 1993)

McCarthy, Conor, *Modernisation, Crisis and Culture in Ireland, 1969–1992* (Dublin: Four Courts, 2000)

McCarthy, Justin P. (ed.), *Irish Literature*, 10 vols (New York: Bigelow, 1904)

McClintock, Anne, 'The Angel of Progress: Pitfalls of the Term "Post-colonialism"', in Patrick Williams and Laura Chrisman (eds), *Colonial Discourse and Post-Colonial Theory* (London: Harvester Wheatsheaf, 1994), pp. 291–304

McCormack, Lily, *I Hear You Calling Me* (London: W. H. Allen, 1951)

McCormack, W. J., *From Burke to Beckett: Ascendancy, Tradition and Betrayal in Literary History* (Cork: Cork University Press, 1994)

MacDonagh, Thomas, *Literature in Ireland: Studies Irish and Anglo-Irish* (Talbot: Dublin, 1916)

McLaverty, Bernard, *Cal* (London: Jonathan Cape, 1983)

Mahaffey, Vicki, 'Sidereal Writing: Male Refraction and Malefactions in "Ithaca"', in Kimberley J. Devlin and Marilyn Reizbaum (eds), *'Ulysses' – Engendered Perspectives: Eighteen New Essays on the Episodes* (Columbia: University of South Carolina Press, 1999), pp. 254–66

Maidment, B. E., *Reading Popular Prints, 1790–1870* (Manchester: Manchester University Press 1996)

Magee, William Kirkpatrick ('John Eglinton'), *Anglo-Irish Essays* (New York: Books for Libraries Press, 1968 [1918])

Maguire, Mark, 'The Space of the Nation: History, Culture and a Conflict in Modern Ireland', *Irish Studies Review*, 6:2 (1998), 109–20

Maley, Willy, 'Postcolonial Joyce?', in Alan Marshall and Neil Sammells (eds), *Irish Encounters: Poetry, Politics and Prose Since 1880* (Bath: Sulis Press, 1998), pp. 59–69

Mattar, Sinéad Garrigan, 'Primitivism and the Writers of the Irish Dramatic Movement' (DPhil Thesis, Oxford, 1997)

Maume, Patrick, *'Life that is Exile': Daniel Corkery and the Search for Irish Ireland* (Belfast: Institute of Irish Studies, 1993)

Meaney, Gerardine, *Sex and Nation: Women in Irish Culture and Politics* (Dublin: Attic, 1991)

Melucci, Alberto, 'The Post-Modern Revival of Ethnicity', in John Hutchinson and Anthony D. Smith (eds), *Ethnicity* (Oxford: Oxford University Press, 1996), pp. 367–70

Memmi, Albert, *The Colonizer and the Colonized* (London: Earthscan, 1990)

Mercier, Vivian, 'An Irish School of Criticism?', *Studies*, 45 (1956), 84–7

Mitchel, John, *Jail Journal* (Dublin: M. & H. Gill, 1918)

Moore, Brian, *Lies of Silence* (London: Bloomsbury, 1990)

Morash, Chris, 'The Rhetoric of Right in Mitchel's *Jail Journal*', in Joep Leerssen, A. H. van der Weel and Bart Westerveld (eds), *Forging in the Smithy: National Identity and Representation in Anglo-Irish History* (Amsterdam: Rodopi, 1995), pp. 207–18

Moriarty, Michael, *Roland Barthes* (Oxford: Polity Press, 1991)

Moroney, Mic, 'Postcards from the Edge', *Cara*, March/April 1998, 20–8

Nolan, Emer, *James Joyce and Nationalism* (London: Routledge, 1995)

Norstedt, Johann A., *Thomas MacDonagh: A Critical Biography* (Charlottesville: University Press of Virginia, 1980)

Ó Ciosáin, Niall, *Print and Popular Culture in Ireland, 1750–1850* (London: Macmillan, 1997)

O'Connor, Frank, 'Introduction to the 1964 Edition', in Eric Cross, *The Tailor and Ansty* (Cork: Mercier, 1999), pp. 7–12

O'Donnell, C. J., *The Irish Future, with The Lordship of the World* (London: Cecil Palmer, 1931)

O'Donoghue, David J., *The Poets of Ireland: A Biographical Dictionary with Bibliographical Particulars* (London: Paternoster Square Press, 1892)

O'Donovan, Patrick, 'Introduction', in *Time Off In Ireland* (London: Hodder and Stoughton, 1966), pp. 11–16

Ó Faoláin, Seán, 'Signing Off', in Sean McMahon (ed.), *The Best from the Bell: Great Irish Writing* (Dublin: O'Brien Press, 1978), pp. 120–3

Ó Faoláin, Seán, 'This is Your Magazine', in Sean McMahon (ed.), *The Best from the Bell: Great Irish Writing* (Dublin: O'Brien Press, 1978), pp. 13–16

Ó Faoláin, Seán, *The Irish* (Harmondsworth: Penguin, 1980 [1947])

Ó Gráda, Cormac, 'The Owenite Commune at Ralahine, 1831–2', *Irish Economic and Social History*, 1 (1974), 36–48

O'Toole, Fintan, *The Ex-Isle of Erin: Images of a Global Ireland* (Dublin: New Island Books, 1996)

O'Toole, Fintan, *The Lie of the Land: Irish Identities* (Dublin: New Island, 1998)

Owens, Rosemary Cullen, *Smashing Times: A History of the Irish Women's Suffrage Movement 1889–1922* (Dublin: Attic, 1984)

Parry, Benita, 'Problems in Current Theories of Colonial Discourse', *Oxford Literary Review*, 9:1–2 (1987), 27–58

Pettitt, Lance, *Screening Ireland: Film and Television Representation* (Manchester: Manchester University Press, 2000)

Pickering, Michael, *History, Experience and Cultural Studies* (London: Macmillan, 1997)

Platt, Len, *Joyce and the Anglo-Irish: A Study of Joyce and the Literary Revival* (Amsterdam: Rodopi, 1998)

Porter, Dennis, 'Orientalism and Its Problems', in *The Politics of Theory*, ed. Francis Barker (Colchester: University of Essex, 1983), pp. 179–83

Pratt, Mary Louise, *Imperial Eyes: Travel Writing and Transculturation* (London: Routledge, 1992)

Radhakrishnan, R., 'Nationalism, Gender, and the Narrative of Identity', in Andrew Parker, Mary Russo, Doris Sommer and Patricia Yaegar (eds), *Nationalisms and Sexualities* (London: Routledge, 1992), pp. 77–95

Rajan, Rajeswari Sunder, *Real and Imagined Women: Gender, Culture and Postcolonialism* (London: Routledge, 1993)

Read, Charles A. (ed.), *The Cabinet of Irish Literature* (Dublin: Blackie, 1895)

'The Real Potato Blight', *Punch*, 9 (July–December 1845), 255

Redmond, Brigid, 'Films and Children', *Studies*, 45 (1956), 227–33

Richards, Thomas, *The Imperial Archive: Knowledge and the Fantasy of Empire* (London: Verso, 1993)

Ricoeur, Paul, *Oneself as Another*, trans. Kathleen Blamey (London: University of Chicago Press, 1994)

Robbins, Bruce, *Secular Vocations: Intellectuals, Professionalism, Culture* (London: Verso, 1993)

Roberts, John H., 'James Joyce: from Religion to Art', in Robert H. Denning (ed.), *James Joyce: The Critical Heritage*, Vol. 2 1928–1941 (London: Routledge & Kegan Paul, 1970), pp. 612–15

Rockett, Kevin, Hill, John and Gibbons, Luke, *Cinema and Ireland* (London: Routledge, 1988)

Routledge, Paul, *John Hume: A Biography* (London: HarperCollins, 1997)

Said, Edward W., *Orientalism: Western Conceptions of the Orient* (London: Penguin, 1991)

Said, Edward W., *The World, the Text, and the Critic* (London: Vintage, 1991)

Said, Edward W., *Culture and Imperialism* (London: Chatto & Windus, 1993)

Said, Edward W., *Representations of the Intellectual: The 1993 Reith Lectures* (London: Vintage, 1994)

Saorstát Eireann Official Handbook (Dublin: Talbot, 1932)

Saussure, Ferdinand de, *Course in General Linguistics*, intro. Jonathan Culler (London: Fontana/Collins, 1978)

Shaw, George Bernard, *John Bull's Other Island*, in Seamus Deane (ed.), *The Field Day Anthology of Irish Writing* (Derry: Field Day, 1991), II, pp. 423–93

'The Shawl Makes a Comeback', *Irish Times*, 27 December 1999, p. 2

Sheehan, Ronan, *Foley's Asia* (Dublin: Lilliput, 1999)

Smyth, Ailbhe, 'The Floozie in the Jacuzzi', *Irish Review*, 6 (1989), 7–24

Smyth, Ailbhe, 'Declining Identities (lit. and fig.)', *Critical Survey*, 8:2 (1996), 143–58

Smyth, Gerry, 'The Location of Criticism: Ireland and Hybridity', *Journal of Victorian Culture*, 2:1 (1997), 129–38

Smyth, Gerry, *Decolonisation and Criticism: The Construction of Irish Literature* (London: Pluto, 1998)

Spivak, Gayatri Chakravorty, 'Subaltern Studies: Deconstructing Historiography', in Ranajit Guha (ed.), *Subaltern Studies*, IV (Delhi: Oxford University Press, 1985), pp. 330–63

Spivak, Gayatri Chakravorty, *In Other Worlds: Essays in Cultural Politics* (London: Routledge, 1988)

Spivak, Gayatri Chakravorty, *Outside in the Teaching Machine* (London: Routledge, 1993)

Spivak, Gayatri Chakravorty, 'Can the Subaltern Speak?', in Patrick Williams and Laura Chrisman (eds), *Colonial Discourse and Post-Colonial Theory: A Reader* (London: Harvester Wheatsheaf, 1994), pp. 66–111

Spivak, Gayatri Chakravorty, *The Spivak Reader*, eds Donna Landry and Gerald MacLean (London: Routledge, 1996)

Steel, Jayne, 'Vampira: Representations of the Irish Female Terrorist', *Irish Studies Review*, 6:3 (1998), 273–84

Sullivan, Moynagh, 'Feminism, Postmodernism and the Subjects of Irish and Women's Studies', in P. J. Mathews (ed.), *New Voices in Irish Criticism* (Dublin: Four Courts, 2000), pp. 243–51

Thirty First International Eucharistic Congress, Dublin 1932: Pictorial Record (Dublin: Veritas, n.d.)

Thompson, William Irwin, *The Imagination of an Insurrection: Dublin, Easter 1916: A Study of an Ideological Moment* (New York: Oxford University Press, 1967)

Ulmer, Gregory L., 'The Object of Post-Criticism', in Hal Foster (ed.), *Postmodern Culture* (London: Pluto, 1985), pp. 83–110

Viswanathan, Gauri, *Masks of Conquest: Literary Study and British Rule in India* (London: Faber & Faber, 1990)

Walker, Brian, 'Ireland's Historical Position – "Colonial" or "European"', *Irish Review*, 9 (1990), 36–40

Ward, Margaret, *The Missing Sex: Putting Women Into Irish History* (Dublin: Attic, 1991)

Wills, Clair, *Improprieties: Politics and Sexuality in Northern Irish Poetry* (Oxford: Clarendon, 1993)

Winseck, Dwayne, 'Contradictions in the Democratization of International Communication', *Media, Culture and Society*, 19:2 (1997), 219–46

Yeats, W. B., *Essays and Introductions* (Dublin: Gill & Macmillan, 1961)

Yeats, W. B., *Fairy and Folk Tales of the Irish Peasantry*, in *Fairy and Folk Tales of Ireland* (London: Picador, 1973)

Yeats, W. B. (ed.), *Representative Irish Tales*, with a Foreword by Mary Helen Thuente (Gerrards Cross: Colin Smythe, 1979 [1891])

Young, Robert J. C., *Colonial Desire: Hybridity in Theory, Culture and Race* (London: Routledge, 1995)

Young, Robert J. C., 'Response', *Journal of Victorian Culture*, 2:1 (1997), 138–51

Zimmern, Helen, *Maria Edgeworth* (London: W. H. Allen, 1883)

Index

Fundamentalism in America
Millennialism, Identity and Militant Religion
Philip H Melling

This important book challenges the idea that religious fundamentalism can adequately be understood as a paranoid, xenophobic faith. It demonstrates instead how it draws upon a long tradition of evangelical and millennialist scripture in its engagement with issues at the spiritual and ethical core of postmodernity in America. The author examines the contradictions of fundamentalism as they appear in prophecy, sermon, film and fiction, including work by Gore Vidal, Peter Matthiesen, Thom Jones, Alison Lurie and Pete Dexter. In its wide-ranging consideration of the rhetoric of the 'New World Order', the literature of prophecy, Cold War films, tele-evangelism, cross-border texts and postnationalist writing, this book provides a vital and compelling account of the present crisis in religious and national identity in the United States.

November 1999 **Pb** 256pp 0 7486 0978 4 £16.95

Race and Urban Space
in Contemporary American Culture
Liam Kennedy

This innovative book looks at representations of ethnic and racial identities in relation to the development of urban culture in postindustrialised American cities. The book focuses on a range of literary and visual forms including novels, journalism, films (narrative and documentary) and photography to examine the relationship between race and representation in the production of urban space. Texts analysed include writings by Tom Wolfe (*The Bonfire of the Vanities*), Toni Morrison (*Jazz*), John Edgar Wildeman (*Philadelphia Fire*) and Walter Mosely (*Devil in a Blue Dress*). Films covered include *Falling Down, Strange Days, Hoop Dreams* and *Clockers*.

May 2000 224pp **Hb** 0 7486 0969 5 £45.00 **Pb** 0 7486 0952 0 £16.95

Memory, Narrative, Identity
Remembering the Self
Nicola King

This book explores the complex relationships that exist between memory, nostalgia, writing and identity. The author examines a range of autobiographical and first-person fictional texts from holocaust literature, women's writing and popular fiction. Texts include Sylvia Fraser's *My Father's House*, Margaret Atwood's *Cats Eye*, Barbara Vine's *A Dark Adapted Eye*, Toni Morrison's *Beloved*, George Perec's *W Or the Memory of Childhood*, and Anne Michael's *Fugitive Pieces*.

March 2000 208pp **Hb** 0 7486 1116 9 £45.00 **Pb** 0 7486 1115 0 £16.95

Order from
Marston Book Services, PO Box 269, Abingdon, Oxon OX14 4YN
Tel 01235 465500 • Fax 01235 465555
Email: direct.order@marston.co.uk

Visit our website www.eup.ed.ac.uk

All details correct at time of printing but subject to change without notice

Narratives for a New Belonging
Diasporic Cultural Fictions
Roger Bromley

Cultural fictions - texts written from the perspective of the edge - are the focus of this exciting and enlightening book. The author examines the formations of narratives of identity in contemporary 'borderline' fictions and films. The work of migrant and marginalised groups located at the boundaries of nations, cultures, classes, ethnicities, sexualities and genders, is explored through an intricate weaving of theory with textual analysis. Organised around the themes of memory, tradition and 'belonging', the book proposes the space of 'migrant' writing - an emerging third space - as one that challenges fixed assumptions about identity.

The cross-cultural range - including texts from British, Caribbean, Chinese-American, Indo-Caribbean, Canadian, Cuban and Indian writers; the original discussion of authors such as Maxine Hong Kingston, Gloria Anzaldua, Amy Tan, Gish Jen, Hanif Kureishi and Chang-rae Lee; and engagement with the work of theorists including Bakhtin, Freud, Lyotard, de Certeau, Deleuze and Guattari, produces a significant contribution to the broadening definitions of ethnicity and the 'post-colonial'.

Works explored include *Jasmine, Borderlands, The Joy Luck Club, The Wedding Banquet, Dreaming in Cuban, My Year of Meat, Buddha of Suburbia* and *East is East*. These contemporary texts and films will make this book accessible to a broad range of readers.

June 2000   182pp   **Pb**   0 7486 0951 2   £16.95

Cruising Culture
Promiscuity, Desire and American Gay Literature
Ben Gove

An extended analysis of the competing understandings of promiscuity within American gay culture, and of the root assumptions and contradictions which contribute to dominant cultural understandings of promiscuous sex and desire. The author challenges the normative dichotomy of 'bad' gay male promiscuity and 'good' heterosexual monogamy and presents a wider overview of American attitudes towards sexual practice and desire. The reader is guided clearly through the maze of competing attitudes towards promiscuity in American gay culture through the autobiographical fiction and memoirs of three highly influential authors from the early 1960s onwards: John Rechy, Larry Kramer and David Wojnarowicz. The author also draws on numerous other queer critical, historical and fictional viewpoints to illustrate the argument.

"Gove's book really packs a punch. Rather than perceiving gay popular fiction as a reflection of society's behavioural patterns, he highlights its importance as a catalyst for change. In doing so, he brings the subject to life and makes it more accessible to everyone."
Time Out

February 2000   224pp   **Pb**   0 7486 1361 7   £16.95

Order from
Marston Book Services, PO Box 269, Abingdon, Oxon OX14 4YN
Tel 01235 465500 • Fax 01235 465555
Email: direct.order@marston.co.uk

Visit our website www.eup.ed.ac.uk

All details correct at time of printing but subject to change without notice